DANCE

About the Editors

LYNNETTE Y. OVERBY, Ph.D., is an Assistant Professor of Physical Education and Director of the Motor Behavior Laboratory at Howard University. She has had wide experience in dance as a teacher, performer, choreographer, and researcher. Her major interests are in the areas of motor development and motor learning. At the present time she is focusing on the role of imagery in learning and performance of motor skills. Currently she serves as Director of Publications for the National Dance Association.

JAMES H. HUMPHREY, Ed.D., Professor Emeritus at the University of Maryland, has published over 40 books and 200 articles and research reports. He is the author of two children's books on dance that have had widespread distribution in the schools of the United States and Great Britain. He is the author of the recently published textbook *Child Development and Learning through Dance* (AMS Press, 1987).

DANCE
Current Selected Research
Volume 3

Edited by

Lynnette Y. Overby
and
James H. Humphrey

With the Cooperation of the National Dance
Association

AMS PRESS
New York

DANCE
Current Selected Research
Volume 3

Copyright © 1992 by AMS Press, Inc.
All rights reserved.

ISSN 0894-4849

Series ISBN: 0-404-63850-3
Vol. 3 ISBN: 0-404-63853-8
Library of Congress Catalog Card Number: 87-47814

MANUFACTURED IN THE UNITED STATES OF AMERICA

AMS Press, Inc.
56 East 13th Street
New York, N.Y. 10003

CONTENTS

BOARD OF REVIEWERS

CONTRIBUTORS

Nancy BrooksSchmitz, Programs in Dance and Dance Education, Teachers College, Columbia University, New York, New York

Sylvie Fortin, Department of Dance, University of Quebec, Montreal, Quebec, Canada

Betsey Goodling Gibbons, Department of Health, Physical Education and Dance, Washburn University, Topeka, Kansas

Dorothy J. Harris, Department of Physical Education and Sport Studies, University of Alberta, Edmonton, Alberta, Canada

Thomas F. Johnston, Department of Music, University of Alaska, Fairbanks, Alaska

Billie Lepczyk, Division of Health, Physical Education and Recreation, Virginia Polytechnic Institute and State University, Blacksburg, Virginia

Sandra Minton, Department of Physical Education and Dance, University of Northern Colorado, Greeley, Colorado

Nelson D. Neal, Department of Physical Education, Health and Recreation, Longwood College, Farmville, Virginia

Robert W. Nicholls, Ph.D., African Studies and Research Programs, Howard University, Washington, DC

A. Brian Nielsen, Department of Physical Education and Sport Studies, University of Alberta, Edmonton, Alberta, Canada

Lynnette Young Overby, Department of Physical Education, Howard University, Washington, DC

Marnie E. Rutledge, Department of Physical Education and Sport Studies, University of Alberta, Edmonton, Alberta, Canada

Jeffrey Steffen, Department of Physical Education and Dance, University of Northern Colorado, Greeley, Colorado

Sheryl Popkin Triebe, Department of Physical Education, University of Wisconsin, La Crosse, Wisconsin

Christalia O. Volaitis, Programs in Dance and Dance Education, Teachers College, Columbia University, New York, New York

Sandra R. Weeks, Department of Health and Physical Education, East Texas State University, Commerce, Texas

Aileene S. Lockhart, Ph.D., D.Sc., Cornaro Professor of Dance, Texas Woman's University, Denton, Texas

Jane A. Mott, Ph.D., Chairman, Department of Dance, Texas Woman's University, Denton, Texas

Ruth Stone, Ph.D., Department of Folklore, Indiana University, Bloomington, Indiana

Nancy Struna, Ph.D., Associate Professor, Department of Physical Education, University of Maryland, College Park, Maryland

Jill Sweet, Ph.D., Department of Sociology/Anthropology, Social Work, Skidmore College, Saratoga Springs, New York

Lynn Wallen, Ph.D., Curator, Alaska State Museum, Juneau, Alaska

PREFACE

This third volume of *Dance: Current Selected Research* presents a variety of papers that are concerned with various aspects of the field of dance. Criteria for the consideration of such papers for publication consisted of: (1) original manuscripts on topics for which valid techniques in experimental, historical, ethnographic, or clinical research have been applied in the collection of data with appropriate analytical treatment of the data; (2) state-of-the-art research reviews on topics of current interest with a substantial research literature base; and (3) theoretical papers presenting well-formulated but as yet untested models.

It is the intention of the editors and AMS Press, Inc., to provide dance researchers and students with an annual series reporting original investigative research that is important to the advancement of knowledge in the various aspects of dance. The volumes are intended to supplement and support journals and annual reviews reporting on similar topics.

The area of dance continues to be characterized by diversity. It is at once a science as well as an art. From a scientific point of view dance involves biological, behavioral, and biomechanical considerations. And as an art form it perhaps has little or no equal as a medium of expression. This third volume is well represented by professionals concerned with these considerations.

This annual series should contribute to communication among those who represent the various aspects of dance. Each volume is meant to serve as a reference for educators investigating similar topics. Courses of study considering topics on dance should find this series useful as a supplement to required readings.

A volume of this nature could not be possible without the cooperation of many individuals. In this regard we wish to thank the contributors for presenting their work for evaluation. In addition, we wish to express our gratitude to the distinguished board of reviewers for giving their time and excellent talents to this endeavor. The enthusiasm and support of the National Dance Association is important to the continuation of this series. The Advisory Board of that association consisted of Mary Alice Brennan, Judith Lynne Hanna, and Sara Chapman, and their suggestions were of great importance in the production of this third volume.

ANNE SCHLEY DUGGAN: PORTRAIT OF A DANCE EDUCATOR

Sandra R. Weeks

The evolution of dance to its present position of academic respectability has taken the contributions and efforts of many individuals, yet the literature is limited in this area. Therefore, it is important to the history of the development of dance in higher education that the pioneers in the field be identified and recognized for their contributions.

The purpose of this study was to make available biographical information about one person, Anne Schley Duggan, a prominent personality in the development of dance in American higher education. The problem undertaken was to study her life during the years from 1936 until her retirement in 1973. The procedures for this study involved the collection of data from both human and documentary sources. Two techniques, the interview and the questionnaire, were used for gathering data from human sources. The data were organized according to selected aspects of the subject's personal and professional life.

On the basis of the investigation, it was concluded that sufficient evidence exists to support the hypothesis that Anne Schley Duggan was influential in advancing dance to its present status in American higher education.

The status of dance in American higher education has been through many stages throughout its historical development. The evolution of dance to its present position of academic respectability has taken the contributions and efforts of many individuals, yet the literature is very limited in this area. Therefore, it is important to the history of the development of dance in higher education that the pioneers in the field be identified and recognized for their contributions.

The purpose of this study is to make available biographical information about one person, Anne Schley Duggan, a prominent personality in the development of dance in American higher education. The problem undertaken was to study her life during the years from 1936 until her retirement in 1973. The investigation was based upon the hypothesis that Anne Schley Duggan was influential in advancing dance to its present status in American higher education. Although it is recognized that she contributed to the whole field of health, physical education, recreation, and dance, only her role as a dance educator was considered for this study.

METHOD

Selection of Human Sources of Data

In developing the current study, certain procedures were followed. The first step involved the selection of human sources of data. The following categories were used for grouping these individuals: (1) family, (2) former student and/or Modern Dance Group member, (3) former Texas Woman's University (TWU) colleague and/or friend, and (4) former professional colleague and/or friend outside TWU. The names of these people were obtained by a preliminary search of documentary sources, by conversations with persons still in Denton, Texas, who were closely associated with Duggan, with the help of Duggan's personal telephone directory, from members of the dissertation committee, and from people responding to the questionnaire or being interviewed.

Methods of Collecting Data

Next, instruments for gathering data were developed. From two master sets of questions (see Appendixes A and B), four questionnaires were designed, one for each of the selected categories of human sources of data. Identical questions were used with those sources who were interviewed and those who were mailed a questionnaire.

An introductory letter, a questionnaire, and a self-addressed stamped envelope were mailed to the questionnaire group. An introductory letter, a set of questions to be used as a guide while conducting the interview, and a self-addressed stamped envelope were sent to those persons in the interview group. Follow-up letters were mailed to those not responding. Further correspondence and personal telephone calls were used in finalizing plans for the interviews. All interviews except one were taped, transcribed, and approved by the interviewees. The one individual requested that the interview be recorded only in written form.

Eighty-four persons were either sent a questionnaire or interviewed. Of those individuals, 62 responded, yielding a 74% total response.

During the time data were being collected from human sources, information was being gathered from documentary sources. Materials that were once a part of the personal and professional files of Duggan were examined in Denton, Denison, and McAllen, Texas. Other documentary materials were examined in the departmental files of the College of Health, Physical Education, and Recreation at TWU, in the TWU library in Denton, and at the New York Public Library Dance Collection at Lincoln Center. These materials consisted of newspaper articles, scrapbooks, books, theses, dissertations, departmental records, periodicals, professional journals, proceedings of professional meetings, and historical records relating to the development of the physical education programs at the TWU.

Organization, Analysis, and Reporting

The next procedure involved organization, analysis, and verification of authenticity of the data. An examination of the data indicated that a topical system for arranging the material was more logical than a chronological grouping. The data, having been submitted to external and internal criticisms, were then organized according to selected aspects of the subject's personal and professional life. Data not relevant to the purpose of this study were eliminated. The final report was organized and presented in the following sections: (1) Introduction, (2) Method, (3) Beginning Sketches, (4) Administrative Tones, (5) Traces of the Dance Teacher, (6) Etchings of the Speaker and Pen, and (7) Finishing Touches.

BEGINNING SKETCHES

The available information pertaining to Duggan's early life, education, dance background, and career beginnings was obtained. Based on the information, it seems probable that these factors influenced her role in advancing dance in American higher education.

Background of Childhood and Youth

Anne Schley Duggan was the daughter of William Young Duggan and Margaret Anna Grafton Duggan. Anne, who was born on October 20, 1902, was one of 10 children. She followed the family tradition of concealing her true birthdate. In the literature several different dates are published, but 1902 is the date on her birth certificate.

Background evidence of the early development of Duggan's interest and training in dance is scarce. It is most likely, though, that Duggan, who displayed a tremendous amount of energy and interest in outdoor activities at an early age, took dance lessons as a child (E. B. Duggan, personal communication, December 1, 1978). These classes were probably in tap, ballet, and acrobatics (J. S. Roosevelt, personal communication, March 10, 1978). Duggan, whose interest and talent for dance can be traced to her childhood, utilized her early gift for teaching by instructing her playmates and schoolmates in dance lessons (cited in Gunnell, 1973, p. 382). As a high school student herself, she directed a group of 10 or 12 girls who presented dance programs in nearby towns (P. D. McDaniel, personal communication, November 26, 1978).

Educational Background and Early Work Experience

Duggan graduated valedictorian from Belton (Texas) High School in 1919. Specific training for her chosen field of teaching began with her earning an undergraduate degree from Baylor College for Women (now Mary Hardin-Baylor) with a major in English and literature. After teaching health and physical education for four years in Belton—one year in public school and three years at Baylor College—she received a master of arts degree from Teachers College, Columbia University, with a major in health, physical education, and recreation. She then taught two years at Lindenwood College in St. Charles, Missouri, before returning to graduate school at Columbia University. She earned a doctor of philosophy degree in 1936 with a major in health, physical education, and recreation.

With its national reputation as a teacher education institution and its strong dance program, Teachers College was most likely responsible for the strongest influence at the beginning stages of Duggan's career. During this time, she formed much of her philosophy of education, particularly physical education, styling it after that of Jesse Feiring Williams, her mentor.

Duggan's interest in modern dance also began to emerge during this period. She took dance classes at Teachers College from Gertrude Colby, one of the pioneers in modern dance in the college and university. Duggan also studied in private studios with the early modern dance leaders such as Doris Humphrey, Charles Weidman, and Martha Graham. In addition, she observed dance classes at Bennington (Vermont) Summer School of Dance and attended dance recitals in New York, including dance performances at St. Mary's-in-the-Bowery.

Duggan's dance lessons were not confined to modern dance. She also studied tap at Columbia with Marjorie Hillas, a noted clog and tap-dance teacher, and at the Ned Wayburn School of Dancing.

During the time that Duggan was working on her doctorate at Teachers College, she studied in the summer at the University of California at Berkeley. While she was studying at the University of California at Berkeley and Teachers College, she took an assortment of dance classes. Among those courses were the following: pageant organization and production, English country dancing, Morris and sword dancing, school pageantry, dramatic and folk dancing for playgrounds and elementary schools, interpretative dancing, Danish gymnastics, clogging anad tap dancing, natural dancing, and theory of dance.

To assist in paying for her educational expenses, Duggan taught classes in tap through the extension center at Teachers College and even had her own school of stage dancing in California while she studied there. In addition, she had some short-term employment during the period 1932–1936—she was a dance instructor at three universities, one school of dance, and two summer camps.

Little documentation could be found regarding specific teaching assignments at all of Duggan's early teaching positions. However, it is likely that she taught some, or all, of the following dance forms when she was employed in Missouri: (1) natural dancing, (2) English folk dancing, (3) folk dancing, and (4) clogging. She did teach folk, clog, and tap, at least in the summer, while she was at Teachers College.

It is clear that Duggan did study dance with many of the then accepted leaders in educational and professional dance. Furthermore, it is evident that her experience in dance teaching was varied and extensive before she began her tenure at the TWU.

ADMINISTRATIVE TONES

Anne Schley Duggan became the director of the Physical Education Department at TWU in Denton, Texas, in 1936. Dr. L. H. Hubbard, the president of the university and Duggan's long-time acquaintance, was the primary reason for her accepting this position. The position allowed her to be near her family and provided her with an opportunity to develop the type of program that her philosophy envisioned. She served as the director until 1954 when her department became the College of Health, Physical Education, and Recreation. Her title was then changed to dean, making her the first female dean of a college of health, physical education, and recreation in the entire nation (cited in Gunnell, 1973, p. 385). She remained in this position until her retirement in 1973.

Background Descriptions

Individuals who knew Duggan over the years provided this background of her as an administrator. Nancy, as she was known by many, was characterized as being a very demanding administrator, one who expected perfection from herself and others. She was an "organizer par excellence" (L. Ellfeldt, questionnaire) who was "strong and indomitable" (W. Terry, questionnaire).

Duggan was considered the instigator and the driving force in the events that established the noted reputation of the College of Health, Physical Education, and Recreation at TWU. Her tremendous capacity for efficiency at work, while exhibiting a seemingly endless source of energy, permitted her to be involved in three or four activities at once (M. Bell, speech, April 7, 1973, Denton, Texas). Her accomplishments were credited to two factors. The first of these was her extraordinary ability to delegate duties and then follow through to see that they were completed. The second contributing factor was her inspirational effect on those around her.

Dance Curriculum Development

As administrator, Duggan was directly involved in curriculum development. She built the dance courses and programs around her philosophical belief that "the well-rounded, broad program of dance in education . . . includes the four types we now designate as folk, tap, ballroom, and modern" (Duggan, 1951, p. 26).

During Duggan's era, course offerings in dance at TWU increased from elementary and intermediate levels of folk, natural, and clog dancing, as well as elementary aesthetic dancing, to include various levels of modern, tap, social, ethnic, jazz, and ballet. Whereas a history and philosophy of dance class was the only lecture course included in the curriculum when she arrived on campus, others such as "Appreciation of Dance," "Current Theories and Practices in the Teaching of Dance," "Accompaniment for Movement," "Theory and Practice of Labanotation," and "Research in Dance" were added.

In addition to the increased number of course offerings, the number of degrees offered in dance was expanded. In the early 1950s, TWU students could earn a master's degree with a dance major. Also, a dance specialization was available in the undergraduate recreation degree. A significant step was taken in 1954 when doctoral degrees became a part of the newly established college and both a dance major and minor were offered. Not only was the doctorate in dance unknown as a major in any other university in the Southwest, it was a rare degree program in the entire nation. Fewer than 10 U.S. universities offered such a program at that time.

In continuing to strive for improvement, the most unique dance major was introduced in 1956, the master of arts degree with a major in dance and related arts. This major was extended to the doctoral level in 1957. This program reflected Duggan's (1951) belief that:

> Teacher education institutions are at fault when they fail to augment the professional education of their graduates in anatomy, kinesiology, fundamentals of movement, etc., with training in music, drama, stage-craft, costume design, and other aspects of related creative arts. Only through such a background of training will the potential teacher of dance integrate his instruction with the various arts to the enrichment of all concerned. (p. 28)

An undergraduate minor in dance was added in 1958. It was not until 1973 before a new dance specialization, a bachelor of arts degree with teaching and nonteaching degree plans, was offered.

Professional Connections

Another aspect of Duggan's administrative role dealt with further-ing the relationship between educational dance and professional dance. She continued the university tradition of engaging nationally acclaimed professional dancers and companies to teach workshops and master classes, perform concerts, and present lecture/demonstrations. Most of the pioneers of modern dance participated in one or two of these activi-ties, with some visiting the campus several times. Among those promi-nent early modern dance figures were St. Denis, Shawn, Graham, Hum-phrey, Weidman, Limon, and Holm (Rallis, 1978).

Authorities in other dance forms also made guest appearances on the TWU campus. Two of these well-known personalities in the areas of folk and ethnic dance were Burchenal and La Meri. These few exam-ples from a long list of prestigious artists are intended to give the reader some idea as to the caliber of contacts that thrived between the dance program at TWU and the world of professional dance. Although this exchange between dance communities is common now, it was used spar-ingly in the past by colleges and universities, especially in the Southwest. However, TWU, with funding from the Women's Athletic Association and the Physical Education Department, provided this valuable experi-ence for its students.

Duggan's expertise in both educational and professional dance pro-vided her with the background to develop a rich curriculum in the dance program at TWU, a program that many individuals subsequently used as a model in developing their own dance programs. She fostered dance as a natural part of the university climate. As a direct result of her efforts, professional dancers were engaged as guest artists for various campus activities. Her expertise and fortitude assisted in obtaining fund-ing for the dance activities. Through graduates of the varying degree programs, she supplied educational institutions across the nation with qualified dance personnel.

TRACES OF THE DANCE TEACHER

In addition to being an administrator at TWU, Duggan was a teacher. Although she taught varied subjects within the field of health, physical education, and recreation, the reader is remainded at this point that this study is limited to the dance-related teaching experiences.

A Descriptive View

Duggan was pictured as a careful, thoughtful, and lucid dance teacher. As a very competent dance teacher, she exhibited high integrity and deep involvement. Utilizing her own vitality, she generated enthusiasm among her students.

Duggan's classes were well organized and concise. She was considered extremely demanding; not only did she expect quality work, her students could always expect many reading assignments and lengthy reports. While her expectations for perfection often caused frustration and sometimes even tears, she was still encouraging and inspiring to her students. She never seemed to forget that she was teaching people, not subjects.

Roosevelt, one of Duggan's former students who became a professional colleague and friend, described quite nicely how many individuals felt about Duggan. She was "a teacher for all seasons, . . . (she) laughed with us, disciplined us, made festivals with us, and wept with us" (Roosevelt, speech, April 7, 1973, Denton, Texas).

As a teacher, Duggan tried to instill in her students the importance of dance at all educational levels and for men and women. At the same time, she discouraged participation in physical education and dance to the exclusion of everything else. She (1951) believed:

> strongly in the wholesomeness of all-round development. She encouraged this point of view in her students and tried to practice it herself by combining recreational interests in worthwhile reading, music, art, the theater, travel, et cetera, with those of hiking, swimming, and various games. (p. 27)

Dance Teaching Experiences

During her career at TWU, the courses Nancy taught in dance were varied; these consisted of both on-campus and off-campus offerings. A partial list of dance courses taught by Duggan include the following:

intermediate clogging, elementary natural dancing, intermediate and advanced tap, elementary modern dancing, advanced modern dancing, history and philosophy of dance, and dance appreciation.

Duggan was an innovator of both tap and modern dance. Considering the time when she began her tenure at TWU, and the stage of development of both of these dance forms, it is easy to see why she is considered a pioneer. Clog dancing was becoming tap dance, and modern dance was evolving from natural dance.

In the dance history classes, Duggan was virtually a "walking encyclopedia." Her incredible memory was filled with many personal experiences based on her close associations with many of the pioneer professional modern dancers—Shawn, St. Denis, and Humphrey. Over the years, Duggan and Shawn corresponded frequently. As it was often mentioned in their letters, they shared a special bond because they had the same birthdate, October 20. Another connection they shared was Mary Campbell. Campbell was the accompanist for Shawn and his dance company (Denishawn) at various times from 1928 through 1965. Between 1942 and 1972, she was also an accompanist at TWU for dance classes and the Modern Dance Group.

During the summers, especially from the 1930s through the early 1950s, Duggan frequently taught as guest instructor: five summers at the prestigious Jacob's Pillow Festival and the University of Dance; three visiting professorships at the Teachers College, Columbia University; one short intensive course at the University of Kansas; one session at June Sports Camps in the Pocono Mountains; one session at Geneva Park on Lake Couching in Ontario, Canada; and one short term at the Margaret Eaton School of Dance in Ontario.

In addition to summer teaching, Nancy presented dance classes at various sessions for several different organizational meetings, including the American Association of Health, Physical Education, and Recreation (now the American Alliance, an organization of which she was the youngest female at that time to hold the office of president). Master classes and lecture/demonstrations in conjunction with the Modern Dance Group tours played a large role in Duggan's teaching of dance. Through these efforts, she reached many high school and university students who might otherwise have had little, or no, contact with modern dance.

Several contributions to the development of dance in higher education were made through Duggan's teaching. She advanced dance by developing well-trained dance teachers; she served as their model and mentor. She was able to extend the field by requiring all physical education majors at TWU to take dance classes. Even though these students were not expected to become dancers, it was hoped that this exposure

would help them see the value of dance and also develop their appreciation of dance from the audience's standpoint. She contributed by es-
pousing her philosophy of dance in education, which required dance to
be taught to both sexes at all educational levels. By teaching master
classes and giving lecture/demonstrations, she was responsible for introducing dance to the Southwest.

OUTLINES OF THE SPONSOR

Texas Woman's University was not without a dance group before
Duggan became the director of the Physical Education Department.
However, it was Duggan who was directly responsible for developing
the design for the group that gained a national reputation, the Modern
Dance Group.

In the capacity of sponsor of the Modern Dance Group, Duggan
was described as excellent. Her activities associated with this organization
were considered very well organized. As the group's tour agent, she was
highly efficient.

For the most part, the actual conducting of rehearsals for this group
was handled by assistants. Graduate students who were former members
of the dance group filled this role at first, but during the end of Duggan's
career, a faculty member was assigned this duty.

As was her tradition, Duggan set high standards for this group,
expecting flawless performances at all times. She actually stopped both
informal presentations and concerts when the dancers were not performing according to her expectations; they would have to start again.
In an effort to maintain her standards of excellence, the dancers spent
many long, hard hours learning and polishing the choreographic works.
The dancers often had to relinquish evenings and weekends for practice.

Duggan's high expectations extended beyond the performances; it
reached into the dancer's personal appearance. For instance, a rigid
dress code was enforced until the late 1960s, or even the early 1970s.
This code mandated that the girls, when on tour, wear hats, gloves,
stockings, and high-heel shoes; these items all had to be worn even when
making a rest stop along the road. Duggan herself always traveled fully
prepared with proper dress. Among her many suitcases was always one
that contained full outfits of clothing for any occasion and another that
housed her complete collection of flowers and ribbons for her hair, items
that served as her trademark. It was important to her that she and these
"young ladies" made a good impression whenever they were visible to
the public.

Duggan was forever attempting to broaden the knowledge of those
who toured with this group, taking every opportunity to develop the

"liberally educated individual." When on tour she always tried to enhance the girls' education by telling stories. The Legend of the Dogwood, one of her favorite stories, was always triggered whenever she saw a dogwood tree.

Through the concert performances, Duggan attempted to develop an appreciation of dance in the theater by people at all educational levels. She hoped that increasing the interest and growth of dance would contribute to the audience's cultural experiences. The annual itinerary of the Modern Dance Group always included extensive touring as well as numerous performances before groups at varying types of local, state, and national conventions. One especially noteworthy engagement was at the Jacob's Pillow Dance Festival.

Duggan made several contributions to the development of dance in higher education in her role as the sponsor of the Modern Dance Group. With the help of this group, she advanced dance by educating audiences to accept dance as an art form. She provided the dancers with excellent educational opportunities in the area of dance management. Many of today's dance leaders in colleges and universities across the nation were trained in the Modern Dance Group, which Duggan sponsored.

ETCHINGS OF THE VOICE AND PEN

The Speaker

The amount of evidence found to support Duggan's contributions to dance in education as a speaker was limited. When she did speak, however, she was excellent. Her presentations were considered well organized and well planned. Her vocabulary was most impressive, appropriately technical when addressing learned groups and yet comprehensible when speaking to lay audiences. Whatever the situation, Duggan had excellent rapport with her audiences.

The Author

As an author, Duggan a prolific writer, was considered to be a good stylist. She had the ability to use clear descriptions that made her works understandable and useful. She covered a wide range of subject areas in her writings. While her books on tap dance and folk dancing were written for the beginning dancer, they were also written for teachers of these dance forms. At the time they were published, these books and her articles were considered relevant and much-needed material; their timelessness is obvious because the contents of many are still useful today. As evidence of this, one of the tap-dance books, *The Complete Book of Tap* (1977), has been revised and is currently on the market.

Duggan's own experiences in writing articles and books for publication sharpened her editorial skills. She directed the writing of numerous theses and dissertations, as well as serving on the editorial boards of several professional journals. She was also a contributing editor in the area of folk dancing to the *Encyclopaedia Britannica*.

Although Duggan's total number of works may be limited, that which she did write is considered valuable. This is especially true of her books. Through her writing, Duggan is credited with actively and significantly promoting dance as an educational form and as an art form.

FINISHING TOUCHES

Although petite in stature, Anne Schley Duggan stands tall among those pioneers whose efforts contributed to the development of dance in higher education. Through her administrative work, a unique model for dance programs was built. As a teacher, her philosophical beliefs, as well as a wealth of personal experiences related to the world of dance, were shared with many individuals who are today's dance teachers. Dance as an art form was vigorously promoted by this energetic, red-headed female. Students and teachers of dance, past and present, have benefited from her writings. As a result of her numerous endeavors, she has left a positive mark on the development of dance in the American college and university, thus supporting the hypothesis that Anne Schley Duggan was influential in advancing dance to its present status in American higher education.

REFERENCES

Duggan, A. S. (1951). The place of dance in the school physical education program. *Journal of Health, Physical Education, and Recreation, 22*, 26–29.

Duggan, A. S. (1977). *The complete tap dance book* (rev. ed. with M. E. Tripplett). Washington, DC: University of America.

Gunnell, R. J. (1973). Biographies of outstanding leaders in health, physical education, and recreation (Doctoral dissertation, Brigham Young University, 1973). *Dissertation Abstracts International, 34*, 605A.

Rallis, K. E. (1978). *Appearances of professional dance artists at the Texas Woman's University, Denton, Texas, between 1926 and 1977*. Unpublished master's thesis, Texas Woman's University, Denton, TX.

Weeks, S. R. (1980). Anne Schley Duggan: Portrait of a dance educator (Doctoral dissertation, Texas Woman's University, 1980). *Dissertation Abstracts International, 41*, 2011A.

APPENDIX A
QUESTIONNAIRE AND INTERVIEW QUESTIONS FOR
RELATIVES AND/OR FAMILY FRIENDS

1. Please indicate Anne Schley Duggan's date and place of birth.

2. Describe any of the following as they might apply to Anne Schley Duggan as a young girl: appearance, grooming, behavior patterns, temper tantrums, and member of "a gang."

3. Did she undertake projects which were meaningful? Were these projects always completed?

4. Describe the types of companionship she sought as she was growing up. Did she seek out peers or did she prefer older companions and/or being alone?

5. What were her specific interests and/or hobbies?

6. To what extent or degree did she pursue these interests?

7. Describe any details pertaining to dance training which she had while growing up, i.e., teachers' names, studio names and/or locations, types of dance studied, and years of study.

8. Was she studious in nature, always maintaining a high grade or scholastic average?

9. What type of literature did she prefer for leisure reading?

10. Did she have specific ambitions with respect to "What she wanted to be" when she grew up? What were these expressed ambitions at different stages in her childhood?

11. Who were the individuals comprising the Duggan household during this period? Describe the home environment.

12. Who were the individuals who may have influenced the development of her special interests and characteristics?

13. Did she like to discuss her ideas and experiences with others? With whom?

14. Do you have any stories, anecdotes, or events illustrative of her personality traits and interests as a child? (Please recall as many as you can.)

15. What is your favorite story about Anne Schley Duggan?

APPENDIX B
QUESTIONNAIRE AND INTERVIEW QUESTIONS FOR FORMER
TEXAS WOMAN'S UNIVERSITY COLLEAGUES AND/OR
FRIENDS

1. Under what circumstances were you associated with Anne Schley Duggan?

2. What is your favorite story about her?

3. Do you know any stories, anecdotes, or events illustrative of her personality traits and interests?

4. What were her specific interests and/or hobbies? To what extent did she pursue these?

5. Do you know when and/or how she became interested in dance?

6. Describe any knowledge you have pertaining to Anne Schley Duggan's dance training in private or educational settings, i.e., teachers' names, studio names and/or locations, and length of study.

7. Did she exert any influence upon the direction of your professional career or upon the professional career of others of your acquaintance? Describe.

8. Please give highlights of special places which you visited together.

9. What words do you find descriptive of Duggan
    a. as a teacher of dance in higher education?
    b. as an administrator?
    c. as an author?
    d. as an individual?
    e. as a performer of dance?
    f. as a choreographer?
    g. as the sponsor of the Modern Dance Group?

10. What was her apparent philosophy
    a. guiding relationships with students and performers of the Modern Dance Group?
    b. of life?

11. What do you consider the major contributions of Anne Schley Duggan
    a. as a teacher?
    b. as an administrator?
    c. as an author?
    d. as a speaker?
    e. as the sponsor of the Modern Dance Group?

12. What were her contributions to the development of dance in higher education in general?

13. What was her role in the development of programs of dance at the TWU in Denton, Texas?

14. What, if any, significant change occurred as she grew and developed as a dance educator?

15. Describe any important achievements or influences in Anne Schley Duggan's life with which you are familiar.

16. Describe any honors or special recognition received by her of which you are aware.

17. What were her expressed reasons for teaching at the TWU?

18. Who were the specific individuals who may have influenced her? How did they influence her?

19. Did she always undertake projects which were purposeful in nature? Did she always complete them?

20. Did she like to discuss her ideas and experiences with others? With whom?

21. Were there any major disappointments or outstanding events in her life during the period with which you are familiar?

22. What specific evidence can you cite to illustrate the breadth of her scope and vision with respect to dance in American higher education?

2

A LOOK AT DANCE IN HIGHER EDUCATION IN THE 1920S, 1940S, AND 1986–87

Christalia O. Volaitis

This paper examines dance in higher education in the 1920s, 1940s, and 1986–87, through a survey of three American universities. I selected these periods in view of noting significant change rather than gradual growth. I chose Teachers College, Columbia University, New York (TC), University of Wisconsin, Madison (UWi), and University of California, Los Angeles (UCLA), for their locations across the United States, and because previous studies in the history of dance in education had often brought them to my attention. I wondered how there could have been uniform developments in a country so large and diverse. The data has therefore been compiled from the bulletins, catalogues, and announcements published by each institution for the years examined, as I was interested in obtaining a more detailed view of the dance in higher education. Observations include the nature and evolution of dance courses, the effects of World War II on the dance programs, the influence of key individuals in disseminating ideas and establishing the orientation of each institution's programs, and a look at each of these school's dance programs in the 1986–87 academic year.

THE 1920S

During the 1920s, dance classes in American colleges and universities were offered through the departments of physical education, generally requiring of the physical education major courses in gymnastics (general, Danish, natural/corrective, therapeutic, or individual); kinesiology; recreation; sports; physiology; games and athletics; and methods and supervision. Dance classes, though segregated for women and men, were characterized by their social nature, that is, folk, national, and social dancing. Natural, interpretive, or aesthetic dance; tap, clogging, or classical; and theory of the dance were the more specialized offerings. The generalities end here.

Teachers College was notable at this time as a hotbed of experimentation and innovation, promoting a learner-oriented, experiential approach reflecting John Dewey's influence. Dr. Thomas Wood was in attendance as college physician and professor of physical education, and it was he who encouraged Gertrude Colby to develop her seminal ideas in the teaching of dance as a creative art. She did so, implementing an unusual selection of courses that highlighted collaborations between the School of Practical Arts and the School of Education. For example, she cotaught "Dramatic Expression in Physical Education" with Madame Alberti, a course that aimed to promote "understanding . . . and appreciation of the art side in Physical Education and the relation it bears to the sister arts Music and Literature" (1920–21, p. 65). Other unique combinations characterized the era, in courses such as *Games, Folk Dancing, and Corrective Gymnastics.* Miss Agnes Burke taught *Dramatic Arts, Plays, Games and Dances of Early Childhood* "from the genetic standpoint beginning with the early instinctive activities from which these originate, tracing their development . . . into the more highly organized and artistic forms" (1920–21, p. 65). Helen Frost and Mary O'Donnell were instructors, the latter teaching *Dances Suitable for Boys* in addition to folk and national dancing (Summer, 1920). The latter two courses provided instruction not only in the forms themselves, but in rhythm, evolution of dance, history, music, interpretation, and composition (1920–21, p. 118).

In the mid-1920s, Marjorie Hillas cotaught *Natural Gymnastics and Dancing for Men* with Mr. Brace (1924–25, p. 82). By this time, Colby's course *Natural Dancing* had been integrated into the curriculum. It was "based upon full and natural movements," offered the "opportunity for music interpretation and pantomimic dancing," and was required for participation in festival and pageant performances (1924–25, p. 82). By the end of the decade, she had seen the need for and added *Problems in Natural Dancing* to the curriculum. It was not described. *Theory of the Dance,* whose content seems to have branched out from the folk and national dance classes, evolved into a study integrating "all rhythmic expression" in its relation to physical education, to education in general, as art, in relation to other arts, and its sociocultural, anthropological significance (1928–29, p. 159). Mabel Ellsworth Todd introduced *Basic Principles of Posture,* broadening the scientific dimension of the curriculum.

Meanwhile, dance in higher education at the University of Wisconsin, Madison, was firmly established as a quality program by the end of the decade. Under the guidance of Blanche Trilling, director of the Women's Gymnasium, one could choose from this selection of dance classes: *Singing Games and Folk Dancing for Elementary Schools; Folk Dancing for Secondary Schools; Theory and Technique of Dancing; Technique of Elementary and Advanced Folk Dancing;* and three levels of *Interpretive Dancing* (Summer, 1924, p. 103). This latter resembled Colby's *Natural Dancing* but excluded the emphasis on festival and pageantry, which was here offered separately. This signals a departure in the teaching of dance as an expressive medium, rather than as attached to performance of a specific nature, although it did remain contingent upon music. Margaret H'Doubler, who had studied with Colby and others in New York, initiated many important changes in this program. While still offering the same dance courses as the previous year, out-of department courses became requirements for the specialty in dance, and included *Dramatic Expression and Production* (Drama); either *Human Traits, Aesthetics,* or *Psychology of Emotions* (Psychology); *Man and Nature* (Philosophy.); *Man and Nature* (Philosophy); and *Appreciation of Music* (1925–26, p. 205). By the end of the 1920s, the first American dance major had been instituted at UWi, and H'Doubler had expanded the program to include *Rhythmic Form and Analysis I & II; Theory of the dance; Dance Composition* (the first among the three universities); and *Seminary* [*sic*] *in Dance Drama,* all of which she taught. *Folk Dancing* and *Festival and Pageant Movements* were still offered. She also established the Orchesis group, described as an "advanced dancing class to give opportunity to go beyond required class work" (1928–29, p. 99). It is striking how sophisticated the program quickly defined itself to be, as she saw the need for, and addressed the needs of, dance specialists.

In contrast to these dynamic contemporaries, the dance program at UCLA in the 1920s under Genevieve Kelso featured *Folk Dancing for Schools and Playgrounds;* three levels of *Aesthetic Dancing; Rhythmic Gymnastics* and *Social Dancing* (1920–21, p. 117). Its unique course was *Dalcroze Eurythmics,* in *Analysis of Posture and Movement,* and in *Pantomimic Expression* (Summer, 1921, p. 116). A paragraph describes in charming detail the special costume required of the women, which was designed by Miss Kelso "to insure the proper color effects in development of dance productions" (Summer, 1921, p. 10). By the middle of the decade, *Natural Dancing* had replaced *Aesthetic* (there is, unfortunately, no descriptions of either). *Clog* and *Theory of Dancing with Practice Teaching* were also offered, taught by Ruth Atkinson and Lucile Grunewald (1925–26, p. 155). The end of the decade showed that Martha B. Deane, who had studied with Colby at Teachers College, had joined the dance faculty; other courses were *Folk; Natural; Theory; Dancing and Pageantry; Character; Games and Rhythms for Elementary Schools;* and *Methods and Character,* the lecture, practice, and study of festival and pageant (1928–29, p. 152).

In summary, the training of teachers highlighted UWi's liberal-arts-oriented program under H'Doubler; experimentation and collaboration characterized Colby's era at TC; and festival, pageantry, and social forms provided UCLA's orientation at this time.

THE 1940'S

The dance program at Teachers College under the direction of Mary O'Donnell numbered fewer courses than in the 1920's, and were distilled into the areas of social dance, specialized classes for teachers, and a shifting range of physical education courses. Classes were no longer segregated for men and women, and included: *Elementary Modern Dance,* consisting of movement and rhythmic components; *Advanced Modern Dance,* theory and practice of teaching; *Dance for Young Children,* stressing traditional and creative aspects of movement and rhythm fundamentals (1941, p. 212); *Arts in Education and Life,* cotaught by Rugg, Mursell, Faulkner, and O'Donnell; and *Survey of Modern Dance for Men and Women,* a course in theory, technique, composition, percussion, accompaniment, and eurythmics, with Elsa Findlay, F. Boas, Doris Humphrey, Charles Weidman, Louis Horst, Mary O'Donnell, and others (1941, p. 213). A new era for dance in education had begun, which brought the professional performing artist to TC as part of its academic-year faculty, in addition to offering the first "modern dance" as such.

By the summer of 1945, military science had become a branch of the Physical Education department, but dance courses continued unabated. *Social and Folk Dance; Elementary and Intermediate Modern Dance* geared to teachers of children; *Accompaniment for Dance; Music for Teachers of Physical Education; Teaching of modern dance;* and *Theory of modern dance*—lectures and discussion of the place of modern dance, its purposes, content, history, and relation to other arts—were listed (Summer, 1945, p. 157–58). Teachers College, while still in the vanguard with such courses as the *Survey of Modern Dance* and the philosophically oriented *Arts in Education and Life,* settled more into aspects of teaching, rather than the exploration, and experimentation of the 1920s.

The end of the decade showed a dramatic reduction in dance offerings: *Elementary Modern Dance; Modern Dance: A tool for Physical Conditioning; Modern Dance for High and elementary Schools; Accompaniment;* and *Folk and Social Dance* were the remnants of the program (1947–48, p. 174).

In 1939–40 the University of Wisconsin catalogue (p. 431) stated that the "demand for teachers who have been trained especially for this field must be recognized." And it was, in this program, which included Orchesis and *Practice in Dancing. Rhythm and Elementary Dance Forms* subsumed previous classes in tap, singing games, and folk dances for younger grades, and required the study of one country's history, art, music, and folklore, in addition to a demonstration of class and original work in clog and tap; *Advanced Forms of Folk Dance; Rhythmic Analysis I & II; Accompaniment for Contemporary Dance I & II* and *Dance Composition:* approaches to content in dance at different age levels. *Theory and Philosophy of Dance* emerged as the study of the "classification of true meaning of dance, its justification as an educational and creative art medium, its place in the school curriculum, a theory of art technique . . . dance in a changing world." *Thesis Course in Dance* was a historical survey of the cultural background of dance in various civilizations with special emphasis on relation of social structure to the existing dance forms (1939–40, p. 451). The content for these latter two courses seems to have derived from the folk, pageantry, and national dance classes of the '20s called *Theory of the Dance,* which examined the sources from which the dances arose. Last is *Seminary [sic] in Dance Drama,* the study of problems of program building and production, with experience in composition, casting, direction, and cost, as well as problems of publicity and expense (1939–40, p. 452).

The 1942–44 catalogue shows that the required hours for physical education had dropped from 5 to 2 hours weekly (p. 46), and that 5 academic years were recommended for the dance major due to the heavy activity program and the need for other related subjects (p. 295). *Modern Dance* and *Integrating Course in Dance II* had been added to the curriculum, and the *Seminary in Dance Drama* became *Seminar in Dance Production* (p. 295).

Contrary to the diminished course offerings at TC by the end of the decade, UWi under Marie Carns, chair, and H'Doubler, director, showed continued evolution and increase in kind of courses offered. *Dance Technique for Majors; Movement and Its Rhythmic Structure—Kinesthesia; Dance Accompaniment (Perc), Improvisation and Composition; Dance Accompaniment (Music), Improvisation for Dance Technique; Teaching Rhythms of Dance to Children; Foundations of Motor Skill;* and *Dance Seminar* were offered, as well as kinesiology, relaxation, thesis, theory, practice, technique, and composition courses (1948–50, pp. 311–15). Louise Kloepper (Wigman trained) and Mary Hinkson (Graham trained) had joined H'Doubler's staff of dance instructors, bringing their professional experience to bear upon a program that combined theoretical aspects with rhythmic, technical, and scientific studies in dance and dance teaching.

Changes in the nature of dance classes were also in evidence at UCLA during the 1940s. The "Group Major in Dance" did not "intend to train professional dancers, but to offer those interested a program of study in contributing fields" (1941–42, p. 97). John Bovard was chair, and Martha Deane continued as director, establishing a program of liberal arts studies around the hub of dance, similar to that instituted by H'Doubler at UWi in the late 1920s. The dance courses listed were: *Character; Dance Fundamentals; Folk; Social; Dancing for Elementary School; Professional Activities (Women) I*, the fundamental rhythmic activities necessary for teaching on secondary and college levels, and music analysis for dance; *Folk Festivals I & II; Dance Composition Workshop; Dance Recital*, the development of dances for a recital program; *History of Dance in America; Organization of Dance; Principles of Teaching Dance*; and *Practice in Dance* (pp. 242–44). Courses in physical education, English, psychology, and philosophy "as related to dance" were required for this broader orientation.

The summer of 1945 catalogue lists *Rhythmic Expression in Elementary School* and *Principles of Teaching Dance*, the analysis of materials and methods of Dalcroze Eurythmics (p. 48). Elsa Findlay, formerly instructor at Vassar and at Teachers College, had joined the staff at UCLA. In 1948–49, the Group Major became "Curriculum in Dance" (p. 129) and consisted of: four courses with rhythmic or musical bases, most of the above, excluding character and social dance, and the addition of *Comparative Study of Materials and Methods in Dance II*, a study of educational ideas and practices as they relate to the various forms of dance (pp. 311–15). By this time, Pia Gilbert had joined Martha Deane's dance faculty.

The general trend of the 1940s indicated specialization toward training teachers of dance. Growth and expansion characterized UCLA and UWi, while a remarkable reduction occurred at TC. The nature of the courses reflected a growing liberal arts orientation with dance as the core of study, with physical education requirements to be met. While professional performing artists were introduced and entered more into the scheme of dance in higher education, the training of teachers was essential to all. By the end of the decade, TC and UWi both had classes called *Modern Dance*, and the concept of "technique" seems to have emerged as a specific concern. All three schools offered composition and history of the dance. Opportunities to create and perform works were encouraged, though least at TC, perhaps due to its location in New York City, which itself provided a stage for those who desired.

1986–87

The 1986–87 catalogue of Teachers College depicts a time of transition for the dance program, one of three branches of the Department of the Arts in Education. Under the direction since 1985 of Nancy

BrooksSchmitz, the dance program, which offers the M.A. (and has since added interdisciplinary M.Ed. and Ed.D. degrees), is being fine-tuned to perfect its single focus as a program in dance education. While it may lack in variety and quantity what UCLA and UWi currently offer, the TC programs in dance and dance education uniquely highlight the concerns of the fine artist in the academic environment, and explore in depth the methods, philosophies, and history of the dance in education (p. 252). The core curriculum includes: *Methods of Teaching Dance; Performance Techniques; Dancer/Artist in Education; Anatomical Analysis of Ballet and Modern Dance;* and *Seminar in Dance Education.* Other courses may be chosen from *Laban Movement Analysis I & II; Choreographic Problems; Rhythmic Structure of Music and Dance; Music for Dance; Movement Concepts in Modern Dance; Choreography;* and *Creative Movement/Drama in the Classroom* (pp. 253–54). Out-of-department requirements contribute to the integrity of the program according to the interests and needs of the individual. Performance, choreographic, and production opportunities are available in the form of the final project, and in the city of New York as the nation's dance capital. Students are encouraged to explore the city's resources, and may teach in a variety of educational milieus. Technique/creative courses for the nonmajor are offered each semester, and numerous noncredit dance classes are offered to the community, both children and adults.

The 1986 dance program at UWi, headed by coordinator Mary Alice Brennan, remained part of the physical education department, while both the TC and UCLA dance programs are now to be found in arts departments. This, however, has not inhibited it from growing into a well-rounded program able to offer its students a choice of degree programs. UWi offers a B.S. in dance, and requires that students arrive with previous training, helping to ensure their readiness for concentrations in Dance Education, Performance/Choreography, or Pre-Dance Therapy. Other degrees offered from among a broad range of courses are the M.S. or M.A. in physical education with a concentration in dance; M.F.A., major in dance, and Ph.D., major in Physical Education (1986, p. 61–63). Requirements include studies in anatomy/kinesiology, physiology, social studies, and humanities, and courses in rhythmic and musical analysis, history, practice in dance, student teaching, and in the teaching of children and adults. Like TC and UCLA, UWi has implemented studies in the work of Rudolph von Laban. Ballet has been added to the technical work, and the folk and square-dance classes continue to be taught. *Dance Performance Workshop, Dance: An Introductory Survey, Theory and Fundamentals of Movement,* and *Introduction to Dance Composition through Improvisation* are among the core courses.

The dance program of the College of Fine Arts at UCLA under Director Pia Gilbert offers B.A. and M.A. degrees in four areas of concentration: choreography/performance, dance ethnology, dance education, and dance therapy (p. 315). Technique classes include modern dance and ballet, as well as ethnic dance from Asia, Africa, the Balkans, American Indian culture, Mexico, Israel, and other European countries. Courses in rhythm, accompaniment, and history abound, enhanced by work in improvisation, choreography, philosophy, research, Laban theories and analysis, aesthetics, anthropology, theater, physical sciences, design, English, art history, and the humanities. This range of progress also reflects the influence of Dr. Alma Hawkins, professor Emeritus, who developed UCLA's program from 1953 to 1974, according to the needs of the times for not only specially trained teachers of the dance, but choreographers, performers, therapists, and ethnologists. UCLA can boast a fine and diverse program of study in the widening field of dance, dedicated to "combining professional training with the liberal study essential to the development of each dancer's own creative potential" (p. 315).

CONCLUSION

I expected to find greater uniformity in dance-program offerings within each time period than the facts indicated, noting, rather, certain trends and concurrence with enough differences to characterize the essential orientation of each institution as unique. Today, each program maintains the identity seminally established early in the century, while reflecting growth and expansion. I had also anticipated that World War II would have had a pervasively negative impact upon dance programs throughout the United States in the 1940s. I found that only Teachers College manifested a dramatic reduction in dance-course offerings at the end of the decade.

The path of communication among dance educators and the changes instigated by particular individuals as their careers took them across the country was significant, for the essence of each program seems to have been determined by the efforts of one key individual who initiated basic philosophical and practical lineages. Specifically, Colby and O'Donnell set the stage for the dance program at Teachers College. Alma Hawkins, who completed both her M.A. and Ed.D. at Teachers College, taught in the Midwest, then moved to UCLA. Margaret H'Doubler taught and studied at Teachers College, interacted with Gertrude Colby in New York at a critical time in her development as a dance educator, then returned to UWi. Martha Deane also studied with Colby, and Elsa Findlay taught at Teachers College, both before going west to UCLA. Closely tracing the influence of these and other instructors could lead to further enlightenment with regard to each era, and to the subsequent evolution of each current program. A search for the texts or any written course material could be equally revealing.

There has been tremendous growth in the field of dance itself, as these 20- and 46-year periods illustrate. Today's students may choose from several areas of specialization, enriching their dance studies with a wealth of liberal arts and administrative courses. The dance programs at Teachers College focus on the dance in education, geared to the training of professional dance artist/educators. UWi and UCLA are able to offer concentrations in dance education, performance/choreography, and dance therapy, while UCLA features a unique specialty in dance ethnology as well. Among other things, these distant and different institutions share a commitment to the growth of the individual, and the belief that dance belongs to the highest quality human experience in the education and training of students.

REFERENCES

School of Education, School of Practical Arts Announcement. (1920–21). New York: Teachers College, Columbia University.

Bulletin, Southern Branch, (1920–21). University of California. Fourth Series, vol. 2, no. 1.

Summer Catalogue. (1924). Madison, WI: University of Wisconsin.

School of Education, School of Practical Arts Announcement. (1924–25). New York: Teachers College, Columbia University.

Announcement. (1925–26). University of California, Southern Branch.

Bulletin. (1925–26). Madison, WI: University of Wisconsin.

Announcement. (1926–27). University of California, Southern Branch.

Announcement of Courses General Series No. 1366, 1928–29. (May 1929). Madison, WI: University of Wisconsin, serial no. 1592.

School of Education, School of Practical Arts Announcements. (1928–29). New York: Teachers College, Columbia University.

Bulletin/Announcement. (1928–29). University of California, Los Angeles. Third Series, vol. 22, no. 4.

Announcement of Courses General Series No. 2197, 1939–40. (August 1939). Madison, WI: University of Wisconsin, serial no. 2413.

Announcement of Teachers College, Columbia University. (1941–42). New York: Teachers College, Columbia University.

Bulletin/General Catalogue. (1941–42). University of California, Los Angeles, vol. 35, no. 9.

Announcement of Courses General Series No. 2392, 1942–44. (August 1942). Madison, WI: University of Wisconsin, catalog serial no. 2608.

Bulletin/Announcement Spring and Summer. (1944). University of California, Los Angeles, vol. 37, no. 14.

Summer Catalogue. (1945). New York: Teachers College, Columbia University.
Bulletin/Summer Session (1945). University of California, Los Angeles, vol. 38, no.
    14.
Announcement of Teachers College, Columbia University. (1947–48). New York:
    Teachers College, Columbia University.
Bulletin/General Catalogue Fall and Spring. (1948–49). University of California,
    Los Angeles, vol. 43, no. 1.
Announcement of Courses General Series No. 2898, 1948–50. (September 1949).
    Madison, WI: University of Wisconsin, catalog serial no. 3124.
Announcement of Courses. (1986–87). Madison, WI: University of Wisconsin.
Bulletin Series 77, 1986/1987. (April 1986). New York: Teachers College, Colum-
    bia University.
Catalogue. (1986–87). University of California, Los Angeles.

3

INFLUENCES AFFECTING K-8 DANCE EDUCATION IN THE UNITED STATES: 1950–1980

Nancy BrooksSchmitz

This research surveys major influences affecting K-8 dance education in the United States from 1950 through 1980. It traces the influence during the 1950s of the National Dance Association and Laban-based movement education programs. It notes the influence of specialized degree programs focusing on dance performance and the more recent alliance with the other arts (music, visual arts, and theater). It identifies the major funding sources and arts programs involving dance (Arts i Education Program, CEMREL, IMPACT, AIS) during the 1960s and 1970s. Finally, the study suggests that dance educators must become knowledgeable about political framework of the arts in order to make dance education and education through dance a viable part of the elementary school program.

The focus of this study is to survey major influences affecting K–8 dance education in the United States from 1950 to 1980. It notes significant programs and resources that developed as manifestations of these influences.

Prior to the mid-1960s the spread of dance education occurred mainly through the efforts of the National Section on Dance, which later became the National Dance Association. This organization, formed in the 1930s as part of the American Association for Health, Physical Education and Recreation (HPER), later became the American Alliance for Health, Physical Education and Recreation. The founding of this group helped to provide an important national professional interchange between dance educators in the field and perspective dance educators in training institutions. The National Section on Dance provided an important support network enabling dance educators to share ideas via publications, meetings, and workshops. During the 1950s the organization became an advocate for improved opportunities for dance within the educational environment and for more thorough and comprehensive teacher education programs in dance.

During the decade following World War II an interest developed in the physical fitness of our youth. This filtered down to the elementary schools and provided an impetus for developing programs especially for this age group. Increasingly, physical education specialists with specific training for the elementary population taught these programs.

This interest led the AAHPER and the Dance Section to discussions of appropriate teaching methods, materials, the relationship of physical education to general education, and the role of the dance specialist within the school framework. Prominent leaders in physical education and dance, including Margaret H'Doubler, Martha Meyers, Delia Hussey, and Elsa Scheider of the U.S. Office of Education, agreed that there was a need in the elementary physical education program for creative exploration of movement and teaching in a guidance style. As a result of study visits to England during 1954 and 1955, Elizabeth Halsey and Freda Miller helped introduce new ideas and methods of elementary physical education into the United States (Chapman, 1974).

In conjunction with the English Ministry of Education, Halsey helped plan the Anglo-American Workshop on Elementary School Physical Education, which took place June 24–July 13, 1956. A group of 15 American educators viewed children's classes and participated in workshops in physical education based on Rudolf Laban's theories for modern educational dance. The materials and methods, observed by the American educators, did not aim at artistic perfection or performance. Instead, it focused on establishing a sense of individual harmony, integrating emotional, spiritual, physical, and intellectual aspects of the individual, developing creativity, and developing expression and communication through movement (Laban, 1975). The methodology espoused a child-centered, teacher-guided exploration of movement using problem-solving strategies maintaining a balance between freedom and discipline (Hussey & Murray, November 1956).

The American educators brought Laban's ideas and those of his protégé, Lisa Ullman, back to the United States. They hoped that similar programs might be established as the primary focus of physical education. In actuality,

> the subsequent growth of movement education in the United States was dependent upon the time, energy, and inclination of individual educators to spread its concepts and implementation. (Chapman, 1974, p. 134)

The result created a mixed bag of teacher preparation and instruction in physical education and specifically in dance. There was no specific adherence to particular content or methodology. Dance instruction around the country included methods and content derived from Laban or the more autocratic studio style.

Some of the problems encountered centered on the United States school political framework in which individual states and/or school systems set their own curricula, standards, and criteria for the quality of instructors that they employed. A split between dance education and physical education programs also contributed to the problem. This split occurred at a time when cooperation might have proved most positive for dance/movement in the elementary and secondary schools. It occurred because of an increasing desire on the part of dance educators, particularly those with professional performance backgrounds, to see dance established as a separate discipline within college and university structures. This entailed either establishing dance programs as separate departments under the physical education and health framework or to realign with fine arts programs in some configuration. This change in teacher preparation changed the framework in which dance appeared within the K–8 school setting.

Today, as a result of this trend, dance typically can be found in the K–8 school as an aspect of the physical education program taught either by a physical education teacher or by a classroom teacher; as a separate subject area taught by a specialist; as part of a fine-arts program taught by a fine-arts specialist or classroom teacher; or as part of a comprehensive or integrated arts or aesthetic education program taught by a combination of classroom teachers, arts specialists, and practicing professional artists.

With the success of *Sputnik* in 1957, educators, politicians, and parents suddenly took a look at the education system and reordered priorities so that science programs took a precedence over movement education, the arts, and the humanities. The passage of the National Defense Education Act provided huge sums of federal money to educational institutions to upgrade their science programs. Interestingly, the precedence that this funding set—government funding for perceived deficits in the educational system—positively affected access to dance education in the mid-1960s (Arts, Education and Americans Panel, 1977).

As college and university dance programs moved further away from the mainstream of physical education or severed their ties completely, certification of graduates to teach dance in the schools became an issue. This came at a time when college and university dance programs had the capability to prepare better qualified dance educators than previously. Unfortunately, movements to get separate dance certification often failed because of poorly timed, poorly articulated, and inadequately documented proposals to state accreditating boards. Grass-roots support appeared to be severely lacking. Certification efforts also failed because the timing of the applications corresponded to various movements for "back to basics" in education, which focused public attention away from perceived frills. Additionally, states that granted certification for students graduating from dance emphasis programs housed in physical education departments did not normally transfer this certification to the independent or newly aligned dance programs. With the dance programs outside the administrative unit of physical education departments, fewer PE majors took dance or dance education courses. As fewer opportunities existed for dance education employment in the school setting, dance programs in higher education ceased preparing students for the special needs of this population and setting. Dance became a smaller and smaller aspect within physical education as fewer PE majors emerged from colleges with dance interest or skills.

In 1960 a new interest in the arts began to emerge nationally. This trend interested major foundations who had provided research funds to education during the 1940s and 1950s. Private-sector dollars began to flow into individual art areas and also into arts in education, a relatively new concept in relating the arts to each other and to the general education curriculum. Soon after private dollars began underwriting arts research and programming, local governments and the federal government began to fund arts programs. The position of dance in alliance with the other art forms allowed it to benefit from this funding.

The Kennedy administration brought strong support for the arts in education (John F. Kennedy, 1962). As a result, a Cultural Affairs Branch (later renamed the Arts and Humanity Program) was added to the Office of Education in 1962. Its purpose included developing ". . . programs and activities aimed at improving arts education at all educational levels" (Arts, Education and Americans Panel, 1977, p. 219). The establishment of this branch indicated the growing support for arts in education by the federal government.

The 1963 Heckscher report, *The Arts and the National Government* recommended that

> further consideration be given to increasing the share of the Federal Government's support to education which is concerned with the arts and the humanities. This should include the same type of across-the-board assistance now given to modern languages, mathematics and science. (Arts, Education and Americans Panel, 1977, p. 218)

Federal funding for arts education began indirectly in 1965 with the passage of the Elementary and Secondary Education Act (ESEA) with a mandate to assist local and state education agencies in the development

of programs to aid disadvantaged children (Title I); to assist development of innovative educational programs (Title III); and to support
education research (Title IV). Arts and humanities programs were specifically included for the first time—if local or state agencies included
them in their proposals (Arts, Education and Americans Panel, 1977;
Bloom & Eddy, 1980).

Eventually the Arts and Humanities program assumed the administration of the Title IV funds for research and development in the arts
and education. Another program, the Emergency School Aid: Special
Arts Project, provided funds for development of special projects in the
arts in areas of multiracial and multicultural populations to help children
appreciate arts and encourage creativity (Imel, 1977).

A second piece of legislation, known as the Arts and Humanities
Act of 1965, created the National Endowments for the Arts and the
Humanities. The Endowment for the Arts set as its general goals the
development of a larger, more informed audience, decentralization of
the arts, encouragement and support of state arts agencies, stimulation
of private sector giving to the arts, federal grants to the arts, and provision of inservice and preservice teacher training (*New Dimensions for the
Arts*, 1973).

Private foundation giving to the arts and to arts education increased
during this period. Most notedly from 1967 through 1979, the Arts in
Education Program of the JDR 3rd Fund focused on discovering and
refining ". . . a process for making all the arts integral to the general, or
basic, education of all children in entire schools and systems" (Bloom &
Eddy, 1980, p. xi). The Arts in Education Program began with a premise
that the arts are important to all. It included music, art, theater, and
dance. It advocated involvement of local artists and arts organizations
as resources. Selection of pilot programs could include newly developed
programs or those already begun. Criteria for pilot programs included
evaluation of the likelihood for success, support, and replication of the
program. Requirements for funding of the project included establishing
parity of the arts with other subjects in the curriculum and a strong
commitment of local resources and interest. Each of the pilot cites, the
School District of University City, Missouri; The Arts and the School—A
Program for Integrating the Arts in an Elementary School at Public
School 51 in New York City and Developing Arts Leadership Teams,
both designed by Bank Street College; and the Integrated Arts Program
at Mineola Public Schools, Mineola, Long Island, received a commitment
of long-term support from the JDR 3rd Fund (Bloom, 1974; Bloom &
Eddy, 1980).

Because of differences in resources and setting, each project site
developed uniquely. They each collected data regarding ". . . essential

ingredients of an arts in general education program, and a variety of procedures that could be used by school systems in developing and implementing such programs" (Bloom, 1980, p. 13). Replication programs began in 1970 in Jefferson County (Colorado) School District, Ridgewood (New Jersey) Public Schools, and the Creative Education Program in Oklahoma City, including the Opening Doors program. The JDR 3rd Fund also provided funding for the New York City AGE (Arts in General Education) program, which became a prototype for expansion to Seattle, Minneapolis, Little Rock, Winston-Salem, and Hartford (Bloom, 1974; Eddy, 1978; Fineberg, 1976; *The Arts in Education,* 1975–1976; W. Kennedy, 1976)

Recognizing the need for advocacy and the sharing of information, the Arts in Education Program linked sites by formation of the League of Cities for the Arts in Education. Another network, the Ad Hoc Coalition, linked state departments of education serving Arizona, California, Indiana, Massachusetts, Michigan, New York, Oklahoma, Pennsylvania, and Washington (Bloom & Eddy, 1980; Remer, 1977).

Numerous other projects received partial funding during this period. CEMREL (Central Midwestern Regional Educational Laboratory) became one of the most important of these (Bloom & Eddy, 1980). The JDR 3rd Fund provided partial funding for CEMREL to develop an aesthetic education program providing teaching material for classroom use by teachers with little or no background in the arts. CEMREL, formed in 1965, received initial support through the United States Office of Education to ". . . improve the quality of education for the nation's children through working cooperatively with many educational agencies to bridge the gap between sound educational practices and actual school practices" (Madeja, 1977, p. xiii). Later the newly established National Institute for Education provided funding for the project.

In 1967, CEMREL began to develop their aesthetic education program for use in kindergarten through grade 6 using a multimedia approach to instruction. The CEMREL program provided curriculum materials that could be flexibly structured to allow local sites and teachers to adapt it to their needs and provided teacher education to facilitate program adoption and follow through. CEMREL's Aesthetic Education Program utilized artist/educators to develop curriculum design and content. Virgina Tanner, noted Salt Lake City dance educator, assisted CEMREL as consultant for the dance activities. The Aesthetic Education Program complemented arts programs currently in place within the school setting. Interchangeable arts forms, styles, and historical periods demonstrate that ". . . all the arts are potential sources of aesthetic experience" (Madeja, 1977, p. xvi). Various views and approaches to aesthetic qualities, creative process, and aesthetic response are presented. University City, St. Louis, and numerous other Missouri school districts helped to pilot the resulting curriculum. Additionally, CEMREL directed advocacy efforts as to the importance of the arts in education in order to build grass roots support for aesthetic education (Bloom & Eddy, 1980; Madeja, 1977; Reinhart & Kerr, 1978).

In 1976, CEMREL established 11 Aesthetic Education Learning Centers for teacher education. One of these, the National Aesthetic Education Learning Center, opened at the Kennedy Center for the Performing Arts. By creating demonstration sites in local school districts, materials could be tested and the program observed by teachers and administrators contemplating initiating similar programs within their schools (Bloom & Eddy, 1980).

The United States Office of Education provided grants of $10,000 to $20,000 to state and local education agencies for the development of innovative in-service training, curriculum development, and service delivery modes for arts in education beginning in 1976. Additionally, grants of $50,000 were made available to urban, suburban, and rural settings for 1979–80. These grants developed an interest in arts in education. Some funded projects provided for surveying practices in the arts (*Arts in Education Survey*, 1979). Much of our data concerning the extent of dance within the school setting resulted from these grant outcomes (Bloom & Eddy, 1980).

The Arts IMPACT Program (Interdisciplinary Model Programs in the Arts for Children and Teachers) received funding in 1969 through a $1 million allocation to the Department of Education as part of the Teacher Retraining authorization of the Education Professions Development Act. The project developed as a cooperative effort by representatives from the four major professional organizations serving arts education: the National Dance Association, the National Art Education Association, the National Music Educators Association, and the American Theatre Association. This cooperative group became informally known as DAMT (Dance, Art, Music, and Theatre) (Joel, 1972).

The IMPACT Model had five broad goals: reconstruct the educational program and administrative climate of the school in an effort to achieve parity between the arts and other instructional areas, and between the affective and cognitive learnings provided by the total school program; develop educational programs of high artistic quality in each art area—visual arts, music, dance and theater; conduct in-service programs; develop methods to infuse the arts into all aspects of the school curriculum; and use professional artists and educators outside the school system as a means to enhance the quality arts experience (Joel, 1972).

IMPACT received funding from July 1970 through December 1972. The advisory committee, consisting of representatives from DAMT, the Arts and Humanities Program, and the National Endowment for the Arts, selected 5 project sites from a total of 60 applications from 30 states. The project sites selected included the Glendale (California) Unified School District; Eastgate and Cranbrook elementary schools in Columbus, Ohio; R. H. Conwell Middle Magnet School in Philadelphia; Edgewood School, Eugene, Oregon; and a group of Troy, Alabama, schools including several city elementary schools, a junior high, and two rural schools (Joel, 1972). The selected sites represented diverse geographical settings, socioeconomic conditions, and school structures.

The National Endowment for the Arts provided funding for residencies for professional artists at each site ". . . to assist teachers to enhance learning through first-hand encounters with working artists" (Joel, 1972, p. 11). According to the 1972 report by NEA project evaluator, Lydia Joel, the involvement of the working artists provided the crucial element in the program's success.

Although IMPACT concluded at the end of 1972, it accomplished its goals as a demonstration project. The Columbus program grew to include 12 schools with local funding. The Glendale program became a model for development of an exemplary multiarts program that spread to 3 other California sites. The IMPACT site in Eugene Oregon, became a magnet arts school because of its strong administrative, parental, community, and teacher support for the arts program developed there (Arts, Education and Americans Panel, 1977).

The Artist-In-Schools program of NEA, an outgrowth of the IMPACT model, continued to provide artists for educational programs. The Dance Component, serving an average of 40 sites per year, continued to operate similar to IMPACT until 1980. It provided a four-week residency by a dance-movement specialist and a two-week residency a professional dance company (Reinhart & Kerr, 1976). Three dance companies, directed by Bella Lewitsky, Murray Louis, and Lucas Hoving, who had participated in the original IMPACT project, continued their involvement in the AIS program. Virgina Tanner and Shirley Ririe worked as dance-movement specialists under both programs. Their continuing involvement in the Dance Component helped prepare other artists for AIS residences. During 1973–74, funds under the Manpower Development and Training Act provided for workshops and seminars as well as artist assistants to the program. The National Endowment Dance Advisory Panel and the National Council on the Arts selected new artist participants, including professional American dance companies and experienced dance/movement specialists as the program expanded (Reinhart & Kerr, 1976).

Each summer the American Dance Festival became the site for an important AIS workshop for teachers, administrators, dance artists, and state arts agency personnel, providing for a sharing of ideas and participation in hands-on experiences (Ririe, 1981). The Dance Component of AIS focused upon presenting dance as an art form, exploring movement as a teaching tool, and employing movement as a means of encouraging self-expression and self-awareness in children through discovery of kinesthetic awareness. A major criteria used in the selection of school sites and artists became the likelihood for continuation and development of dance activities in the schools after the conclusion of the AIS residency (Reinhart & Kerr, 1976). Charles Reinhart, coordinator of the Dance Component, stated:

> The program's intent is to explore the joy of movement, to offer possibilities for teachers to discover new approaches for exploring all subject areas of the curriculum, to demonstrate how movement can provide a richer learning experience and to augment the teachers' skills in applying these components (Reinhart & Kerr, 1978, p. 3).

The regular AIS program administered by each state arts agency assumed aspects of the Dance Component in 1980 (*Artist-in-Schools Program*, 1980). This benefited rural and urban schools with fewer financial resources by allowing for shorter dance residencies by movement specialists, companies, or some combination. Although the emphasis slowly shifted from catalyst for development of arts in education programs to enrichment program, the AIS program still provided an important interface of the working artist with the school community, including the arts educators.

Project IMPACT and the AIS Dance Component increased the demand for dance both inside and outside the educational setting. The projects encouraged the use of movement specialists for teacher and student workshops and increased the acceptability of dance within the school (Arts, Education and Americans Panel, 1977). The status of dance within a comprehensive arts approach was enhanced. This approach used dance as one of the art forms contributing to general education. Comprehensive arts programs have an overall philosophy that lend themselves to exploration and child-centered strategies. Although the availability of these programs to all children is a long way off, the spread of such programs in the last 15 years is encouraging. Child-centered and problem-solving dance and arts education programs continue to develop and grow as universities provide resources for preservice training and as educational systems embrace in-service education utilizing trained consultants in the arts.

The Educational Program of the John F. Kennedy Center for the Performing Arts has contributed to the spread of comprehensive arts programs and arts in general education. In 1973 the Kennedy Center and the Department of Education formed the Alliance for Arts Education. The goal of the AAE is advocacy for the arts through maintaining ". . . a network of individuals and organizations for communication, co-operation, and promotion of arts education at the local, state, regional and national levels" (*Alliance for Arts Education 1985 Program Guide*, 1985, p. 3). Subsequently, the Kennedy Center Education Program, serving as a flow-through agency for federal and private funding, provided initial support to 53 state and territorial committees. State AAE committees develop and implement state plans for comprehensive arts education programs and assist in advocacy efforts for the arts including dance (*Alliance for Arts Education 1985 Program Guide*, 1985).

The Kennedy Education Office/AAE also sponsors Imagination Celebrations, which are children's arts festival that ". . . provide community visibility to existing arts education programs and provide seminars, workshops and performances" as an outreach (*Alliance for Arts Education 1985 Program Guide*, 1985, p. 3).

The National Committee, Arts with the Handicapped (now Very Special Arts), formed in 1974 as an affiliate of the Kennedy Education Program, acts as a coordinating agency for creating and promoting arts programs for the disabled, which serve as a means to integrate the disabled into mainstream arts education programs. Numerous special projects provide development of innovative content, methods, and materials such as the New Visions Dance Project for the visually impaired piloted by the Alvin Ailey American Dance Center (*Alliance for Arts Education 1985 Program Guide*, 1985; *The New Visions Dance Project*, 1984).

Beginning in the 1960s, state and local governments began to provide funding for arts education programs. Local school boards, likewise, provided funding for arts education programming, first matching monies with the IMPACT program, then as a requirement of the AIS program, finally not specifically linked to either of these programs. The various projects during this period demonstrated the value of using community resources in the arts to enhance the school program. Many new organizations focusing upon the arts in education emerged during the mid 1970s to assist the schools in providing quality arts programs to their students. Dance became a highly visible and valued part of these programs.

While government and agency support of arts in education and arts education programs is higher than ever before, it is clear that this funding will never provide all that is needed. Increasingly, funding of arts programs in education, especially of an innovative nature, must turn to additional resources in the private sector. According to Jack Kukuk, education director of the Kennedy Center, funding for arts education programs suffered in the late 1970s and early 1980s, but he adds that the pendulum is swinging back again. More people see the arts as a basic subject. Private funding is increasing, as is funding from state sources (personal communication, November 21, 1984). The new initiatives in arts education programs by the NEA seem likely to assist the development of programs, with long-term effects. It seems to be the right time for a surge of new programs in the arts and a renewed effort on the part of dance educators for their proper place in school programs.

Dance has survived the past 30 years within the educational environment. The involvement of dance in arts in education projects has allowed many teachers, administrators, and parents to see and acknowledge for themselves that dance should rightfully belong with the more traditional art forms of the visual arts and music taught within the school setting. Renewed interest in dance education is informing and causing change in dance programs in higher education. Regardless of their particular setting within the college or university framework, these programs are challenged to develop new teacher preparation programs in dance and to focus upon curriculum and methodology appropriate to the school setting.

It seems important for dance educators of today to be knowledgeable about the political framework within which dance education exists, whether taught as an art form, as a means to aesthetic literacy, as recreation, or as physical education. This knowledge can provide the means to make dance education and education through dance a viable part of the elementary school program. Dance educators must become more politically savvy and make use of both the alliance with the arts and the connection with physical education to develop dance education and to examine current practices and materials in dance. We must, however, understand the political framework in order to take appropriate actions when necessary to maintain the integrity of dance and its value within the education environment.

REFERENCES

Alliance for arts education 1985 program guide. (1985). Washington, DC: The John F. Kennedy Center for the Performing Arts, Education Office.

Artists-in-schools program information. (1980, February). Washington, DC: National Endowment for the Arts.

Arts, Education and Americans Panel. (1977). *Coming to our senses.* New York: McGraw-Hill.

Arts in education survey. (1979). Helena, MT: Office of Public Instruction.

Bloom, Kathryn. (January 1974). *Arts organizations and their services to schools: Patrons or partners?* New York: JDR 3rd Fund.

Bloom, Kathryn, & Eddy, Junius. (1980). *An arts in education source book.* New York: JDR 3rd Fund.

Chapman, Sarah. (1974). *Movement education in the United States.* Philadelphia: Movement Education Publications.

Eddy, Junius. (1978). *Seattle's arts for learning project.* Seattle, WA: Seattle Public Schools.

Fineberg, Carol. (1976, December). *New York City arts in general education project up-date.* New York: Division of Educational Planning and Support, Board of Education.

Hussey, Delia, & Murray, Ruth. (1956, November). Anglo-American workshop in elementary physical education. *Journal of Health, Physical Education and Recreation,* pp. 22–23.

Imel, E. Carmen, ed. (1977). *Focus on dance viii: Dance heritage.* Reston, VA: National Dance Association.

Joel, Lydia. (1972). The impact of IMPACT: Dance artists as catalysts for change in education. *Dance Scope.*

Kennedy, John F. (1962). The arts in America. In *Creative America.* New York: Ridge Press.

Kennedy, Wallace. (November 14, 1976) *Minneapolis arts in general education network progress report.* Minneapolis, MN: Public Schools.

Laban, Rudolf. [Lisa Ullman, ed.] (1975). *Modern educational dance* (2d ed.). London: Macdonald and Evans.

Madeja, Stanley S., with Onuska, Sheila. (1977). *Through the arts to the aesthetic.* St. Louis, MO: CEMREL.

National endowment for the arts: 1977–78 artists-in-schools/dance component. (1977–78). Washington, DC: NEA.

New dimensions for the arts 1971–1972. (1973). Washington, DC: National Endowment for the Arts.

Reinhart, C. L., & Kerr, J. H. (1976, December). *National endowment for the arts: 1977–78 artists-in-schools/dance component program information.* Washington, DC: NEA.

Reinhart, C. L., & Kerr, J. H. (1978). *National endowment for the arts 1978–79 artists-in-schools program: Dance component program information.* New York: Charles Reinhart, Management. Washington, DC: NEA.

Remer, Jane. (1977). *The league of cities for the arts in education.* New York: JDR 3rd Fund.

Ririe, Shirley Russion. (1981). Contemplating a dance program K-12. In Martin Engel and Jerome J. Hausman (eds). *Curriculum and instruction in arts and aesthetic education.* St. Louis, MO: CEMREL.

The arts in education: Seattle reflections. (1975–76). Seattle, WA: Seattle Public Schools.

The New Visions Dance Project. (1984). Washington, DC: Very Special Arts.

4

ERICK HAWKINS: A NEW PERSPECTIVE

Sheryl Popkin Triebe

The intention of the study is to present a new perspective on Hawkins's work by showing the influence of Eastern ideas on Hawkins's point of view and thus in his choreography. Eastern, as used here, refers to a culture reflecting a way of thinking and knowing the world, rather than a reference to a specific geographic area or particular country. It is the basic premises of Eastern thought that impacted Hawkins's thinking. Contemporary life in the East was outside the concern of the research.

Research sources for the presentation include interviews, lectures, classes, and writings by Hawkins and his associates. Dance philosophy and history books, periodicals, and newspapers provided relevant data. Study of Eastern thought and aesthetics, Western thought and aesthetics, and comparative philosophy was undertaken to enhance analysis and interpretation. The articulation of the Western characteristics of Hawkins's dance was outside the purpose of the study. It is recognized, however, that they play an important part in a complete analysis of his work.

In order to show the reflection of the Eastern influence in Hawkins's dance, evidence of the emergence of his interest in Eastern thought is given. It is shown that there were preconditions for the changes that took place in Hawkins's thinking and dancing and that his search for alternative ways of thinking and feeling led him to Eastern literature. Discussion and analysis of the choreography and dance style reveals that the values reflected in the dance of Erick Hawkins have been influenced by Eastern thought. Hawkins's own acculturation being Western, the Western basis of his dance, coupled with the evidence of the study, points to a perspective of Hawkins's art as a synthesis of Eastern and Western premises.

Significantly, the study makes a contribution to the limited dance literature of a unique art form and point of view. Its importance lies in promoting understanding of a significant figure in dance who has been exploring issues of contemporary intellectual interest, a figure significant to dancers and scholars alike in the furthering of movement understanding and dance appreciation.

Erick Hawkins is one of the least understood among the important figures in the dance world today. A controversial figure, he both baffles and intrigues the best of the critics. This lack of understanding has led to inadequate documentation of Hawkins's work in dance literature, consequently overlooking an approach important to the field in the integrations it has made.

There are reasons for the confusion that Hawkins's work generates. This is a man who takes a reflective approach to his art. He is an explorer, and avid reader, and highly receptive to the influence of philosophical ideas. In his search for knowledge and understanding, he investigated alternative ways of thinking and feeling. Hawkins's search resulted in his looking to literature on Eastern thought. Inspired by the unfamiliar ideas, he incorporated them into his own sensibility and consequently, his dance. Thus infused with characteristics akin to Eastern ways, Hawkins's dance presents qualities and problems difficult to accommodate within habitual schemes.

Hawkins's work, when viewed from this new perspective, is not so perplexing. To dispel the bewildering nature of Hawkins's dance, an analysis follows of the emergence of his interest in Eastern thought. The emergent notions are integrated with the affects they were having on his thinking and, consequently, on his work, thus in turn revealing their developing power as a primary source for his artistry.

BACKGROUND

Hawkins's background among dancers is rather unique. He pursued literary and philosophical ideas throughout his academic life, intially studying music and Latin, then Greek philosophy, literature, and art, leading him ultimately to a major in Greek civilization at Harvard. His response to his inclination toward the study of Greek civilization was his belief in its being the beginning of ideas. He understood it as the starting point of all Western art, the only Western culture that accepted and admired the human body, and the one having the strongest aesthetic sense. Hawkins's lectures and writings, as well as his background, show him to be a man of education who has read extensively, and continues to do so. He often mentions the book he picked up the evening before, or the one he reread or discovered during his last vacation. Hawkins is constantly scanning literary sources. It is this proclivity for knowledge and its results that help answer questions as to why, with all the already existing directions in modern dance, one should bother with a new technique, and why Hawkins was the one to discover it.

There are other reasons as well. In addition to a mental keenness and a penchant for learning, there was also a physical stimulus. Having sustained two serious injuries, first of the knee and then of the lower back, Hawkins came to question the dance training he received. This message from his own body led him to seek another body discipline, and one that trained with wisdom.

Another precondition to this change is Hawkins's predisposition to curiosity. As Hawkins himself says:

Sometimes I find there seems to be no alternative but to divide all of us individuals into two groups. I hate to do it, but it seems inevitable, really necessary. Really everybody has already placed himself into one or the other of these two groups. Some of the people of the world seem to be curious. They look on everything in human nature and non-human nature with curiosity. The other group just plain isn't curious about anything, really curious. These are the two groups. It is too bad, but it seems so.

So when we talk about anything like art, I guess we have to reckon with this division of everybody into two groups, the curious and those who aren't curious. (I guess by way of parenthesis I should say that the people who are most curious to me are the people who aren't curious) (Hawkins, 1959).

Accompanying Hawkins's curiosity is his predilection for adventure, and he calls his search for a new body discipline, in fact modern dance itself, "a voyage of discovery." "To be a discoverer generally means, doesn't it, to be curious about something, and you go toward it . . . a real discoverer keeps going on to have the fun of discovering. Some people just like to adventure and I guess I am one of them" (Hawkins, 1959).

There were also "psychological hassles," as Hawkins calls them, that influenced the search for a new way, not only to dance, but to live. All of these factors—mental, physical, and psychological, encompassing emotional and social causes—led to Hawkins's readiness to discover the Eastern ideas that contributed to the change in his thinking, feeling, living—dancing.

EXPOSURE TO THE EASTERN IDEAS: CHRONOLOGY

Hawkins's first exposure to the Orient was through his mother's missionary magazines. (His mother was not a missionary). The main thing he remembered was the disease in India called elephantiasis. Distortions of the body, such as the legs being enlarged, affected him very much. Neither young Hawkins nor his parents did much traveling. The only trip Hawkins remembers was to California at the age of eight. So this finding in a magazine constitutes Hawkins's first awareness of the existence of another place where things were very different.

The second time he was exposed to the East—what he refers to as his first knowing about the Orient—was when he was attending Harvard. He went to the Boston Museum of Fine Arts, where they had an extraordinary collection of Oriental art, and saw some Japanese pottery. So he claims, he was "bowled over" by its irregularity. At first he disliked the asymmetry, though now he thinks it very beautiful.

While attending Harvard, a classmate gave him a copy of Okakura's *Book of Tea,* written in 1906, "as a first little aesthetic introduction to the West of Oriental ideas" (Hawkins, 1976b). This was the first time that Hawkins saw the word *Zen* and so he says, "I could smell that the idea was very different from anything I had known" (Hawkins, 1976b).

The artist's next exposure was when he first came to New York. He attended a performance of Uday Shankar and was so intrigued that he saw him perform 23 times that winter.[1] The real turning point, however—when the impact of the East was in terms of the ideas and not just what Hawkins calls the synthetic—came during a time when Hawkins was having some troubles.

> As I was growing up, I got into some very bad psychological hassles. I had put myself into a very difficult personal situation which had many virtues, but it was also a very troubling one. . . . I was just wanting to find out about my own life, 'cause I was dancing very nicely and all, a kind of what you'd call a success, but I wasn't happy (Hawkins, 1976b).

At the time of his search for new alternatives, a friend passed on to him Suzuki's *Essays on Zen.* Looking at the three volumes, as he says out of intellectual curiosity, he was intrigued by the illustrations of the Chinese and Japanese paintings. The Zen ideas that Suzuki was writing about were totally unfamiliar. "But," as he says, "I kept literally digging for it" (Hawkins, 1976b). Just as it was Okakura's *Book of Tea* that served as Hawkins's introduction to Eastern culture, it was Suzuki's work that contributed to Hawkins's awareness of Eastern *ideas*.

The next phase evolved out of reading R. H. Blythe's book on Zen and his translations of Japanese Haiku poems. At the time that Hawkins was reading these volumes, he was not under any pressure, and so he says, "I could just kind of go back into myself and see what my instinct was." This led him to begin some dances called "openings of the (eye)," a series of five progressional solos, based on the Buddhist notion of the third eye,[2] and Jesus' notion, also, of let thine eye be single. He used this notion "as a kind of metaphor" (Hawkins, 1976b).

---

[1]About this time was the choreography, in 1938, of his first dance called "Show Piece."

[2]The third eye is a single "eye," imagined to be in the center of the forehead (actually the pineal gland), through which one receives divine or intuitive insight, as opposed to mundane visions.

It was about this time that Hawkins claimed, "I just awakened up. Naturally, I was stimulated and excited about for the first time a kind of seeing the image of not trying to go to heaven but staying right here." The first dance that Hawkins choreographed based on this image was "Goat of the Gods," one of the dances of "openings of the (eye)." "It was the first time that I did a dance where I just wanted to show the immediacy of physical movement and without any daydreams." He used the image of the goat and the goat's existence because the goat lives only in the present, and as Hawkins says, it has no ego, that can plot to kill you, in revenge. The "animal-like existence of the moment by moment I coupled then with my growing understanding of just the immediacy of movement and the correctness of the body" (Hawkins, 1976b).

What has begun to happen here is that Hawkins's new awareness, attained through exposure to Eastern thought and aesthetics, led him to begin choreographing dances that were a reflection of his new understanding. He felt a new orientation had taken place. His aesthetic principles were changing because he was arriving at new basic premises. Hawkins makes the point that "once you've come to certain philosophical ideas, then your aesthetic will change" (Hawkins, 1976b).

What has begun to happen here is that Hawkins's new awareness, attained through exposure to Eastern thought and aesthetics, led him to begin choreographing dances that were a reflection of his new understanding. He felt a new orientation had taken place. His aesthetic principles were changing because he was arriving at new basic premises. Hawkins makes the point that "once you've come to certain philosophical ideas, then your aesthetic will change" (Hawkins, 1976b).

This was the period of Hawkins's experimenting with the application of immediacy to the dance; the time in Hawkins's developing art process that he was exploring movement for the sake of beautiful movement, pure and immediate. The discovery of F. S. C. Northrop's book *The Meeting of East and West* gave credence to this process. The concern with the immediately experienced materials Northrop defines as art in its first function. Furthermore, Northrop's comparative investigation of philosophy, East and West, clarified for Hawkins the distinction between the two culture's ways of knowing and, additionally, showed the complementarity of these two ways.

With Hawkins's curiosity still alive, more of the Eastern ideas continued to filter in. While teaching at his studio, a student gave him a copy of Herrigel's *Zen in the Art of Archery*. Hawkins, wondering what information this little book had to give him, took it into his dressing room and was so intrigued by what it had to say that he did not go to dinner until he had finished it. The fascination was with "the most extraordinarily beautiful goal" put forth in the book as to the achievement of a "oneness of the inner and outer, the body and soul." Hawkins, very much in tune with the beauty of this idea, and receptive to its possibility, has said, "That kind of a goal, which is egoless, that I knew would be the most beautiful quality of the dancing" (Hawkins, 1976b).

Thus began a voyage into the creation of works where quality was more important than quantity and where effortlessness became the predominating motivation. It was in regard to viewing these pieces of the late 1960s that Clive Barnes had told Hawkins, "Erick, yours is the one work in America I don't understand" (Barnes quoted in Hawkins, 1976b). Hawkins, however, understood that this could be so, for he said, "I was going from another starting point" (Hawkins, 1976b). Furthermore, Barnes had not given up, for he later acknowledged that "I saw something" (Barnes, quoted in Sabin, 1972).

Clearly the philosophical ideas and the artistic methods of the East have had a great impact on Hawkins, and not only on his thinking process, but also, consequently, on his dance process. Important also is the influence it has had in his life. Of this he himself says: "This is the point. In trying to understand my own, I didn't go to the Oriental aesthetic ideas just out of trying to rob somebody else's bag artistically. I went because I wanted more complete philosophical ideas so that I could live my life with happiness" (Hawkins, 1976b).

Hawkins was now aware of the importance and relevance to Westerners of this other way of thinking. He saw that it offered a way to perceive and understand one's life with more meaning and depth. For the artist, as well, this alternative view offers something very valuable: a view of his function as important, that function being to reflect the best thinking of his time.

It cannot be overlooked that thinking goes on in both hemispheres, that the thinking is different, and that both ways have their value. Hawkins, now recognizing his aim to be completeness, of the Greek way complementing the Oriental way, combines in his work these two ways. "That's why they don't get it" (Hawkins, 1977). Hawkins and his work had changed because his views had changed.

THE EASTERN INFLUENCE IN THE CHOREOGRAPHY

Hawkins's exposure to Eastern ideas not only transformed his philosophical beliefs and his point of view but also resulted in changes in his dancing and his choreography. This further consequence of Eastern influence was the result of Hawkins's applying his theory to create the kind of dance he envisioned. As Hawkins said, "Once you accept certain notions, why of course then the goal of the art will be different" (Hawkins, 1976b). Hawkins's goal for the art was the result of the influence of Eastern ideas transforming his philosophical beliefs, and his dance was an embodiment of this influence in an objective form.

In dance, in general, as well as in Hawkins's dance in particular, the artist's goal reveals itself in two ways: through the movement style; and the choreographed dances, reflecting values. What we discover upon analysis of Hawkins's dance is that the qualities that emerge out of the objective form, as well as the values embodied, reflect Eastern influence.

Hawkins has choreographed many dances, but there is no need to look at all of them individually because a few will serve quite well as a representative cross-section. As a preview to discussing a selection in detail, what follows is an overview of the choreography in a chronological perspective that was suggested by Robert Yohn (a dancer with the Hawkins' Company for many years).

Prior to Hawkins's establishment as an independent choreographer, there were solos experimenting with art in both its first and second functions.[3] Works choreographed in relation to other dancers constitutes the early category of dances, which were duets—including "Here and Now with Watchers" and "Eight Clear Places." These dances were primarily concerned with art in its first function—that is, where the movements, sounds, colors, and shapes were there just to be perceived for their own sake. A middle category of dances are mostly quartets—composed to the music of Lucia Dlugoszewski. In this category fall "Early Floating," "Cantilever," "Geography of Noon," and "Lords of Persia." Basically, they are abstract dances dealing with the beauty of shape, form, and flow.

A later category of dances includes pieces for small orchestra and pieces for large orchestra. The first division includes "Of Love," "Tight Rope," "Greeks Dreams with Flute," "Angels of the Inmost Heaven," and "Black Lake." Many of these dances are sextets with six to eight sections and begin moving into deeper themes. Materials are now appearing that reflect aspects of Hawkins's life experience. There are the dances where he has drawn from his background in Greek literature,

---

[3]In "The Body is a Clear Place," Hawkins put forth a theory of aesthetics, derived from Northrop, that divides art into two functions.

Art in its first function uses the aesthetic materials to convey the materials themselves for their own sake. . . .

Art in its second function, on the other hand, uses these aesthetic materials not primarily for their own sake, but analogically to convey some theoretically conceived factor in the nature of things, of which the aesthetic materials alone are the mere epistemic correlates or signs (Northrop quoted in Hawkins, 1969).

male-female polarity dances, and new link-with-nature dances. The large orchestra pieces all use existent music as accompaniment and include a wide array of theme and movement variations.

Typically, Hawkins's dances reflect a progression from solos to larger group dances, studies to masterworks; but there is something unique about Hawkins's dances, so well captured in the words of Walter Sorell:

> Before entering Erick Hawkins' world, I always feel like taking off my shoes and leaving them in the check room with all the street noises and insulting sights of the daily dirt. I feel like reclining in my chair and letting him guide me into his imaginary world where time is of no duration and the West is as close to the East as it ever can be.
>
> Based on the philosophy of the Tao-Te-King which says, "By non-action everything can be done," Hawkins and his company move with utter tranquility, seeking an expression of purity, the feeling of movement rather than the movement itself. I once said that like the lines of a haiku poem, Hawkins' movements evoke, instant by instant, a sensation of poetic significance, a sensuous impression, a fleeting thought (Sorell, 1972).

The following review of the dances suggests some of their unique qualities and their relation to Eastern essence.

"Geography of Noon"

Along with "Early Floating," "Cantilever," and "Lords of Persia," "Geography of Noon" is one of a series of quartets choreographed in the early 1960s. In "Geography of Noon" the four dancers are two men and two women representing characters with the names of real butterflies (Spring Azure, Variegated Frittilary, etc.). The title is interestingly appropriate because it is indicative of the mix of the geometric and the organic that begins to appear, here, in Hawkins's work. "Noon" is a very feeling-laden word, it being "the fullest, brightest, hottest midday" (Yohn, 1976). This feeling is also captured in the music. Geography, described by *Webster's Dictionary* as the science of the earth and its life, implies a scientific investigation. Its juxtaposition with noon aptly foreshadows Hawkins's approach here.

Hawkins, describing this dance, says, "I use the geometry very exactly at the beginning and the end" (Hawkins, 1976). The form that results from the geometrical-diagrammatic way of thinking in choreography is the use of straight lines in space, as well as in the body itself—body line. "Geography of Noon" is very shape oriented, a thematic structure being the dancers in a square. Hawkins's justification for using the geometrical-diagrammatic approach is so acceptably straightforward. "I use it all the time. Because it's there" (Hawkins, 1976a). In this piece, in particular, where the intention was for it to be a dance about the metaphor of butterflies, the problem arose that one could not be

> naively realistic all the time and show just the becomingness. Therefore, I wanted to counteract that with something that was strangely different, and so . . . the formality of form, and then go into the becomingness of the butterfly metaphor, and then [to] come back to that again [the form] I think was more beautiful (Hawkins, 1976a).

Hawkins makes the point that there is nothing wrong with the diagrammatic approach but indicates that

> it is very partial and [also that] what it is is very Western. And what it has done is denied the immediately sensed moment by moment experiencing that is done when you are living with more emphasis on the concept by intuition way of knowing. And it's that theoretical side that made the Protestants take all the color out of the churches. They thought that the good life was only on the theoretical side. . . . So the task is that we have both (Hawkins, 1976a).

"Geography of Noon" could be viewed as a work reflecting the synthesis of the theoretic and aesthetic components, of the West and East, in their mutual complementarity. "Geography of Noon" could aptly be called an adventure in totality.

"Lords of Persia."

Another quartet of this period, choreographed in 1965, "Lords of Persia" consists of "three scenes of polo-playing Persian gentlemen, picturing the game in a most ceremonial manner" (Sorell, 1971). It is apparently a Hawkins favorite, having appeared many times in concert programs. Choreographed for four men, "Lords of Persia" is a particularly important piece. It depicts Hawkins's special sense of subtle balance, grace, and ease and, at the same time, shows that men can be beautiful dancing and still be virile. Strength need not be portrayed by being powerful, overbearing, or domineering. Large, free-flowing, sweeping movements characterize the dance, along with quick shifts of weight, weightless leaps, lingering balances, and clear, sharp, rhythmic phrases that, here, all represent very noble, very manly qualities.

"Black Lake."

"Black Lake," choreographed in 1969 for six dancers and four musicians, falls into Hawkins's later category of dances for small orchestra. The piece "is a series of tableaux with a ritualistic quality alluding to such natural shapes and phenomena as sun, moon, clouds, night birds, or deep midnight" (Sorell, 1971). Having eight sections, it is in the tradition of earlier works. Deborah Jowitt once remarked that she thought a good title would be "Eight Clear Places in the Sky." Having been described as ceremonial, metaphoric, Oriental, intense, austere, interpretive, and so on, "Black Lake," despite, or perhaps because of these qualities, is a most impressive work—visually and aurally, as well as effectively. A large part of its visual impressiveness is in the costumes and the props, both of which, in this dance, play an important role.

If one were to speak of the virtuosity of Hawkins's dancers, one area of reference would be to the use of dynamics, of which "Black Lake" displays a huge range. Lucia Dlugoszewski refers to Hawkins's originality in regard to dynamics resulting from "his daring use of fluid energy."

> His delicacies seem to have all the energies of the universe fiercely locked inside them. *Sun setting, night birds, longcomet hair, summer thunder, milky way,* all 'Black Lake" dances move in this way.
> The individual quality of Hawkins' dancing seems to defy analysis until one understands his dynamics. All that lightning speed in shifting back and forth between strong and delicate, all the mysterious changes of direction, one strong, one elusive, all at different lengths of time, are expressions of his extensive constructing with dynamics (Dlugoszewski, 1972).

Time is another particularly important element in Hawkins' dance—his unique use of it again evident in "Black Lake," both durationally and rhythmically. What is significant to recognize, however, is that the unique way that the timing unfolds and, as well, that the dynamics emerge, is due to Hawkins's "relating to nature in a completely fresh way that brings a new time experience into play" (Dlugoszewski, 1972).

"Black Lake," along with "Eight Clear Places," "Geography of Noon," and "Naked Leopard," falls into another classification of Hawkins's dances—new link-with-nature dances. It is an instant-by-instant awareness—the basis of Eastern knowledge—that characterizes a Hawkins dance. *Black Lake* is sensitivity to nature, an instant-by-instant alertness, gravity experienced rhythmically; and also a depiction of the sheer wonder of nature's components. It is this combined sensitivity and immersion in the sense of contemplation that evokes all of the allusions to Hawkins's dances being "Oriental." Captured in the words of Deborah Jowitt, "Black Lake" is ceremonious; it is Oriental in several other ways too." It is "excellent Hawkins, a quietly magic experience" (Jowitt, 1969).

"Dawn Dazzled Door."

Choreographed in 1972, "Dawn Dazzled Door," belonging to Hawkins's later category of dances for large orchestra, is performed to

Toru Takemitsu's "Dorian Horizon," a score for string orchestra. Here is another example of Hawkins's choreography, which

> also goes . . . to the nature of things, not solely of people. He who has arrived, says Chuang-Tzu, knows that all things are One and identifies himself with them in their essential activity. And just as that pre-Zen philosopher used the Chinese language as it had never before been used, so does Erick Hawkins use stillness, flow, intensity of dance movement as never before, as seen in the precise subtleties of "Dawn Dazzled Door," . . . to the end of divining and penetrating nature. . . .
>
> But then the simplicity, the power of his approach lies not in rhapsodizing or intellectualizing on the lightning forces of nature but merely in being them, . . . (Woodworth, 1972)

Like "Black Lake," "Dawn Dazzled Door" is a "nature" dance, but whereas "Black Lake" deals with aspects of the sky at night, "Dawn Dazzled Door" is simply a dance about the beauty of the heavens. More specifically, it thematically depicts the natural order of the cosmos and man's contingency in the midst of it. It has in its cast a pair of "moons" (women), two "stars (women), and two "suns" (men), dressed in stylized Japanese kimonos, their headdresses identifying them in their roles.

The dance is ceremonial and gestural, consisting of very formal patterns. "The dancers entered slowly, gracefully, one by one, like some strange Oriental academic procession" (Quarm, 1974). They formed two lines across the stage, facing the audience—the movement, "reminiscent of the traditional Japanese Kabuki dances" (Gilbert, 1972), leaving and returning to these lines. "Bows, turns, lunges, the kinds of small gestures Hawkins loves, moves of the kimonos or sharp attacks of the bare feet, all build within narrow space and carefully defined time to great power" (Steele, 1974). Review after review speaks of the dance as a "facsimile of an Oriental ritual."

The American Dances.

Despite the continual reference to the Oriental nature of Hawkins's dance, it is noteworthy and appropriate to mention that there are works that could aptly be called American pieces. "Classic Kite Tails," choreographed in 1972, is set to David Diamond's "Rounds for String Orchestra." Significantly, despite the American character that typifies the piece, the Eastern references still appear:

> In this dance the playfulness of pure movement and David Diamond's exuberant string writing are in the spirit of Toju Nakae's belief that "the natural state of man's mind is delight" and Chuang Tzu's saying "Never be at a loss for joy, and make it spring with everything" (Lyons 1976).

"Hurrah" (1975) is Hawkins's contribution to America's Bicentennial. Along with "Classic Kite Tails," "Parson Weems and the Cherry Tree, Etc.," and a number of later works, "Hurrah" indicates that Hawkins's Eastern influences do not obliviate his feeling for his own country's history and specialness and the idealism behind its founding. Naima Prevots—in a review of a Hawkins concert in Washington DC featuring "Agathlon," "Plains Daybreak," and Heyoka"—reiterates the point. These "three dances . . . were all different but they had a common core—a metaphoric expression in dance for the spiritual reaches of the American dream" (Prevots, 1982).

"Death is the Hunter."

Two months after "Hurrah," Hawkins premiered "Death is the Hunter," presenting his viewers with the more familiar Hawkins idiom. Unlike "Hurrah," "Death is the Hunter" has the "inexorable pace, the ceremoniousness of a Noh play" (Jowitt, 1975). "The motif is Oriental and there is even a Nohlike tree to the side. . . . Sure enough this is Mr. Hawkins in his Japanese mood again. . . ." (Kisselgoff, 1975). Thematically, the piece portrays a reverence for death as the natural fulfillment of life. "It is an Eastern view of mortality, consonant with Hawkins' larger esthetic outlook" (Kriegsman, 1977).

The work, when I first saw it, had Hawkins himself, as masked death, entering from the back of the stage and, ever so slowly—garbed in a robe with a long pleated train—making his way toward downstage. His pace, drawing one into the present moment, and his attention to the shift of weight was reminiscent of the Buddhist meditation "Now I am walking." Upon reaching downstage, he encounters the six dancers. One by one, "death 'shoots' each dancer, and they move from birth (tying on the mask) to death (taking off the mask) . . . [and] peacefully lie down on their gravestone pillows" (Kisselgoff, 1975).

Hawkins has said of this piece, "In the silence what I want is for everybody in the theatre to maybe sense, 'Yes, I too am going to die.' Even young people need to have a kind of perspective about the fact that we don't live forever so we'll have to treasure the moment-to-moment existence" [Hawkins, quoted in Clurman, 1976].

An important aspect to recognize in "Death is the Hunter" is that "the Hawkins' death-figure is not the medieval one of terror . . . the victims regard their meeting with Death as a natural encounter . . . [and so the last dancer 'shot'] stares death calmly in the face" (Kisselgoff, 1975).

The 1980s.

A brief sketch of the most recent works reveals that the pattern continues. "Going to see Erick Hawkins can be a strangely reassuring experience. He marked out his territory long ago, and although he may look at something with new eyes, or extend its boundaries, he never pulls up stakes" (Jowitt, 1986). "Within the ever-widening spectrum of modern dance, the art of Erick Hawkins remains steadfast" (Gruen, 1987).

The controversy and mixed views live on as well, and so do the continual references to Hawkins's "Eastern modality. "Ahab" (1986) has been cited as "the contemporary equivalent of a Japanese Noh play" (Mazo, 1986), and "The Joshua Tree, or, Three Outlaws" (1984) has been said to have "more in common with Japanese classical theater than it does with a real Wild West yarn" (Kisselgoff, 1984). The examples continue.

ANALYSIS

Analysis of Hawkins's choreography reveals certain qualities and forms and these qualities and forms, as well as the values they embody, have Eastern characteristics.

Amongst the notable characteristics of Hawkins's dance is the quality of effortlessness. The East realizes that for a most peaceful existence in the midst of natural forces, man must flow with them, and not try to oppose them. Gravity, for instance, is a force to which dancers must respond. The effortless quality reflected in Hawkins's dance becomes unique through adhesion to this Eastern value, through cooperation with gravity [rather than the way effortlessness sometimes displays itself in the ballet when gravity appears to be defied]. Sometimes such cooperation is interestingly translated into Hawkins's harmonizing the opposition of resisting and yielding to gravity. This is the method that produces his unique rhythms. The belief in cooperation has led to Hawkins's method of letting the movement happen and not forcing it to happen, relative to the Eastern view of "letting" things happen. (For example, in Eugen Herrigal's *Zen in the Art of Archery*, he speaks of "letting" the arrow go, and "it shoots.")

Fluid energy, the mainspring of Hawkins' dynamics, characterizes his dances. It is the source, as well, of the quality of harmony that pervades his work, and, too, the root of his mystery. At a performance at Wolftrap (June, 1977) someone in the audience, upon seeing "Cantilever," said, "I seem to have a problem with it—the lack of tension."

Westerners are so accustomed to seeing tension that when it's not there, it's as though something is missing. A history of domination has led to the inability of Westerners to appreciate effortlessness. "Our cultural tendency is to ally ourselves rather to strife, suffering and work of which effort is the most excellent metaphor" (Sabin, 1972). The psychological resistance to effortlessness and fluidity is, therefore, understandable. Eastern audiences would be more receptive in Hawkins's theater.

Consonant with effortlessness is the quality of serenity in Hawkins's dance. Hawkins sees nature as an object of contemplation, as in the East, and not something to be dominated, as in the West. The movement response, therefore, is calm, resolving in forms that are tension free, flowing, centered, and curvilinear. The body being no different than any other of nature's components, its natural response is to travel in arcs—like light waves and sound waves. Hawkins makes apparent these natural paths of man's limbs in space. His dances are metaphors of the planets orbiting in space and arrows curving to their marks.

The quality of purity also appears in Hawkins's dances, but along with a sense of celebration, or joy—not seriousness. There is also a related sense of ritual. Ceremoniously, Hawkins's dances "seek to culminate their effect slowly and evenly over a period of time" (McDonagh, 1970). It is a unique manipulation of time that creates the ritualistic nature of Hawkins's dances. It is also a characteristic of Eastern dance and gives there the same effect. Hawkins's use of time is clearly connected to an Eastern sense of time and its contingent reverberations.

In Hawkins's dances, immediacy can also be seen to be of utmost importance. Hawkins remarks that

> When the immediacy and pure existence of movement is the prime concern, time is a much more serious problem of dance than space. Time is also a much richer material of dance than space. Actually if time is sensed intuitively instant-by-instant, the space is created automatically point by point. The liveliest excitement of Flamenco and Hindu dance lies not in its emotional impact, dazzling structure and virtuosity, but in its instant-by-instant sensing of time (Hawkins, quoted in Olinsky, 1959).

Hawkins's dances reflect this instant-by-instant sensing of time. Kisselgoff speaks of a Chinese dancer in the audience commenting that Mr. Hawkins had a remarkable understanding of the timing that makes Asian drama so compelling for many (Kisselgoff, 1975). Don McDonagh (1970) has said, "Hawkins' pacing is measured in units that have more in common with Eastern conceptions of time than Western." And in 1986, Kisselgoff mentions this point again, when she speaks of Hawkins being "particularly susceptible to certain concepts in Asian theatre. The unhurried time sense, the distillation of gesture beyond abstraction to communicate sensation, the acknowledgment that not doing is equated with doing—all these elements frequently find their way into his dances."

Stillness is another important element in Hawkins's dance, serving the function of bringing attention to details that in other circumstances might have been overlooked. McDonagh points out that such a concern with isolating elements is better known in Eastern societies than in Western theater. Stillness also heightens the awareness of the moment-to-moment sensing of time and "gradually induces a sense of quietude and contemplation of things for themselves." McDonagh further points out that the use of stillness in the dancing "creates a form of theatre that calls for a type of patience that has to be cultivated and is not normally indigenous to the United States" (McDonagh, 1970). The stillness in Hawkins's dance is a partial reason for its often poor reception by Western audiences.

Oriental-sounding music, costumes of floor-length robes (even kimonos), the use of masks, and the simplicity of his props and sets all enhance the Eastern aestheticism of his dances.

COALESCENCE

It is explained by aesthetic theory that the qualities and components in relation constitute the form. The particular form that evolves, in turn, signifies the values expressed. It is a unique combination of the qualities and components discussed above that produces a Hawkins' dance. And when these elements are reintegrated, it is seen that their relationship signifies values that also have been influenced by Eastern thought. Hawkins's dance depicts an Eastern sense of truth in its inculcation of sensitivity to nature, its conveyance of the ritual theme of death and rebirth as the natural order of the universe, and its deliverance of essence rather than action.

In conclusion, it can be seen that the values reflected in the dance of Erick Hawkins haave been influenced by Eastern thought. Furthermore, in addition to the kinship of the internal components to the Eastern characteristics, these components are also significant in their presentation of what is symbolized. The foremost area of Eastern affinity is the impact and import of the whole—greater now than the sum of its parts.

REFERENCES

Clurman, I. (1976, April 7). Poetry and drama of dancer Erick Hawkins. *Rocky Mountain News* (mimeograph).

Dlugoszewski, L. (1972). Heir to new tradition. In M. L. Gordon Norton (Ed.), *On the Dance of Erick Hawkins* (pp. 26–38). New York: Foundations for Modern Dance.

Gilbert, E. (1972, July 17). "Dazzled Door" first rate. *Detroit News* (mimeograph).

Gruen, J. (1987, November 29). Less strain, more gain. *New York Times*, pp. 18, 26.

Hawkins, E. (1959, June 1). *Modern dance as a voyage of discovery.* Lecture presented at the San Francisco Museum of Art.

Hawkins, E. (1969). *The body is a clear place* (mimeograph).

Hawkins, E. (1976a, July 23). Lecture, American University, Washington, DC.

Hawkins, E. (1976b, August 7). Interview with Sheryl Popkin, Washington, DC.

Hawkins, E. (1977, May 24). Interview with Sheryl Popkin, New York.

Herrigel, E. (1971). *Zen in the art of archery* (R. F. C. Hull, Trans.). Vintage Books, Random House. (Original work published 1953).

Jowitt, D. (1969, November 6). Dance: Dance flood. *Village Voice* (mimeograph).

Jowitt, D. (1975, September 29). Dance: Erick Hawkins dazzles Carnegie Hall. *Village Voice* (mimeograph).

Jowitt, D. (1986, February 18). The dragon lashes its tail. *Village Voice* (mimeograph).

Kisselgoff, A. (1975, September 13). Dance: Erick Hawkins. *New York Times* (mimeograph).

Kisselgoff, A. (1984, October 28). Erick Hawkins transforms American folk themes. *New York Times* (mimeograph).

Kisselgoff, A. (1986, February 6). Dance: Erick Hawkins Company. *New York Times* (mimeograph).

Kriegsman, A. (1977, June 20). In touch with nature: "Busting loose" in the warmth and greenery. *Washington Post* (mimeograph).

Kriegsman, A. (1987). Hawkins' haunting vision. *Washington Post* (mimeograph).

Lyons, M. (1976, July 17). Notes on the program. Kennedy Center, Washington, DC.

Mazo, J. (1986, September 24). Innovative ritualized dance drama works in "Ahab." *The Record* (mimeograph).

McDonagh, D. (1970). *The rise and fall and rise of modern dance.* New York: New American Library.

Olinsky, L. (1959, March). The uncommunicating choreography of Erick Hawkins. *Dance Magazine* (mimeograph).

Prevots, N. (December 1981–January 1982). Hawkins: Redefining America. *Washington Dance Review* (mimeograph).

Quarm, J. (1974, March 28). Beauty unfolds at Hawkins, E. P. Symphony Show. *El Paso Herald Post* (mimeograph).

Sabin, R. (1972). What comes after the avant-garde. In M. L. Gordon Norton (Ed.), *On the Dance of Erick Hawkins* (pp. 44–60). New York: Foundations for Modern Dance.

Sorell, W. (1971, April). Reviews: Hawkins . . . The Erick Hawkins Dance Company, Anta Theatre, N.Y.C. *Dance News* (mimeograph).

Sorell, W. (1972, December). Erick Hawkins Dance Company, Anta Theatre, N.Y.C., October 26, 27, 28, 1972. *Dance News*, pp. 7, 12.

Steele, M. (1974, April 1). Dance: Erick Hawkins. *Minneapolis Tribune* (mimeograph).

Woodworth, M. (1972). Opening the eye of nature. In M. L. Gordon Norton (Ed.), *On the Dance of Erick Hawkins* (pp. 6–15). New York: Foundations for Modern Dance.
Yohn, R. (1976). Interview with Sheryl Popkin, Washington, DC.

5

A COMPARISON OF NOVICE AND EXPERIENCED DANCERS' BODY AWARENESS

Lynnette Young Overby

The primary purpose of this study was to ascertain whether or not a relationship exists between dance experience, body awareness, and imagery. Twenty experienced female dancers 18–30 years of age (with 5 or more years of dance training) and 20 novice female dancers 18–30 years of age (with one year or less of dance training) were utilized. Each subject performed two body-awareness tasks; the directionality (D) body-awareness task and the reflective body-perception body-awareness tasks. In both tasks the subjects viewed the criterion movement on a large-screen video monitor and were then videotaped as they reproduced the movements both sighted and blindfolded. A MANOVA 2 × 2 × 2 repeated measures analysis revealed that the body awareness (D and R) of experienced dancers was significantly better than the body awareness of novice dancers. The effect of sight was also significant. For both groups, performance of the task sighted resulted in better performance than blindfolded. The results of a follow-up ANOVA on directionality revealed a main effect for dance experience that the experienced dancers performed the directionality tasks better across the two sighted conditions. On the reflective body-perception task the experienced dancers performed better across both sighted conditions, and the effect of sight did not affect performance in the R task for either group. In a subjective questionnaire on the strategy utilized by each subject to facilitate remembering each task, both groups reported utilizing an imaginal strategy.

After years of training, dancers develop an awareness of their bodies that enable them to move competently in a variety of directions and floor patterns, and to replicate complex body positions. Dancers seemingly have the ability to grasp visual images and transform them into actions. Although the dance literature (Hawkins, 1964; Hayes, 1964; Hays, 1981; Sherbon, 1975) describes the changes in dance ability that occur as a result of dance experience, there are few empirical studies dealing with the nature of the dancers body awareness and its relation to dance ability and imagery.

Dancers ability to move easily in many directions and initiate various postures is indicative of the perceptual motor process—body awareness. Body awareness is defined as the conscious awareness and identification of the location, position, and movement of the body and its parts, and the relationship between the body and its parts (moving or stationary) to the external environment (Williams, 1983). The construct of body awareness includes internal and external subcomponents.

The internal subcomponents consist of awareness of the body and its parts. Included are laterality, awareness of spatial dimensions of the body, and identification of body parts. The external subcomponents are those concerned with the interaction and interrelationship of the body and its parts with the environment. Dance training emphasizes body awareness in space as one of the key elements of successful movement. Modern dance texts give many explorational activities to enhance the dancer's ability to move in space (Chaney, 1969; Hawkins, 1964; Hays, 1981; Lockhart, 1977; Sherbon, 1975). A dancer's training entails an increasingly complex utilization of space. Some of the elements of space that directly relate to the external elements of body awareness are direction, floor patterns, levels, and body shape. Objectives of a beginning-level modern dance class might include the identification of spatial elements and the execution of simple movement patterns in specified spatial areas. Objectives of an advanced dance class might include not only the utilization of all areas of the space, but also the composing and choreography of movement into personally unique designs that would unify all elements of space into an aesthetically pleasing design. In all of these experiences, it is hypothesized that dancers develop a kinesthetic sense that enhances their body awareness in space. The specific elements of space studied by dancers include levels, direction, focus, and body shape.

The specific components of body awareness used in this study were directionality, spatial orientation, and reflective body perception. These three components were chosen because they directly relate to the elements of space, studied by dancers. Directionality is the capacity to identify various aspects of external space and the ability to project outward the spatial dimensions of the body. "The identification of the dimensions of external space involves directional labels such as right-left, up-down, front-back—the same directional labels used in identifying spatial dimensions of the body" (Williams, 1983, p. 311).

Another component of body awareness is spatial orientation. Spatial orientation refers to the position of the body in space without reference to another object or another person. External referents are not a necessity in spatial orientation as they are in directionality. The integration of the somatosensory system and visual information provides the basic information needed for perception of spatial orientation. Studies have shown that a relationship exists between spatial orientation and field independence or dependence (Witkin, 1954, 1959). Gruen (1955) utilized spatial orientation tests developed by Witkin et al. (1954) to test male and female professional dancers. Gruen concluded that in general, the perceptual performance of dancers does not differ from that of a control group.

Reflective body perception, the third component selected, is defined as the individual's ability to spontaneously and accurately imitate body positions (Arnheim & Sinclair, 1979). Reflective body perception or imitation of postures has mainly been studied with children. The child's ability to accurately imitate postures has been measured by utilizing a model who assumes various positions with the body and performs different gestures. The child must then replicate the position or gesture. Studies of imitation tests have shown there is an age-related improvement in the child's ability to replicate simple and complex movements (Ayers, 1969; Berges & Lezine, 1965). The data also suggests that the capacity to imitate body postures is not fully developed until some time after the age of eight years (Ayers, 1969).

In a study by Housner (1981), imitation tasks were developed and utilized with adult subjects. These tasks included 12 movement sequences consisting of 8 head, arm, trunk, or leg positioning movements. The movements were performed by a male dancer, filmed on super 8-mm film relative to the subjects lateral plane and viewed from the rear of the model. Housner classified the two groups of subjects as high and low imagery and found that the high imagery recalled the movements significantly better than the low imagery in a free recall condition.

The present experiment was designed to test the hypothesis that the body awareness of experienced dancers would differ significantly from that of novice dancers. To test this notion the subjects observed a model performing directionality tasks, and reflective body perception tasks. After observing the modeled behavior, they were tested on their ability to reproduce it, blindfolded and sighted. The rationale for the unsighted condition was that blindfolding subjects would encourage them to use kinesthetic information and an imaginal coding system to recall movement. Following the experiment a questionnaire was utilized to test the hypothesis that an imaginal coding strategy was used to enhance the retention of the movement tasks by both novice and experienced dancers.

A second objective of the present study was to examine the effect of high imagery patterns versus lower imagery pattern on the accurate reproduction of modeled activity. Previous research by Hall (1980) indicated that the higher the imagery value of a movement pattern, the better the pattern is remembered.

METHODS

Subjects

The sample consisted of 20 experienced female dancers 18 to 30 years of age, with 5 or more years of dance training in modern dance and/or ballet, and 20 novice female dancers 18 to 30 years of age with 1 year or less of dance training. The novice dancers also had not participated in any varsity-level athletics or gymnastics. All subjects were volunteers, and the majority were students at the University of Maryland. The experienced dancers were current dance majors or recent graduates of the dance program at the University of Maryland. The novice dancers were volunteers from a variety of classes on the College Park Campus. In the initial briefing subjects were told that the purpose of the study was to explore differences between novice and experienced dancers in body awareness and imagery ability. Subjects were guaranteed complete privacy of response.

Body Awareness Tasks

There were two body-awareness tasks—(a) directionality (D) and (b) reflective body perception (R). In the D task, the subjects stood in the center of a taped rectangle on the floor. (A sketch and dimensions of the area are presented in Figure 1.) The subject viewed a videotaped presentation of four floor patterns and one sequence of three floor patterns. The four floor patterns were the ○ , △ , ⌐, and ⌐ The sequence consisted of the ○ , △ , ⌐ , and ⌐ The directionality tasks developed for this study included components of directionality and spatial orientation. The specific design of the tasks required the subjects to view a model of the criterion movement pattern. Subjects were subsequently videotaped as they moved in a specific direction (i.e., forward, backward, or sideward) in a specific floor pattern (i.e. ○ , △ , ⌐, or ⌐) in a specific area of the floor space.

The floor patterns included in the directionality task were based on Craig Hall's work. In 1980, Hall conducted three experiments designed to investigate imagery as a stimulus characteristic of movement patterns.

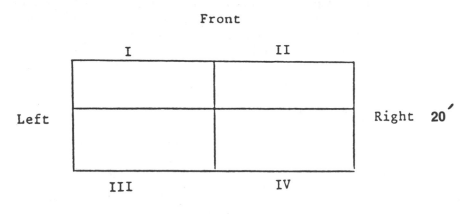

281′

Front

Figure 1

He hypothesized that patterns with higher imagery value would be easier to remember. He based this theoretical position on the dual-coding model of imagery proposed by Paivio (1971). The dual coding model assumes that verbal and nonverbal information are represented and processed in independent but interconnected symbolic systems, and that the nature of the symbolic information differs qualitatively in the two systems. In Hall's experiments, a panel of three judges selected 18 movement patterns from a set of 36 possible patterns. Two major conclusions were drawn from these experiments: (1) movement patterns are a direct function of the imagery value associated with the pattern (i.e., the higher the imagery value, the better the pattern is remembered), and (2) conditions that encourage nonverbal imagery, such as instructions in image, generally result in higher levels of recall of memory for movements.

The four single floor patterns and one sequence of three floor patterns were performed by a female dancer and filmed on videotape. All subjects performed the tasks sighted and blindfolded. Their reproduction was videotaped.

The reflective body perception tasks consisted of a series of eight head, arm, trunk, and leg positioning movements. Six sequences of positioning movements were constructed by combining the alternative responses associated with each body part listed in Table 1. Eight moves were selected from this list and combined to form a sequence. Each of the six sequences, though novel, resembled those types of movements encountered in naturalistic settings such as cheerleading. These sequences were based on descriptions of motoric stimuli by Housner (1981, 1984). Complete descriptions of both body-awareness tasks are available from the author. The subjects reproduced four sequences with eyes open and four sequences with their eyes closed. The subjects' reproduction attempts were videotaped.

Experimental Sessions

Directionality Task. A standard set of instructions was read to subjects upon entering the dance studio. They were given two practice attempts at reproducing movement sequences not used in the experimental trials. Subjects assumed the anatomical position, positioning their feet on markings placed on the studio floor. A trial commenced with the cue "ready," which indicated that the large-screen video monitor was about to be activated. Immediately following a single presentation of a criterion floor pattern on the monitor, subjects were instructed to reproduce this floor pattern, while moving in the correct direction and in the correct spatial area. In the blindfolded condition, the subjects viewed the criterion movement shown on the monitor, then immediately put on a pair of plastic safety goggles with black lenses. They were then instructed to reproduce the floor pattern. After completing the pattern they removed their goggles and returned to the starting position, ready to view the next floor pattern. The subjects performed the directionality task first. This required approximately 15 minutes. The time of presentation of each floor pattern was as follows: floor pattern 1—6 seconds, floor pattern 2—6 seconds, floor pattern 3—26 seconds, floor pattern 4—12 seconds, and sequence—39 seconds. There were 7 seconds between each pattern.

Reflective Body Perception Task. Subjects assumed the anatomical position, positioning their feet on markings placed on the dance studio floor. Subjects were given two practice attempts at reproducing movement sequences not used in the experimental trials. A trial commenced with the cue "ready," which indicated that the video monitor was about to be activated. Subjects reproduced four sequences. After the fourth sequence, subjects were instructed to watch the next sequence, then close

Table 1.
Alternate Responses Associated with Body Parts Used for Construction of Criterion Positioning Sequences

I. Arm Positions (Humerus) (Right or Left Arm)
    A. Vertical (Arm Down)
    B. Vertical (Arm Up)
    C. Horizontal
    D. 45° Above Horizontal
    E. 45° Below Horizontal
II. Head Positions
    A. Head Rotated 90° Right
    B. Head Rotated 90° Left
    C. Head Rotated to Center (from Right or Left)
III. Arm Position (Radius) (Right or Left Arm)
    A. Flexed to 90° (up) from Humerus
    B. Full extension
IV. Trunk Positions
    A. Trunk Positions
    B. Trunk Flexed Left
    C. Trunk Extended to Upright (Right or Left)
    V. Leg Position
    A. Step Sideways Open (Right or Left)
    B. Step Close (Right or Left)
    C. Flex Legs to Squat
    D. Extend Legs to Upright

their eyes before reproducing the movement. After each attempt the subjects opened their eyes to view the next sequence.

The subjects performed the reflective body perception task second. The time of presentation for each sequence was 7 seconds, with 7 seconds between each sequence. Testing for the body awareness tasks took approximately 25 minutes.

Dependent Variables

Analyses of Videotapes. In rating the directionality, task decision rules were employed. A possible 3 points was awarded for each floor pattern. No errors was awarded 3 points, 1 error in floor-pattern direction or spatial orientation was awarded 2 points. Two errors in floor-pattern direction or spatial orientation was awarded 1 point. Three or more errors in floor-pattern direction or spatial orientation was awarded zero points. A total of 15 points was possible in the sighted condition, and 15 points in the unsighted condition.

In rating the reflective body-perception tasks, decision rules were developed and utilized. A protractor was employed to measure each position. A total of 8 points per sequence was possible, 32 points per condition. A subject was given credit for accurately reproducing a position regardless of the order in which it appeared in the modeled response.

In order to determine the reliability of the scoring system, the primary investigator and a second observer independently viewed and judged a random sample of 20 trials of the directionality tasks, and 16 trials of reflective body-perception tasks. Intra-rater agreement was determined by comparing the scores from 20 trials of the directionality task and 16 trials of the reflective body-perception task to the same scores generated two weeks earlier by the primary investigator.

The degree of intra-rater agreement was found to be 94% for the directionality tasks and 98% for the reflective body-perception task. Inter-rater agreement was found to be 90% for the directionality task, and 93% for the reflective body-perception task. The second observer was a dance teacher with many years of performance and teaching experience.

Experimental Design

The experimental design tested the hypotheses that (a) the body-awareness task (D and R) scores of novice dancers would differ significantly from the experienced dancers in both sighted and unsighted conditions, (b) the experienced dancers and novice dancers would utilize an imaginal strategy to enhance retention of the movement tasks, and (c) the higher imagery directionality pattern of both groups would be recalled and reproduced more accurately than the lower imagery directionality patterns in both sighted and unsighted conditions. The experimental design of the body awareness tasks was a $2 \times 2 \times 2$ MANOVA (experience $\times$ body awareness task $\times$ sight condition) with repeated measures on last factor. A questionnaire was utilized to subjectively assess the subjects use of imagery as a strategy for recalling the movement tasks. The t-test was utilized to determine any significant differences between the performances of the higher imagery directionality patterns and the lower imagery directionality patterns in both sighted and unsighted conditions.

RESULTS

Descriptive Analyses

The range, mean, and standard deviation for each dependent variable are presented in Table 2 for novice dancers and Table 3 for experienced dancers.

Body Awareness

The hypothesis stating that the experienced dancers would differ significantly from novice dancers on body awareness tasks D and R in sighted and unsighted conditions was supported. Experienced dancers were more proficient than novice dancers in both tasks. The omnibus multivariate analysis (MANOVA) with repeated measures yielded significant main effects for experience, Wilk's Lambda = .488 $F(4, 75)$ = 9.195, $p < .001$, for sighted condition, Wilk's Lambda = .648, $F(4, 75)$ = 10.29, $p < .001$. The interaction of the group and sight condition was not significant, $p > .1$. Follow-up univariate ANOVAS were performed to examine the appropriate hypotheses.

Directionality (D). Results of the follow-up ANOVA on directionality revealed a main effect for dance experience, $F(1, 38) = 14.03, p < .001$, in which the experienced dancers performed the directionality tasks better across the two sighted conditions. The effect of sight was also significant, $F(1, 38) = 18.84, p < .001$. For both groups, performance of the task sighted resulted in better performance than blindfolded (see Figure 2).

Reflective Body Perception (R). The follow-up ANOVA on reflective body perception produced the following: (1) a significantly higher score for the experienced dancers across both sighted conditions, $F(1, 38) = 32.81, p < .001$, and (2) the effect of sight did not affect performance in the R task for either group ($p > .5$ main effect of sight, and $p > .3$ for the interaction; see Figure 3).

Strategy. The second hypothesis stated that the experienced and novice dancers would utilize an imaginal strategy to enhance the retention of the body-awareness tasks. This hypothesis was supported as illustrated in Tables 4 and 5.

Imagery Rating. For both the novice and experienced dancers the high imagery directionality patterns in the sighted condition were reproduced more accurately than the lower imagery patterns, $\underline{T} = 6.19$, df = 39, $\underline{p} = < 10\ (-6)$. In the unsighted condition, the higher imagery

Table 2.
Descriptive Analyses—Group 1: Novice Dancers
Range, Mean, and Standard Deviation in Each Dependent Variable

Group	D(S)	D(U)	R(S)	R(U)	HID(S)	HID(U)	LID(S)	LID(U)	P(S)	P(U)
Range	06–14	06–12	15–25	14–27	4–6	5–6	1–6	1–6	0–3	0–2
Mean	10.15	9.25	19.30	19.10	5.45	5.35	3.95	3.35	0.75	0.60
Standard Deviation	2.00	1.80	3.59	4.29	0.75	0.67	1.31	1.26	0.85	0.82

Table 3.
Descriptive Analyses—Group 2: Experienced Dancers
Range, Mean, and Standard Deviation in Each Dependent Variable

Group	D(S)	D(U)	R(S)	R(U)	HID(S)	HID(U)	LID(S)	LID(U)	P(S)	P(U)
Range	09–14	07–13	19–31	18–31	5–6	4–6	3–6	3–5	0–3	0–3
Mean	12.25	10.45	24.40	25.30	5.85	5.60	4.85	3.60	1.55	1.30
Standard Deviation	1.51	1.43	3.36	3.70	0.36	0.68	0.93	0.68	0.94	0.78

Notes: S = sighted
U = unsighted (blind-folded)
D = directionality
R = reflective body perception
HID(S) = high imagery directionality (sighted)
HID(U) = high imagery directionality (unsighted)
LID(S) = low imagery directionality (sighted)
LID(U) = low imagery directionality (unsighted)
P(S) = pattern (sighted)
P(U) = pattern (unsighted)

Table 4.
Strategies for Remembering Body Awareness Tasks: Novice Dancers

	Visual Image Only	Verbal Label Only	Both	Neither
D	7	5	6	2
R	7	7	4	2

Table 5.
Strategies for Remembering Body Awareness Tasks: Experienced Dancers

	Visual Image Only	Verbal Label Only	Both	Neither
D	16	1	2	1
R	16	2	1	1

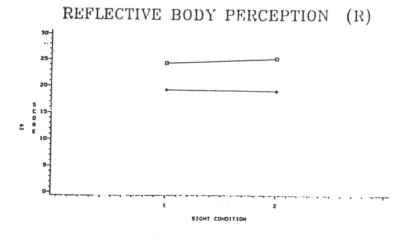

REFLECTIVE BODY PERCEPTION (R)

SIGHT CONDITION

1 = SIGHTED   2 = UNSIGHTED
SQUARE-EXPERIENCED   STAR-NOVICE

Figure 2

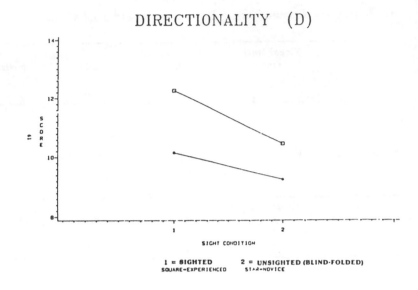

DIRECTIONALITY (D)

Figure 3

patterns were reproduced more accurately than the lower imagery patterns, $\underline{T}$ = 11.90, df = 39, $\underline{p}$ = < 10 (−6) (see Figure 4).

DISCUSSION

This study yielded several interesting findings that corroborate the influential role played by experience in the accurate replication of modeled movement. Experienced dancers scored significantly better on body awareness tasks (D and R) than novice dancers. These results add support to the assertion of dance theoretical literature that dance training positively affects an individual's ability to move through space (Hawkins, 1964; Hayes, 1964; Hays, 1981; Sherbon, 1975).

The perceptual motor literature categorizes the ability to move through space as body awareness abilities. The results of this present experiment support evidence of Williams (1983), Ayers (1969), and Cratty (1979), who report an improvement in body awareness that is directly related to development and experience with spatial concepts. Experienced dancers performed significantly better in body awareness (D and R) than novice dancers in the sighted and unsighted conditions.

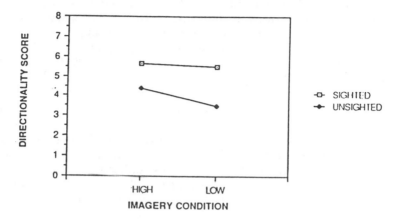

Figure 4

These results further support the contention that dance experience increases the ability to affect kinesthetic responses.

In a subjective questionnaire on the strategy utilized by each subject to facilitate remembering each task, both groups reported utilizing an imaginal strategy. They reported (1) remembering the shapes (visual coding) and counting the steps (verbal coding) (see Tables 4 and 5). However, the increased level of performance of the experienced dancers could be attributed to a combination of imagery ability and experience with movement. As noted by Sternberg and Weil (1980) a relationship exists between ability and strategy. That is "the effectiveness of a given strategy depends on one's pattern of abilities" (1980, p. 234), cited in Yuille, 1983), and one's choice of strategy may be predictable from a knowledge of psychometrically tested abilities (Macleod et al., 1978; Matthews et al., 1980; both cited in Yuille, 1983).

In the directionality task the experienced dancers made fewer directional, floor pattern, and spatial orientation errors in both the sighted and blindfolded conditions. Both groups performed better in the sighted condition than in the blindfolded condition. The directionality task was composed of movements in a specific-direction floor pattern and spatial location of the space. The floor patterns included two high imagery patterns, floor patterns 1 and 2 and two lower imagery patterns, floor patterns 3 and 4 (Hall, 1980). An expected trend toward higher scores for both groups in the high imagery pattern was revealed (see Figure 5). These results provide support for Hall's 1980 assertion that movement patterns can be scaled on imagery and recognition memory. The results of the directionality experiment provided support for the contention of Hall (1980), that movement patterns are a direct function of the imagery value associated with the pattern—the higher the imagery value, the better the pattern is remembered, and in this case, the more accurately the pattern in reproduced.

The reflective body-perception tasks included movement sequences consisting of eight distinct head, arm, trunk, or leg positioning movements. A free-recall scoring system was utilized with the subjects. This was based on Housner's studies (1981, 1984), wherein his findings suggested that visual imagery may have played a functional role in the free recall of modeled movements. The results revealed a significantly higher score for the experienced dancers across both sighted conditions.

One possible explanation of the increased performance of the experienced dancers based on the responses of the subjects to the questionnaire is that because of their experience with movement they were able to form more pertinent visual images of the novel movement sequences. The results of the R tasks in the unsighted condition revealed a small decline for the novice and a small gain for the experienced dancers. However, the effect of sight did not significantly affect performance in this task for either group. Unlike the D task, where the subjects were moving their entire body through general space, in the R task the subjects remained in their personal space as they moved body parts. This movement in one location in the unsighted condition did not affect performance as radically as movement through space in the unsighted condition.

The present study points to the need for continued research in the areas of body awareness. Developmentalists could study the body-awareness changes that occur throughout the lifespan. Data on body awareness changes are primarily confined to young children. The amount of research is sparse, even for children. Accompanying the need for research is the need for standardized tests of body awareness. Few exist presently. This information could lead to measures that could assess body awareness of novice, expert, and developmentally delayed movers.

REFERENCES

Arnheim, D. C., & Sinclair, W. A. (1979). *The clumsy child*. St. Louis: The C. V. Mosby Company.

Ayers, A. J. (1969). *Southern California perceptual motor tests.* Los Angeles: Western Psychological Services.

Berges, J., & Lezine, I. (1965). *The imitation of gestures* (Arthur. H. Parmelee, Trans.). The Spastics Society Medical Education and Information Unit in Association with William Heineman (Medical) Books Ltd. London.

Chaney, G., & Strader, J. (1969). *Modern dance.* Boston: Allyn and Bacon, Inc.

Cratty, B. J. (1979). *Perceptual and motor development in infants and children.* Englewood Cliffs, NJ: Prentice Hall, Inc.

Ellfeldt, L. (1971). *A primer for choreography.* Palo Alto, CA: National Press Books.

Fleishman, E. A., & Rich, S. (1963). Role of kinesthetic and spatial-visual abilities in perceptual motor learning. *Journal of Experimental Psychology, 66,* 6–11.

Gruen, A. (1955). The relation of dancing experience and personality to perception. *Psychological Monographs: General and Applied, 69,* 1–16.

Hale, B. (1982). The effects of internal and external imagery on muscular and ocular concommitants. *Journal of Sport Psychology, 4,* 379–387.

Hall, C. R. (1980). Imagery for movement. *Journal of Human Movement Studies, 6,* 252–264.

Hall, C. R., & Buckolz, E. (1983). Imagery and the recall of movement patterns. *Imagination, Cognition and Personality, 2,* 251–260.

Hann, V. (1973). *A comparison of experienced modern dancers to nondancers in self-image, body image, movement concept and kinesthetic arm positioning.* Unpublished masters thesis, Washington State University, Pullman, WA.

Hawkins, A. M. (1964). *Creating through dance.* Englewood Cliffs, NJ: Prentice Hall.

Hayes, E. R. (1964). *An introduction to the teaching of dance.* New York: The Ronald Press Company.

Hays, J. F. (1981). *Modern dance: A biochemical approach to teaching.* St. Louis: C. V. Mosby Company.

Housner, L. D. (1981). The role of imaginal processing in the short term retention of visually-presented sequential motoric stimuli, *University Microfilms International.* DAI 421 12A, p. 5055. Publication No.: AACB208680.

Housner, L. D. (1984). The role of imaginal processing in the retention of visually-presented sequential motoric stimuli. *Research Quarterly for Exercise and Sport, 55,* 24–31.

Housner, L. D., & Hoffman, S. J. (1978). Imagery and short term motor memory. In G. C. Roberts and K. M. Newell (Eds.), *Psychology of motor behavior and sport* (pp. 182–191). Champaign, IL: WASPA Human Kinetics Publishers.

Housner, L., & Hoffman, S. J. (1981). Imagery ability in recall of distance and location information. *Journal of Motor Behavior, 13,* 207–223.

Jones, L. S. (1972). *The construct of body awareness in space as reflected through children's ability to discriminate directions, levels and pathways in movement.* Unpublished doctoral dissertation, University of Wisconsin, Madison.

Lockhart, A. S., & Pease, E. (1970). *Modern dance building and teaching lessons.* Dubuque, Iowa: William C. Brown Company.

Long, A. B., & Looft, W. R. (1972). Development of directionality in children. *Developmental Psychology, 6,* 375–380.

Marteniuk, R. G. (1976). *Information processing in motor skills.* New York: Holt, Rinehart and Winston.

Montoye, H. (1970). *An introduction to measurement in physical education.* Indianapolis: Phi Epsilon Kappa Fraternity.

Paivio, A. (1971). *Imagery and verbal processes*. New York: Holt, Rinehart and Winston.

Posner, M. I. (1967). Characteristics of visual and kinesthetic memory codes. *Journal of Experimental Psychology, 75,* 103–107.

Sage, G. H. (1984). *Motor learning and control: A neuropsychological approach*. Dubuque, IA: William C. Brown.

Sheets, M. (1966). *The phenomenology of dance*. Madison: The University of Wisconsin Press.

Sherbon, E. (1975). *On the count of one: Modern dance methods*. Palo Alto, CA: Mayfield Publishing Company.

Shick, J., Stoner, L., & Jette (1983). Relationship between modern-dance experience and balancing performance. *Research Quarterly for Exercise and Sport, 54,* 79–82.

Stelmach, G. E. (1974). Retention of motor skills. In J. H. Wilmore (Ed.), *Exercise and sport sciences reviews*. New York: in press.

Sweigard, L. (1974). *Human movement potential: Its ideokinetic facilitation*. New York: Dodd, Mead and Company, 1974.

Williams, H. (1983). *Perceptual and motor development*. Englewood Cliffs, NJ: Prentice-Hall, Inc.

Witkin, H. (1965). Development of the body concept and psychological differentiation. In S. Wapner and H. Werner (Eds.), *The body percept*. New York: Random House.

Witkin, H. A. (February 1959). The perception of the upright. *Scientific American,* pp. 51–56.

Witkin, H. A., Lewis, H., Hertzman, M., Machover, K., Bretnall-Meissner, P., & Wapner, S. (1954). *Personality through perception*. New York: Harper.

Yuille, J. C. (1983). *Imagery memory and cognition*. Hillsdale, NJ: Lawrence Erlbaum Associates.

6

THE DEVELOPMENT OF A SPATIAL KINESTHETIC AWARENESS MEASURING INSTRUMENT FOR USE WITH BEGINNING DANCE STUDENTS

"Sandra Minton, Jeffrey Steffen"

The purpose of this research was to develop an instrument for measuring selected aspects of kinesthetic ability of dance students. A survey of kinesthetic assessment tests was conducted. The instrument designed in this study was derived from the Hill Performance Test of Selected Positional Concepts published in 1981. Eight items were constructed using poses to emphasize body shape. Another eight items emphasized placement/ position of body parts. The Spatial Kinesthetic Awareness Measuring Instrument was tested for reliability and validity in fall of 1987. The test/retest method was used to determine reliability. Validity was established using a panel of judges' scores as criterion measure. Subjects were 22 college students enrolled in beginning modern dance at the University of Northern Colorado. The panel of judges was composed of experienced dance teacher-performers. Judges rated each student from a class video-tape on a scale of 1–5 on shape and placement/position. The 16-item instrument was administered during the following two class periods. The investigator then viewed videotapes of subjects performing the test and scored each subject on a scale of 1–5 for each item. Validity derived from a correlation of judges' scores with the test scores was shape (r = .67) and placement/position (r = .74). Reliability was r = .81.

This investigator began to realize the need for developing a better understanding of the kinesthetic sense after many years' experience teaching beginning dance at the college level. It seemed as though beginning students needed to be introduced to a more basic understanding of the body and its movement potential before engaging in the learning of the more complex patterns traditionally taught in a dance class. Experience showed, for example, that students were often confused about the direction of a movement of a body part or of the entire body through space, and that they did not tune into or remember the feeling of tension or energy that was an important part of the accurate performance of a particular sequence. These abilities are important in the training and development of a skilled dancer.

The above observations led to a desire first to understand kinesthetic awareness in order to improve dance teaching techniques and then to construct a test for this trait or characteristic. Such a kinesthetic test instrument, once proven to be reliable and valid, could be used as part of the screening process for entrance into dance major and minor programs. This would establish a basic level of kinesthetic ability as a prerequisite. The test could be an objective tool used to complement the more subjective opinion of the dance faculty during the audition process. Base-level kinesthetic testing is not currently part of dance auditions, although some college dance programs are now using other types of elementary screening procedures before placing a student at a specific class level (Plastino, 1987).

KINESTHETIC AWARENESS TESTING

The topic of kinesthetic ability or awareness has long been the basis for research studies, particularly in the field of physical education. Some dance educators were also interested in investigating kinesthetic ability testing.

The Kinesthetic Sense Organs

The kinesthetic sensory organs include several different structures: muscle spindles or fluid-filled capsules within the muscles and parallel to muscle fibers; golgi tendon organs found in tendons near muscle; and several kinds of joint receptors located within the joint (Sage, 1977). These structures collectively provide an individual with kinesthetic sensory feedback, and operate in conjunction with the vestibular apparatus located adjacent to the inner ear. Schmidt (1982) believes that kinesthetic sensing operates with remarkable accuracy, but that any one type of receptor is ineffective in isolation; rather, sensations from all types of receptors are integrated in the central nervous system to produce an ensemble of information. Much research is needed to describe the functioning of the kinesthetic sense more accurately. One unsolved problem is whether kinesthesis is a specific or general factor, and how kinesthetic sensations integrate with vestibular, visual, and pressure cues to create a total perception of movement (Cratty, 1973). One researcher concluded that individuals could not accomplish motor learning on the basis of kinesthetic information alone, but needed other forms of sensory input (Drowatzky, 1975).

Kinesthetic Ability

Gladys Scott (1955, 1959) felt that the kinesthetic sense enables an individual to (1) perceive position and movement of the total body and its parts; (2) sense gradations of effort; (3) have knowledge of rate, extent, and direction of movement; (4) have both dynamic and static balance; and (5) duplicate movements as performed. According to other authorities, rhythm is also closely associated with the kinesthetic sense (Johnson & Nelson, 1974), as is the perception of body tensions and movement (Wiebe, 1954). Christina (1967) worded his definition of kinesthesis in a slightly different manner, saying that this sense made one aware of the force and extent of muscular contraction and the orientations of the body and body parts in space. This variety of definitions has led to conflict and confusion in the development of previous kinesthetic awareness tests.

The Kinesthetic Sense and Motor Learning

Many of these investigators also felt that it was necessary to establish a connection between kinesthetic ability and motor learning. An early study by Phillips (1941) had variable results. It showed that efficiency of kinesthesis could have either a positive or negative relationship to success of performance depending on which phase of kinesthesis was being evaluated. In another study, specific manual tasks were used as a test of basic kinesthetic ability with the result that those more skilled in athletic performance scored higher while doing these manual tasks (Wiebe, 1954). Roloff (1953) said that individuals with a higher level of basic kinesthetic awareness showed a greater ability to learn movement skills. Scott (1959) agreed that a high degree of kinesthetic acuity is closely related to general motor ability. She felt that those with greater kinesthetic awareness, when given the opportunity to practice, demonstrated greater motor accomplishments than those without such a high degree of acuity.

Survey of Kinesthetic Tests

Many of the investigators already mentioned researched the reliablity and validity of various kinesthetic tests. These tests included a variety of tasks presented in a battery commensurate with the various skills that make up kinesthetic awareness. Some of these tasks included accuracy in raising an arm or leg a specific number of degrees; ability to grip a dynamometer repeatedly with the same amount of tension;

ability to push or pull an object a designated distance; measurement of the amount of time one could balance on a stick (static balance); skill in balancing following the performance of a side leap (dynamic balance); and walking in a geometric pattern such as a triangle (Scott, 1959). Other tests such as accuracy in pointing or throwing at a target were often included in these batteries (Roloff, 1953).

Weibe (1954) found that 15 of the kinesthetic tasks had reliability coefficients high enough to recommend them as a useful test, while Scott (1955) found the tests for balance consistently reliable and fairly valid. In general, however, the investigators recommended the use of a test battery rather than a single test since none of the validity coefficients for separate tasks were high enough to merit their use as a single test (Roloff, 1953; Scott, 1955; Wiebe, 1954). Low intercorrelations between tasks led to the conclusion that there is no general kinesthetic ability, but that there are probably numerous functions that make up kinesthesis (Phillips, 1941; Scott, 1955; Wiebe, 1954; Young, 1945). Scott (1959) felt that kinesthetic ability is like other movement abilities in that it is highly specific to particular areas of the body; tests must be selected so as to supplement rather than duplicate others in a battery.

Christina investigated the Side Arm Positional Test of the Kinesthetic Sense. In this test, the subject is blindfolded and asked to raise his or her arm to the side. After the arm is dropped, the subject is asked to duplicate the position held earlier. This test was found to be reliable from day to day, but more precise with the nondominant arm; accuracy also improved as the size of the joint angle under the arm was increased (Christina, 1967).

Studies Involving Dancers

Various forms of kinesthetic testing have been used in research done on dancers and on dance-related movement disciplines. Many of these studies were designed to compare groups that differed in terms of kind or amount of movement experience. Carter (1965) had two groups of women as her subjects, those highly skilled in dance and those highly skilled in sports. When using static and dynamic balance tests as one criterion of comparison, she found that the dance group scored better on the balance tests. Hann (1973) also designed a study comparing two groups—modern dancers and nondancers. She had her subjects perform the Side Arm Test as a measure of kinesthetic ability and found no significant difference between the two groups. Brennan (1967) compared four groups (gymnasts, dancers, sports-proficient individuals, and the untrained) on selected characteristics using tests such as arm circling, leg lifting, and weight shifting. The selected variables served to discriminate each of the four groups, but failed to do so to the same degree for each group. The dance and gymnastic groups had closely related test scores. The scores of the sports proficient and untrained were clearly defined but had little relationship to each of the other three groups (Brennan, 1967).

In a study done by Frial (1965), the goal was to use kinesthetic tests as a predictor of ability in modern dance. The result here was that kinesthetic tests such as those already described did distinguish good dancers from both poor dancers and nondancers, but it was hard to use these same tests to separate nondancers from poor dancers.

Other researchers tried to show that dance training improved performance on kinesthetic tests. Ludwig (1971) concluded that training in modern dance increased ability to balance, while Schneider (1977) had the opposite results after exposing subjects to mime and movement exploration. Barrack, Skinner, Brunet, and Cook (1984) sought to determine what effects ballet training had on the sense of joint position and motion. In this instance, it was found that dancers, when compared to a control group of nondancers, detected slight changes of joint position earlier and with more consistency.

DESIGN OF THE SPATIAL KINESTHETIC AWARENESS TEST

This test was limited to the spatial aspects of kinesthetic ability, and did not include construction of tests to measure tension, balance, or any of the other components of kinesthesis. The measuring instrument designed here was derived from the Hill Performance Test of Selected Positional Concepts (Hill, 1981). The Hill Test has been proven a reliable and valid kinesthetic test for blind children, so it was necessary to formulate an instrument that was more complex and could be used with adults. The investigators also wanted this test to have more items that were like dance movement.

Methods

The two sections of the Hill Test used in developing items on the Spatial Kinesthetic Awareness Test were (1) identifying positional relationships of body parts and (2) demonstrating positional concepts by moving body parts in relation to each other. Eight items were constructed using poses to emphasize body shape. An additional eight items were devised emphasizing placement/position of body parts. Shape was defined as the actual shape (curved or angular) of a body part. Placement/position referred to the relationship between body parts. These items were demonstrated and recorded on a videotape. The spatial aspects of direction, level, and size were not included in the final form of this test, although they had been a part of earlier instruments.

The final form of the Spatial Kinesthetic Awareness Measuring Instrument was tested for reliability and validity during the fall of 1987. The test/retest method was used to determine the reliability of the instrument. The time between testing was less than 10 days. Validity was established using a panel of (3–4) judges' scores as a criterion measure. Subjects were 22 college students enrolled in beginning modern dance at the University of Northern Colorado. The panel of judges was composed of experienced dancer-teacher-performers from the same institution. Each subject was videotaped while taking a dance class. The judges rated each student in the class videotape on two aspects of spatial kinesthetic awareness: shape and placement/position. Rating was on a scale of 1–5. The 16-item videotaped test was administered during the following two class periods. Each item (shape, placement/position) was demonstrated on a big-screen television in front of the students. Following the demonstration on the videotape, the subjects were asked to duplicate the body shape or position shown on the screen. While the students duplicated the movement demonstrated, they were filmed again. One of the investigators then viewed the videotapes of the subjects performing the 16 items and scored each of the 22 subjects on a scale of 1–5, using the Spatial Kinesthetic Awareness Measuring Instrument. Originally, all rating and test scoring was done with verbal instructions, but this was found to be confusing for both judges and subjects alike.

Results

Validity derived from a correlation of judges' scores and subject scores on the test instrument was shape ($r = .67$), and placement/position ($r = .74$). Test-retest reliability calculated for the Spatial Kinesthetic Awareness Instrument was $r = .81$.

DISCUSSION

A survey of the literature revealed that kinesthetic ability is actually a grouping of many individual sensory skills including perception of body position or shape; movement speed, direction, and size; muscular contraction, effort, and tension; and orientation in space. The kinesthetic sense also is important in rhythmic ability and in static and dynamic balance.

Past research showed that tests for kinesthetic ability were as varied as the sense itself and that most, but not all, investigations demonstrated a higher level of kinesthetic ability among more skilled performers. Those subjects with varying kinds of skills such as dance or a sport activity also appeared to score differently on these tests.

The solution to kinesthetic ability testing seems to be found in devising a battery of separate tasks, each of which deals with a different aspect of kinesthesis. The instrument designed and tested in this study is an attempt to provide for one such test. It includes items to test for the spatial awareness of shape and placement/position. The Spatial Kinesthetic Awareness Instrument takes only 15 minutes to complete and is easy to administer through the use of the videotape format. Dance is movement performed in an open environment, making it difficult to control during assessment periods. The use of the videotape helps give the dance researcher the advantage of having more control of environmental variables. Additional tests would have to be constructed to assess the other components of kinesthetic ability besides body shape and placement/position in order to measure all aspects of this human ability.

REFERENCES

Barrack, R., Skinner, H., Brunet, M., & Cook, S. (1984). Joint kinesthesia in the highly trained knee. *Journal of Sports Medicine and Physical Fitness, 24,* 18–20.

Brennan, M. (1967). *A comparison of skilled gymnasts and dancers on thirteen selected characteristics.* Unpublished master's thesis, University of Wisconsin, Madison, WI.

Carter, F. H. (1966). Selected kinesthetic and psychological differences between the highly skilled in dance and sports. (Doctoral dissertation, University of Iowa, 1965). *Dissertation Abstracts, 26,* 5850.

Chin, D. L. (1985). The effects of dance movement instruction on spatial awareness in elementary visually impaired students, and self-concept in secondary visually impaired students (Doctoral dissertation, University of Northern Colorado, 1984). *Dissertation Abstracts International, 45A,* 3111-A.

Christina, R. (1967). The sidearm positional test of kinesthetic sense. *The Research Quarterly, 38,* 177–183.

Cratty, B. (1973). *Movement behavior and motor learning* (3rd ed.). Philadelphia: Lea & Febiger.

Drowatzky, J. (1975). *Motor learning: Principles and Practices.* Minneapolis: Burgess.

Frial, P. (1965). *Prediction of modern dance ability through kinesthetic tests.* Unpublished master's thesis, Iowa State University, Ames, IA.

Hann, V. (1973). *Comparison of experienced modern dancers to non-dancers in self-image, body image, movement concept and kinesthetic arm positioning.* Unpublished master's thesis, Washington State University, Pullman, WA.

Hill, E. (1981). *The Hill performance test of selected positional concepts.* Chicago: Stoelting.

Johnson, B., & Nelson, J. (1974). *Practical measurements for evaluation in physical education* (2nd ed.). Minneapolis: Burgess.

Ludwig, A. (1971). *An evaluation of modern dance as an educational process incorporating physical creative and psychological changes within the individual.* Unpublished master's thesis, University of Kansas, Lawrence, KS.

Phillips, B. (1941). Relationship between certain phases of kinesthesis and performance during early stages of acquiring two perceptuomotor skills. *The Research Quarterly, 12,* 571–586.

Plastino, J. G. (1987). The university dancer: Physical screening. *Journal of Physical Education, Recreation and Dance, 58,* 49–50.

Roloff, L. (1958). Kinesthesis in relation to the learning of selected motor skills. *The Research Quarterly, 24,* 210–222.

Sage, G. (1977). *Introduction to motor behavior: A neuropsychological approach* (2nd ed.). Reading, MA: Addison Wesley.

Schmidt, R. (1982). *Motor control and learning.* Champaign, IL: Human Kinetics.

Schneider, F. J. (1978). The effect of movement exploration and mime on body-image, self-concept, and body-coordination of seventh grade children (Doctoral dissertation, Boston University, 1977). *Dissertation Abstracts International, 38A,* 5335-A.

Scott, G. (1955). Measurement of kinesthesis. *The Research Quarterly, 26,* 324–341.

Scott, G. (1959). *Measurement and evaluation in physical education.* Dubuque, IA: Wm. Brown.

Wiebe, V. (1954). A study of tests of kinesthesis. *The Research Quarterly, 25,* 222–230.

Young, O. (1945). A study of kinesthesis in relation to selected movements. *The Research Quarterly, 16,* 277–287.

7

ATTITUDES TOWARD DANCE AMONG STUDENTS ENTERING UNIVERSITY PHYSICAL EDUCATION PROGRAMS

A. Brian Nielsen
Marnie E. Rutledge
Dorothy J. Harris

The purpose of this study was to investigate the concerns that those choosing professional training in physical education lack positive attitudes toward dance. Since the presentation of dance in schools is usually part of the physical education program, a lack of commitment to dance among future instructors has been projected as problematic (Kraus & Chapman, 1981; Weeks, 1986). To date, there has not been substantial empirical evidence for these basic assumptions. Students (N = 265) entering a university physical education program completed one of five randomly assigned instruments in order to assess their attitudinal commitment to dance in general, or as a specific form (folk, jazz, creative, and social). Another group of subjects (N = 102) were assessed on their commitment to physical activity in general. Results indicated that commitment to dance was substantially below commitment to physical activity among these students. Furthermore, commitment to jazz, folk, and creative dance were lower than to social dance or dance in general. Males' attitudes to dance, in all forms, were less positive than those of females. In addition, males were more likely to feel uncoordinated while dancing and were less accepting of dance requirements in education curricula.

Recreational participation in dance has been, and is presently, substantial and will likely remain so in the future (Kelly, 1987). In fact, in North America, the place of dance as a worthwhile physical activity is sufficiently entrenched so as to ensure its official inclusion in the vast majority of school curricula, usually as part of the physical education program (Gingrasso, 1989; Kraus & Chapman, 1981). At the same time, there is concern that actual practice will reflect diminished inclusion of high-quality dance programs due to inappropriate materials, lack of informed upper-level supervision, and the inadequate preparation of instructors of dance for the school systems.

The fact that dance in the schools is usually taught by the physical education teacher has elicited an expressed concern for some time (Kraus & Chapman, 1981; Weeks, 1986). In addition to receiving a very small amount of preparation in the area of dance, it has also been suggested that those preparing as physical education teachers may have attitudes toward dance that are actually negative, or at best neutral (Weeks, 1986). If this is the case, then there must be serious concern regarding their ability and willingness to deliver dance experiences in a confident, meaningful, and well-designed manner. Gingrasso (1989) suggested that, "Left to the optional use by classroom teachers, physical education teachers and district administrators, dance . . . will lie on the shelf unused except by the initiated, the enlightened, the curious, or by those setting up arts curricula for mandated gifted and talented programs" (p. 33).

Therefore, the effective provision and teaching of dance in the school systems may be obstructed by several barriers, which interact with each other to compound and complicate the situation even more. On one hand the role of teaching dance is presently, and will likely remain, with the physical education teacher. On the other hand, the professional preparation of physical education teachers includes a minimal, often token, dance component that is embedded within a degree focusing primarily on games and sports activities. Finally, the self-selection that takes place prior to entry into physical education programs may yield future teachers who have large discrepancies in their attitudes toward physical activity in general versus dance. Although Sanderson (1988) reported that, among adolescents, dance enjoyed a low status compared to other forms of physical activity, no such studies have been completed that have focused on those initiating their preparation in a physical education program (Rae, 1986).

The purpose of this study was to assess the commitment to dance among students entering a degree program in physical education. A second purpose was to compare dance commitment to physical activity commitment. A final purpose was to compare general dance commitment with commitment to several specific forms of dance.

METHOD

Subjects

Subjects (N = 265) for this study consisted of 141 males and 124 females entering the first year of a bachelor-of-physical-education program at a large Canadian university over a 2-year period. The mean age of the subjects was 19.7 years with a range from 17 to 36 years. A second group of subjects (N = 102), previously drawn from the same program, completed an instrument assessing commitment to physical activity.

Instruments

Commitment to physical activity was measured utilizing an instrument entitled "Feelings about Physical Activity." This scale (CPA) had received substantial use (Deeter, 1989; Gruger, 1981; Nielsen & Corbin, 1986) as an assessment of attitudinal commitment. The scale was originally modified from Carmack and Martens' (1979) Commitment to Running scale. Nielsen and Corbin, 1986) reported a Cronbach's alpha of .91 (n = 859), indicating good internal consistency. A test-retest correlation coefficient of .91 and a split-halves coefficient of .92 also supported the reliability of the CPA instrument (Nielsen, Corbin, Borsdorf, Laurie, & Gruger, 1984). In addition, a split-half coefficient of .90 was reported by Nielsen and Corbin (1986), as was a test-retest coefficient of .93 over a 2-week period with 236 subjects.

The CPA scale contains 12 items, and utilizes a Likert-type format with 5 choices from strongly agree to strongly disagree. One-half of the items are worded in the negative sense and are appropriately reverse scored. The possible range of scores can vary from a low of 12 to a high of 60, representing extremely positive commitment.

Commitment to dance in general was assessed using an instrument (CDANCE) that contained the same items as the CPA except that the word "dance" replaced the term "physical activity" as the attitude object (see Appendix). The CDANCE had been employed by Nielsen (1985), who reported a Cronbach's alpha of .95 and split-half coefficient of .95 with 232 subjects. Furthermore the CDANCE successfully discriminated between students who were voluntarily involved and those who were not involved with dance (Nielsen, 1985). The CDANCE further discriminated between three levels of commitment as reflected by the degree of voluntary involvement in dance activities. Therefore, the CDANCE has been shown to reflect good internal consistency and construct validity as an indicator of commitment attitudes toward dance in its general form. Finally, Nielsen (1985) also found that when the two instruments, CPA and CDANCE, were randomly mixed and administered to subjects, that the response patterns were significantly different. This addressed any concerns that dancers may perceive the term "physical activity" as synonymous to dance and respond in an overgeneralized manner.

Commitment to four specific dance forms was also assessed by modifying the attitude object on the CDANCE scale to reflect either creative dance (CCREATIVE), folk dance, (CFOLK), jazz dance (CJAZZ) or social/ballroom dance (CSOCIAL). Although these particular versions of this instrument had not been employed prior to this study, the usefulness of other activity-specific alternatives was established for running (Carmack & Martens, 1979) and for soccer and lacrosse (Nielsen, Borsdorf, & Corbin, 1984). In fact it was suggested that the more specific the attitude object the better able the instrument is to discriminate between commitment levels. Certainly, even though the term "dance" is more specific than "physical activity," it is still comparatively general to the four instrument versions that focus on specific dance forms.

Procedure

Prior to beginning their physical education programs, all subjects completed one of five randomly assigned dance versions of the commitment instrument. Participation was voluntary, but no subjects declined to complete the questionnaire. A second group of subjects, drawn from the same program, completed the CPA scale. All subjects were given identical verbal instructions and assurances that responses would be confidential. In fact, the investigator administering the instruments was always someone other than the instructor(s) for the courses in which the testing took place.

Those completing a dance commitment scale ($N = 265$) provided demographic information concerning age, gender, and self-estimated dance experience. They also responded to four statements concerning confidence in dance and other physical activities, their desire to take a required dance course, and the place of dance in school programs. The Likert scale was used to assess these responses.

RESULTS

The results indicated that, with the exception of dance in general, attitudes to dance in the form of commitment scores ranged from low-moderate to neutral (see Table 1). On the other hand, commitment to dance in its most general form was more positive, and commitment to physical activity in general was very strong. In addition, the values of male scores on all dance instruments were exceeded by those of females.

Table 1
Means and Standard Deviations of Commitment Scores

Instrument	Males			Females			Total		
	n	M	SD	n	M	SD	n	M	SD
CDANCE	24	37.7	6.1	28	46.0	6.4	52	42.1	7.5
CCREATIVE	25	33.1	6.3	22	37.9	9.8	47	35.3	8.4
CFOLK	28	35.1	5.0	25	36.8	6.5	53	35.9	5.8
CJAZZ	31	34.9	6.3	20	41.2	9.2	51	37.4	8.1
CSOCIAL	33	36.1	5.6	29	42.3	8.0	62	39.3	7.4
CPA	43	50.7	5.4	59	51.8	5.0	102	51.3	5.2

In order to further assess the effects of attitude object and gender upon commitment scores in dance, a 2×5 ANOVA (Gender $\times$ Attitude Object) was performed. Analysis did not yield a significant interaction; however, the main effect for gender was significant, $F(1,260) = 38.55$, $p < .0001$, with females scores (M $= 41.0$, SD $= 8.4$) exceeding those of males (M $= 35.5$, SD $= 6.0$). There was also a main effect for attitude object, $F(4,260) = 7.28$, $p < .0001$, indicating different levels of commitment for different forms of dance. A post hoc Sheffé analysis indicated that commitment to dance in general (CDANCE) was significantly ($p <$ .05) higher than for creative, jazz, or folk dance forms.

Over 70% of the subjects reported that they do not lack confidence when approaching new physical activities, while a small number (14%) confirmed that they do suffer some lack of confidence in such situations. On the other hand, 26% of the subjects agreed that they felt uncoordinated while dancing, compared to 36% who did not report that feeling. Opinion was evenly divided on whether or not dance should be taught in all schools, with an identical 32% expressing agreement and disagreement. In response to the fact that a dance course was a mandatory part of their program, about 24% objected while a majority (52%) registered no such objection.

When the responses to these four statements were analyzed according to gender, several significant differences were detected (see Table 2). Males and females did not differ significantly with respect to the confidence with which they approach new activities. However males were more likely than females to feel awkward when dancing, and less likely to accept dance as a course requirement for their personal academic program or for school curricula in general.

Subjects were generally quite inexperienced in dance activities, with

Table 2

Comparisons between Males and Females on Response Scores to Questionnaire Items

Item	Males (N = 141)		Females (N = 124)		
	M	SD	M	SD	t
I generally approach new activities with confidence	3.67	.88	3.51	.88	1.47
I wish I did not have to take a dance course	3.02	1.01	3.82	.98	−6.53**
Dancing makes me feel uncoordinated	3.04	.82	3.27	.99	−2.08*
Dance should be taught in all schools programs	2.73	.89	3.25	.88	−4.82**

Degrees of freedom = (263).
*$p < .05$; **$p < .0001$.

almost one-fifth (19.6%) reporting not even moderate experience in any form of dance. The largest numbers of subjects indicated they had at least moderate experience in either one (29.8%) or two (26.8%) forms of dance, with decreasing proportions of subjects reporting such experience in three (11.3%), four (7.6%), and five or more (4.9%) dance forms. The relationship between experience and gender was moderate ($r = .42$), with females indicating a greater variety of dance involvement. Social dance was the most commonly cited dance experience.

DISCUSSION

Concerns and assumptions regarding the attitudes of physical education students toward dance are common in the literature despite a lack of substantial empirical support. The intent of this study was to determine the validity of those concerns for students just entering a university physical education program.

The results of this investigation provide support for the contention that attitudes among physical education students toward dance not only lag far behind their attitudes toward physical activity in general, but also that those dance attitudes clearly are not positive. Furthermore, attitudes toward several specific common dance forms are even lower than to dance in general.

Finally, dance attitudes among males are consistently lower than among females, supporting the often-reported but seldom-tested experiences of those instructing dance at the secondary and post-secondary levels of education.

Attitudes to Dance versus Physical Activity

The discrepancy between commitment to physical activity and commitment to dance should not be surprising. The role of sport and personal physical skill as factors affecting students' selection of physical education careers has been documented (Johns, 1983). Consistent with this focus is the evidence here that although these subjects expressed a very confident approach to trying new physical activities they also found it relatively difficult to reject the notion of feeling awkward during dance activities. Hence, the very strong commitment to physical activity of those choosing to enter physical education programs at the university level almost seems to be a sensible attitudinal prerequisite for such entry but is not reflected in a similar commitment to dance. In fact, as Weeks (1986) stated, "The current attitude which many physical education majors have towards dance is almost a negative one . . ." (p. 34).

Attitudes to Different Dance Forms

Examination of the results of this study further showed that subjects reflect attitudes that vary somewhat according to the dance form in question. Although dance in general, as measured by the CDANCE commitment scores, yielded the most positive scores, those of most other dance forms (jazz, creative, and folk) were significantly lower. Only social-dance attitudes were not statistically different from the general scores, suggesting the possibility that, when allowed to do so, subjects interpreted the attitude object "dance" as closely related to *social* dance, relating to their most recent and positive experience in secondary school. The fact that the students entered the program reporting very limited dance experience, coupled with the evidence that social dance comprised *most* of that experience, strengthens the possibility of a generalizing effect between social dance and dance in general. Consequently, a lack of experience with other dance forms could help to explain the lower attitudinal commitment toward folk, jazz, and creative dance. Attitude formation in a vacuum of first-hand experience may be based upon stereotypes, misinformation, or a lack of information concerning those dance forms. This same point has been made by others (Kraus & Chapman, 1981; Posey, 1988; Weeks, 1986) who contend that the present inclusion and delivery of dance in secondary schools suffers under the traditional auspices of physical education. The assertion is that dance is often considered a peripheral physical activity by the physical education instructor and is consequently presented with a narrow scope and in a reluctant manner. In such a setting it is no wonder that attitudes such as those reflected in this study are developed toward dance forms that are rarely, if ever, encountered through personal activity experiences. It would be of interest to speculate as to whether the inclusion of additional dance forms in the secondary school curriculum would lead to the development of more positive attitudes toward those forms, as suggested by Griffith (1986) and Posey (1988). It is important to note that even for social dance, the one form most familiar to students in this study, the attitude was not highly positive, especially among males. It would therefore appear that the simple existence of the experience may be superceded, as an influence on attitudes, by other factors concerning the nature of that experience.

Gender and Dance Attitudes

The evidence in this study provides strong empirical support for the contention of others (Kraus & Chapman, 1981; Posey, 1988) that the attitudes of males toward dance are substantially lower than those of females. This was the case for dance in general and for each of the specific dance forms. Posey (1988) stated that even when males express an interest in dance forms such as modern and jazz they are still not encouraged to study dance. She further maintained that if folk dance is taught, it is usually primarily for socializing purposes and is not given credibility as an art form or as having activity value unto itself. If such instruction takes place at a time more suited to female social development than that of males, even the potential social impact could be lost on males. Yet the results of this study indicate that, of all of the specific dance forms, the attitudes of male and females are most closely aligned in the folk-dance form. The reasons for this are unclear, but it could be that folk dance includes so many specific forms that the perception of the term itself is equally diffuse for males and females, resulting in undifferentiated responses. A fuller understanding of this question may require research that allows for the description of the perceptions of terms such as "folk dance."

It is also apparent that, despite the fact that they are equally, and strongly, committed to physical activity and profess to approach new activities with similar confidence, males and females do not exhibit such uniform attitudes about dance activities. Males not only felt less coordinated than females, but they were less supportive of the inclusion of dance in school programs or, in fact, as a portion of their own professional preparation. Weeks (1986) warned that to avoid such dance experiences would only compound the problem by encouraging students to exclude dance from their curricula when they become instructors. Gross (1989) also asserted that it is the lack of experience among physical educators that causes suspicion or hostility toward dance. The gender-related experiential differences reported in this study would imply that the lack of experience among males may be one factor contributing to their lack of positive attitudes.

Future research is needed to determine if the attitudes expressed by these subjects accurately reflect those of students entering programs other than physical education or if, in fact, they differ in any way. It is also important to determine how dance experiences might be most effectively presented in order to alter the specific and general dance attitudes of future instructors. The design and delivery of such interventions will, in the light of the findings of this study, need to proceed carefully, and the effects should be subject to precise and systematic investigation. Finally, it will be important to determine if the attitudes to dance revealed in these findings actually have any effect upon the decisions and practices of these subjects as they graduate to become physical educators. As Brennan (1986) described, the field of dance is a relative novice in the research world. Therefore, the posing and investigation of relevant research questions is crucial if the field is to advance and long-held assumptions and beliefs concerning that field challenged or confirmed. This study has provided an empirical test of several such assumptions concerning the attitudes of university physical education students. These findings can serve as a beginning for further investigation in this area.

REFERENCES

Brennan, M. A. (1986). A look ahead, dance research needed. *Journal of Physical Education, Recreation and Dance, 57*(5), 49, 53.

Carmack, M. A., & Martens, R. (1979). Measuring commitment to running: A survey of runners' attitudes and mental states. *Journal of Sport Psychology, 1,* 25–42.

Deeter, T. E. (1989). Development of a model of achievement behavior for physical activity. *Journal of Sport and Exercise Psychology, 11,* 13–25.

Gingrasso, S. H. (1989). Dance—on paper. *Journal of Physical Education, Recreation and Dance, 60*(5), 32–33.

Griffith, B. R. (1986). New approaches, dance for general education students. *Journal of Physical Education, Recreation, and Dance, 57*(5), 36, 55.

Gross, M. B. (1989). Gaining equal status, dance in physical education. *Journal* of Physical Education, Recreation and Dance, 60(3), 79–81.

Gruger, C. E. (1981). *Measuring commitment to physical activity.* Unpublished master's thesis, Kansas State University, Manhattan, KS.

Johns, D. (1983). Factors affecting students' selection of professional preparation in physical education. *CAHPER Journal, 49*(6), 16–19.

Kelly, J. R. (1987). *Recreation trends, toward the year 2000.* Champaign, IL: Management Learning Laboratories Ltd.

Kraus, R., & Chapman, S. A. (1981). *History of the dance in art and education.* Englewood Cliffs, NJ: Prentice-Hall.

Mason, J. H. (1986). Working ideas, teaching dance to high school students. *Journal of Physical Education, Recreation and Dance, 57*(6), 22–24.

Nielsen, A. B. (1985). *Commitment to physical activity.* Unpublished doctoral dissertation, Arizona State University, Tempe, AZ.

Nielsen, A. B., Borsdorf, L. L., & Corbin, C. E. (1984). Commitment to general and specific physical activity. *Motor Development—Sport Psychology and Motor Learning—Scientific Program Abstracts: Olympic Scientific Congress.* Eugene, OR: Microform Publications.

Nielsen, A. B., & Corbin, C. B. (1986). Physical activity commitment. *Psychology of Motor Behavior and Sport Abstracts—1986.* Scottsdale, AZ: NASPSPA.

Nielsen, A. B., Corbin, C. B., Borsdorf, L. L., Laurie, D. R., & Gruger, C. (1984). Commitment to physical activity. *Abstracts of Research Papers, 1984.* Anaheim, CA: AAHPERD Publications.

Posey, E. (1988). Discipline-based arts education—developing a dance curriculum. *Journal of Physical Education, Recreation, and Dance, 59*(9), 61–64.

Rae, C. (1986). From scratch, a dance program emerges. *Journal of Physical Education, Recreation, and Dance, 57*(5), 37–38.

Sanderson, P. (1988). Secondary school pupils' attitudes to dance. *Proceedings of the D.A.C.I. Conference.* London: Roehampton Institute.

Weeks, S. (1986). Teaching dance, involving the physical education major. *Journal of Physical Education, Recreation, and Dance, 57*(5), 34–35.

Appendix
Commitment to Dance Instrument

FEELINGS ABOUT DANCE

The following statements may or may not describe your feelings about dancing. Read each statement and then circle the most appropriate letter to indicate how well the statement describes *your feelings most of the time*. There are no right or wrong answers. Do not spend too much time on any one item, but give the answers which best describe how you *generally feel* about dancing.

SD   =   STRONGLY   U = UNCERTAIN   SA = STRONGLY AGREE
DISAGREE

D = DISAGREE   A = AGREE

1. I look forward to dancing	SD	D	U	A	SA
2. Dancing is not an enjoyable way to stay fit.	SD	D	U	A	SA
3. Dancing is drudgery.	SD	D	U	A	SA
4. I do not enjoy dancing.	SD	D	U	A	SA
5. Dancing is vitally important to me.	SD	D	U	A	SA
6. Life is so much richer as a result of dancing.	SD	D	U	A	SA
7. Dancing is pleasant.	SD	D	U	A	SA
8. I dread the thought of dancing.	SD	D	U	A	SA
9. I would arrange or change my schedule to dance.	SD	D	U	A	SA
10. I will not dance unless forced to do so.	SD	D	U	A	SA
11. To miss a session of dance is sheer relief.	SD	D	U	A	SA
12. Dancing is the high point of my day.	SD	D	U	A	SA

DOMAIN DISCRIMINATION IN DANCE ATTITUDE RESEARCH

Nelson D. Neal
Sylvie Fortin

The primary purpose of this study was to discover if attitudinal research should discriminate between psychological domains. A secondary purpose was to discover any differences between the dance attitudes of French Canadian children who were taught either by a French-speaking female or male or an English-speaking male. A pretest-posttest design using Neal's Dance Attitude Inventory (1985) was used to collect data. The 30 questions were composed of 12 in each the affective and cognitive domains and 6 in the behavioral domain. Intervention consisted of participation in four modern dance classes. Significant shifts between pretest and posttest scores were found in the affective domain for girls in the English group and for boys in all treatment groups; in the behavioral domain for boys in the English group; and in the cognitive domain for girls and boys in the French female group, and boys in the control group, p < .05. The results lend support to attitude research that discriminates between domains because a shift in one psychological domain does not mean there will be a shift in the other domains. This study also provides support for a shift in subjects' affective dance attitudes due to direct participation whether or not the teacher speaks the native language of the subjects.

It is generally agreed that attitudes are composed of elements from the affective, behavioral, and cognitive domains (Breckler, 1984; Katz, 1960; Morris & Stuckhardt, 1977). Recent attitude research suggests discriminating between the three domains, either by measuring each or by specifying which one is the focus of concern (Breckler, 1984). Discrimination appears to be necessary because it has been found that directing change at any one of the psychological domains may affect a shift in the other two (Cialdini et al., 1976; Katz 1960). Further, it is possible that attitudinal differences between groups of subjects may fall within one or two of the domains rather than all three (Quattrone, 1985).

For this reason a significant shift in one of the domains may not be great enough to indicate a significant shift in the subject's total attitude. Conversely, a significant shift in total attitude may not mean a significant shift in all three domains.

If discrimination is to be effective, then the subjects must be exposed to the domain of concern in a way that will enhance recognition or recall of the attitude object. Once an individual can recall experiences related to the attitude, she or he can express that attitude (Wood, 1982). Motor learning theorists have shown that using verbal labels made it easier for subjects to remember movement skills they had performed (Magill, 1985; Schmidt, 1982), whereas music has been shown to improve recall of serial ballet movements (Starkes et al., 1987).

Directing change at three of the six major characteristics of attitudes—they have a specific social referent, they are learned, and they are interrelated (Morris and Stuckhardt, 1977)—may assist the individual in recalling an attitude object. Lord and Petiot (1985) used verbal labels as specific social referents in the recall of dance activities.

Verbal labels may also prove beneficial for interrelating attitudes. If subjects have positive attitudes about physical activity—running, jumping, skipping, and sliding, and dance movements are related to these movements—then the subjects may develop positive attitudes toward dance through exposure (Carroll & Bandura, 1985; Watts, 1967; Zajonc, 1968). Exposing children to an environment where attitudes can be learned and interrelated has been shown to effect change in an individual's attitude toward dance (Allison, 1976; Burton, 1977; Halsted, 1980; Neal, 1983, 1985; Neal & Laakso, 1987), visual art (Mittler, 1972, 1976; Morris, 1975), and a combination of arts (Howard & Greenwald, 1972; Tilton, 1983).

Children will develop attitudes toward dance based on cultural practices, stereotyping, and peer pressure with little or no exposure to dance activities (Thompson, 1985/1986). For positive dance attitudes to be developed, exposure should begin early in life (Anderson, 1976) and not be taken for granted or assumed to occur automatically (Ecker, 1971). If attitudinal development is assumed to take place, then negative attitudes may develop and prevail through adulthood (Harris, 1970; Smoll & Schutz, 1980). For exposure to occur a teacher is necessary, and the subject's perception of the qualities of the teacher add another dimension to attitudinal development.

Research has shown that a subject's perception of the qualities of the teacher make a difference. It has been suggested that a person who is perceived as an expert or knowledgeable is more likely to be persuasive than one who is perceived as a nonexpert (Wood et al., 1982). Previous dance attitude research found significant positive attitudinal shift when subjects were taught by a teacher from a foreign country (Neal & Laakso, 1987). Since the Neal and Laakso study did not include a teacher from the subjects' home country, there was no way to tell if the attitudinal shift was due to the subjects' perception of a foreign teacher or to the treatment.

The purpose of this study was to discover if attitudinal research should discriminate between psychological domains. The purpose was also to discover any significant differences between the dance attitudes of subjects taught by a "home" teacher (French-speaking) or by a "foreign" teacher (English-speaking) after participation in four dance sessions.

METHOD

Subjects

The subjects ($N = 106$) were girls ($n = 50$) and boys ($n = 56$) enrolled in coeducational third grade classes at St. Marc and St. Marie schools in Granby, Quebec, Canada. The mean age of the girls was 8.88 years, and of the boys, 9.05 years. All subjects were French-speaking.

Materials

The subjects' attitudes were measured by Neal's Dance Attitude Inventory (1985), which had been translated into French. The questions were worded so that the meaning and intent of the statements were not lost in the translation. Using the Chronbah alpha test (Brown, 1970) the questionnaire pretest had previously been found to be internally consistent for Finnish girls and boys with values of $r = .80$ and $r = .93$ respectively, and for American girls and boys with values of $r = .89$ and $r = .91$ respectively. The pretest was administered to the subjects by their classroom teachers the third week of May 1987, and the posttest was administered the second week of June 1987, one week after the final treatment.

All 30 questions were scored for the analysis, and any subject who did not answer every question was eliminated from the subject pool. Each question was scored from one to four with four as the most positive score. Half the questions were worded positively and half negatively. The total score range was 30 to 120, with scores of 12 to 48 in the affective and the cognitive domains and 6 to 24 in the behavioral domain.

Procedure

Exposure to dance was through direct participation in four 45-minute dance sessions during the physical education class meetings on four consecutive days. The affective domain was the focus of attention during the dance sessions even though all three domains were measured. All subjects, by classroom, participated in the same four dances, one modern, one jazz, and two sport style. The three dance teachers taught the dances in the same order, with the same music, using the same terminology and verbal labels for each dance. Each of the three dance teachers taught a different classroom of students. The control group, a separate classroom, did not participate in or watch any of the dance classes. The "home" female teacher and the "foreign" male teacher taught in one school while the "home" male teacher and the control group were in a different school.

RESULTS

A repeated measures analysis of covariance (SPSS, 1986) was conducted to examine the effects of the treatment by group, sex, and psychological domain. Mean scores for dance attitudes are listed in Table 1.

The girls taught by the "foreign" male teacher and the boys in all three treatment groups showed significant shifts in their affective dance attitude. In the behavioral domain only the boys taught by the "foreign" male teacher showed a significant shift. In the cognitive domain only the girls and boys taught by the "home" female and the boys in the control group showed a significant shift. There was a significant shift in total attitude score for the girls and the boys in the "home" female group and the "foreign" male group, but no significant difference was found in total attitude for the "home" male group or the control group. (See Table 2.)

DISCUSSION

It would appear that domain discrimination is necessary because a significant shift in the subjects' mean total attitude score did not indicate a significant shift in each of the three domains. Also, focusing attention on the affective domain did not create a significant affective attitudinal shift in all three treatment groups.

The lack of affective shift by the girls in the "home" female teacher group may have been due to a ceiling affect from their pretest mean

Table 1
Mean Attitude Scores by Sex, Treatment Group, and Psychological Domain

GROUPS	N PRE/POST	AFFECTIVE		BEHAVIORAL		COGNITIVE		TOTAL	
		PRE	POST	PRE	POST	PRE	POST	PRE	POST
					GIRLS				
1	15/14	40.57	43.36	17.57	18.57	38.00	44.21	96.14	106.14
2	11/12	33.73	38.27	14.09	15.54	36.27	38.91	84.09	92.72
3	11/11	37.18	41.00	16.64	16.36	39.36	39.18	93.18	96.54
4	10/11	38.80	38.04	13.80	15.20	35.00	39.20	87.60	92.80
					BOYS				
1	11/11	37.46	43.64	14.91	17.46	39.91	44.46	92.27	105.54
2	12/11	34.00	39.27	9.91	15.73	39.09	41.46	83.00	96.45
3	11/13	37.91	42.09	15.82	16.36	40.73	43.27	94.45	101.72
4	15/13	34.08	37.08	12.39	12.00	39.92	40.92	86.38	90.00

Group 1—Home female
Group 2—Foreign male
Group 3—Home male
Group 4—Control

Table 2.
Shift in Attitude Toward Dance by Treatment Group, Sex, and Psychological Domain

	Home female	Foreign male	Home male	Control
AFFECTIVE DOMAIN				
Female	+2.79	+4.54	+3.82	−0.76
Male	+6.18*	+5.27*	+4.18*	+3.00
BEHAVIORAL DOMAIN				
Female	+1.00	+1.45	−0.28	+1.40
Male	+2.54	+5.82*	+0.54	−0.39
COGNITIVE DOMAIN				
Female	+6.21*	+2.64	−0.18	+4.20*
Male	+4.54*	+2.37	+2.54	+1.00
TOTAL ATTITUDE				
Female	+10.00*	+8.63*	+3.36	+5.20
Male	+13.26*	+13.46*	+7.26	+3.61

*significant $p < .05$

score of 84.5%. Conversely, the girls in the "foreign" teacher group started with an affective mean score of 70.3%, allowing sufficient room for improvement. The positive affective shift by boys in all three treatment groups may have been the result of using verbal labels and social referents to sports movements aiding in recall of their recent dance experience. These same sports labels may have kept the affective attitude of the girls in the "home" male teacher group from shifting significantly. Music, too, may have contributed to some subjects' ability to recall the attitude object that enhanced the likelihood of a significant shift.

The subjects' perception of the qualities of the teacher may also have had an effect on attitudinal development. Although two treatment groups had "home" teachers, neither was the regular teacher. Therefore, subjects in these two treatment groups may have perceived the teacher as "foreign," or at least new, which may have added to the subjects' perception of the teacher as knowledgeable and the activity as acceptable or fun.

Teacher experience and language may have played a significant roll in the development or lack of development in cognitive attitudes. The "home" female teacher had an advantage in years of experience, including teaching young children, over the "home" male teacher. This may have made it easier for her to present cognitive elements while making the dance sessions fun. Because the two "home" teachers had learned the four dances only a few days prior to teaching, the "home" male teacher may have been concentrating on teaching correct movements with specific verbal labels without improving the cognitive development of the subjects and detracting from his spontaneity. The lack of a significant shift in cognitive attitudes in the "foreign" teacher group was not unexpected since he could not communicate concepts to the subjects in their language. As for the unexpected significant shift in cognitive attitude of the boys in the control group, it is possible that they spoke with treatment subjects after some or all of the sessions and learned from their peers as suggested by Thompson (1985/1986).

The only significant behavioral shift was by the boys in the "foreign" male group, for which there may be two explanations. The shift may have occurred because the boys had a male role model who participated with them in an activity that had been interrelated to sports movements or because their pretest mean score was quite low, 41.2%. This low score had a much greater chance of showing a significant shift than scores that started above 80%. Since the classes were coeducational and the subjects in the "home" and "foreign" teacher groups had the same physical education teacher during the year, no explanation can be given for the marked difference between the pretest scores of the boys in these two treatment groups.

The results support the premise that domain discrimination may be necessary. A shift in total attitude did not mean a corresponding shift in all three domains, and a shift in one domain did not consistently mean a corresponding shift in total attitude. The results also support the premise that a shift in dance attitudes may occur whether the instructor is a "foreign" or "home" teacher.

The results also illustrated that when targeting the affective domain participation in four dance sessions, that was sufficient to produce a positive shift in the affective attitudes of most of the treatment groups. They also illustrated that two exposures to the attitude questionnaire was not sufficient to produce a significant shift in affective or behavioral attitudes toward dance in a control group.

Further study in the area of domain discrimination should be pursued in an attempt to discover how many exposures are necessary to shift the behavioral attitudes of subjects. Also, if increased exposure has an effect on behavioral attitudes, will this increased exposure have a positive or negative effect on subjects' affective attitudes? It may also be necessary to reevaluate the questionnaire that was used because of the ceiling effect in pretest and posttest mean scores of some treatment groups.

REFERENCES

Allison, P. (1976). An instrument to measure the creative dance attitudes of grade five children (Doctoral dissertation, University of Alabama, 1976). *Dissertation Abstracts International, 37,* 7065A. (University Microfilms No. 77-12164).

Anderson, F. E. (1976). The arts and the elderly: An assessment of interests and attitudes. *Studies in Art Education, 18*(1), 61–71.

Breckler, S. J. (1984). Empirical validation of affect, behavior, and cognition as distinct components of attitude. *Journal of Personality and Social Psychology, 47,* 1191–1205.

Brown, F. G. (1970). *Principles of educational and psychological testing.* Hinsdale, IL: The Dryden Press Inc.

Burton, C. (1977). Influence of instructional media on attitudes of modern dance students toward movement (Doctoral dissertation, University of Georgia). *Dissertation Abstracts International, 38,* 6599A.

Carroll, W. R., & Bandura, A. (1985). Role of timing of visual monitoring and motor rehearsal in observational learning of action patterns. *Journal of Motor Behavior, 17,* 269–281.

Cialdini, R. B., Levy, A., Herman, C. P., Kozloski, L., & Petty, R. E. (1976). Elastic shifts of opinion: Determinants of direction and durability. *Journal of Personality and Social Psychology, 34*(4), 663–672.

Ecker, D. W. (1971). The structure of affect in the art curriculum. *Art Education, 24,* 26–29.

Halsted, C. E. D. (1980). An analysis of attitudes and definitions by selected teachers and pupils toward dance in general and dance in the classroom (Doctoral dissertation, Wayne State University). *Dissertation Abstracts International, 41,* 4330A.

Harris, D. V. (1970). Physical activity history and attitudes of middle-aged men. *Medicine and Science in Sports, 2*(4), 203–208.

Howard, J. R., & Greenwald, H. J. (1972). *Measurement of changes in children's atitudes toward the performing arts.* (Final Report). Education Collaborative for Greater Boston, MA. (ERIC Document Reproduction Service No. ED 063 614.)

Katz, D. (1960). The functional approach to the study of attitudes. *Public Opinion Quarterly, 24,* 163–204.

Lord, M., & Petiot, B. (1985, August). *A characterization of recreational dance classes.* Presentation at AIESEP World Conference, New York.

Magill, R. A. (1985). *Motor learning concepts & applications* (2nd ed.). Dubuque, IA: Wm. C. Brown, Publishers.

Mittler, G. (1972). Efforts to secure congruent and incongruent modifications of attitude toward works of art. *Studies in Art Education, 13*(2), 58–70.

Mittler, G. (1976). An instructional strategy designed to overcome the adverse effects of established student attitudes toward works of art. *Studies in Art Education, 17*(3), 13–31.

Morris, J. W. (1975). An alternative methodology for researching art attitudes and values. *Studies in Art Education, 17*(1), 25–31.

Morris, J. W., & Stuckhardt, M. H. (1977). Art attitude: Conceptualization and implication. *Studies in Art Education, 19*(1), 21–28.

Neal, N. D. (1983). *The effects of a modern dance workshop on the attitude of fourth grade boys and girls.* Final report (83-209), Commission for the Arts, Richmond, VA.

Neal, N. D. (1985). Assessment of attitude change and position shift in fourth graders after participation in modern dance (Doctoral dissertation, University of Virginia, 1985). *Dissertation Abstracts International, 47,* 2962A.

Neal, N. D., & Laakso, L. (1987). Amerikkalaisten ja suomalaisten peruskoululaisten tanssiasenteista. *Liikunta ja Tieda, 24,* 197–199.

Quattrone, G. A. (1985). On the congruity between internal states and action. *Psychological Bulletin, 98*(1), 3–40.

Schmidt, R. A. (1982). *Motor control and learning.* Champaign, IL: Human Kinetics Publishers.

Smoll, F. L., & Schutz, R. W. (1980). Children's attitude toward physical activity: A longitudinal analysis. *Journal of Sport Psychology, 2,* 137–147.

SPSS Inc. (1986). *SPSSx User's Guide* (2nd ed.). Chicago.

Starkes, J. L., Deakin, J. M., Lindley, S., & Crisp, F. (1987). Motor versus verbal recall of ballet sequences by young expert dancers. *Journal of Sport Psychology, 9,* 222–230.

Tilton, C. L. C. (1983). A comparison of the attitudes of fourth, fifth, and sixth grade students toward the arts (Doctoral dissertation, University of Southern California, 1983). *Dissertation Abstracts International, 44,* 1395A.

Thompson, D. C. (1985/1986). A new vision of masculinity. *Educational Leadership, 43*(4), 53–56.

Watts, W. A. (1967). Relative persistence of opinion change induced by active compared to passive participation. *Journal of Personality and Social Psychology, 5,* 4–15.

Wood, W. (1982). Retrieval of attitude-relevant information from memory: Effects on susceptibility to persuasion and on intrinsic motivation. *Journal of Personality and Social Psychology, 42,* 798–810.

Wood, W., Kallgren, C. A., & Priesler, R. M. (1982). *Access to attitude-relevant information in memory as a determinant of Persuasion: The role of message and communicator attributes.* Presentation at Midwestern Psychological Association, Minneapolis, MN.

Zajonc, R. B. (1968). Attitudinal effects of mere exposure. *Journal of Personality and Social Psychology Monograph Supplement, 9*(2, pt. 2) 1–27.

9

TOWARDS A QUANTITATIVE ANALYSIS OF CLASSIC BALLET: THE UPPER-BODY TECHNIQUE VIEWED THROUGH CHOREUTICS

Billie Lepczyk

Rudolf Laban devised a method of identifying the pathways and forms of human movement through modeling the kinesphere in accordance with the forms of crystalline structures. The purpose of this study was to identify the spatial organization of the upper-body movement of classic ballet technique. The findings indicated that the arm positions and basic ports de bras *adhere readily to the crystalline form of the octahedron. The fundamental movements of* épaulement, croisé, *and* effacé *create diagonal tension. The* épaulements *evident in the positions of the body create a variety of spatial tensions, including octahedral, planal, diagonal, and cubic.*

Ballet masters have agreed that the upper body movement, which includes the *ports de bras* and *épaulement,* lends the artistry to classic dance and is the most difficult part of technique to master. Cecchetti (Beaumont, 1975, p. 25) states that it demands the most serious study and attention. Vaganova (1946, p. 38) explains that its mastery requires the greatest amount of work and concentration. In addition, Lawson (1960, p. 19) states that styles of ballet are distinguished through the *ports de bras.* Therefore, to increase understanding of the nature of ballet's upper-body technique, its spatial organization is viewed through the Laban framework.

METHOD

Rudolf Laban (1974) coined the term "choreutics" to signify the study of the spatial aspect of human movement. This encompasses the forms of movement, their pathways, and harmonic relations. Through the study of crystals, Laban devised a method of identifying the choreutic aspect. He found that lines and forms could easily be understood and described using the terminology of mathematics and geometry. Therefore, he modeled the imaginary personal sphere immediately surrounding the body in accordance with the geometric forms evident in the crystalline structures. Laban (1974, p. 10) named this zone within which the limbs and torso move the "kinesphere." It relates to the axial movements of the body as distinguished from the locomotive movements through the general space of the dancing area.

Laban (1974, p. 4) contends that space is a hidden feature of movement and movement is a visible aspect of space. Therefore, the visible spatial relationship between the body and the space both reveal the form of the movement and distinguish the unfolding movement in a sort of trance-form through the kinesphere. Laban (1974, p. 195) found the cystalline form of the icosahedron the most comprehensive structure for defining the multitude of forms created by human movement. Other basic models of orientation include the dimensions, the dimensional planes, the diagonals, and the crystalline forms of the octahedron and cube. The trace-forms that connect, like a scaffold, one zone of the kinesphere with another are central or transverse paths through the crystalline structures or peripheral paths on the edge of these structures.

PROCEDURE

There are three distinct methods of instruction in classic ballet technique. These are the Cecchetti Method (Italian School), the French School, and the Russian School. These schools basically teach the same movements; however, the same movement may have different names or be executed slightly differently. All three schools were considered in this study.

The procedure entailed the analysis of the positions of the arms, the basic *ports de bras,* and the positions of the body that instruct in the refinement of *épaulement.* The variety of forms and pathways defined by the upper-body technique were classified according to the Laban framework. Therefore, the ordering was the most simple paths, the dimensions, to the most complex choreutic form, the icosahedron.

FINDINGS

With the exception of second position, the three schools have their own system for ordering and numbering the arm positions. According to Vaganova (1946, p. 36), there is a preparatory position and three basic positions of the arms. She considers all other positions variations of these. Although Cecchetti (Beaumont, 1975, p. 22) and Mme. Nicolaeva-Legat (Kirstein, 1978, p. 79) agree that there are five fundamental positions of the arms, the positions they identify are not the same (Grant, 1982, pp. 23–24). Although these differences exist, general statements can be made. First, there is a closed position, an open position, and a combination of these. Second, there are four fundamental spatial directions from which the positions of the three schools are based. These are the arms *en bas* (low), *en avant* (forward), *en haut* (high), and *à la seconde* (side). These correspond to the directions of the three dimensions.

In the Laban perspective, a direction is considered a spatial pull. Therefore, *en haut* corresponds to the high pull and *en bas* to the low pull of the vertical dimension. *En avant* corresponds to the forward pull of the sagittal dimension. *À la seconde* corresponds to the right and left pulls of the horizontal dimension (Figure 1).

Within the framework of choreutics, the crystalline form of dimensional orientation is the octahedron. When the three dimensions lie perpendicular to each other within the reach zone of the arms, they intersect at the center of the chest. The octahedron is then established by connecting the six spatial pulls of the three dimensions. In this study, the center of the octahedron coincides with the center of the chest.

When the arms move, the pathways are oriented to the octahedral form. The *ports de bras* create peripheral paths on the edge of this form as they pass through and connect the dimensional pulls. Within the basic framework of the octahedron, a great variety of *ports de bras* is possible. There are, however, two set exercises that are most fundamental and used most often (Hammond, 1984, p. 89). These will serve to illustrate the octahedral orientation. Both exercises have the identical starting position: face downstage left in fifth position with the right foot front, the head rotated slightly to the left and lowered, and the arms *en bas* (low pull of the vertical dimension).

In the first exercise, the arms raise *en avant* (forward pull of the sagittal dimension) as the torso tilts slightly forward from the waist. Then, the arms open *à la seconde* (left and right pulls of the horizontal dimension) as the head rotates and tilts along with the torso slightly to the right. The arms lower and as they return to their starting position, the head and torso do likewise (Figure 2).

In the second exercise, the arms continue to raise *en haut* (high pull of the vertical dimension) while the torso straightens and the head lifts and tilts slightly to the right. Then, the arms open *à la seconde* as the torso tilts slightly to the right. The arms lower, and as they return to their starting position, the head and torso do likewise (Figure 2).

EN HAUT   **EN AVANT**

EN BAS   **À LA SECONDE**

Figure 1. Dimensional orientation of the arm positions.

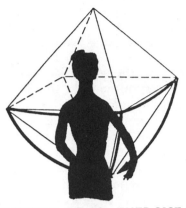

PORT DE BRAS, EXERCISE I

PORT DE BRAS, EXERCISE II

Figure 2. Octahedral orientation of the *ports de bras*.

Épaulement means shouldering and refers to the oblique angle of the head and shoulders in relation to the legs. The fundamental positions are *croisé*, which means crossed, and *effacé*, which means shaded. According to Vaganova (1946, p. 14), this is the first suggestion of future artistry of the classic dance that is brought into beginner's exercises. The fundamental characteristic of *croisé* is the crossing of the legs, and of *effacé* is the opening of the legs (1946, pp. 15–16). Therefore, when facing downstage left with the right foot in front, the *épaulement croisé* would have the right shoulder forward, head tilted right, with the upper body at a slight oblique angle towards downstage. Facing downstage right with the right foot in front, the *épaulement effacé* would have the left shoulder forward, head tilted left, with the upper body at a slight oblique angle to downstage. The oblique angle of the *épaulement* is created by a twist and sometimes a tilt of the upper torso along with a rotation and tilt of the head. In general, the oblique angle of the épaulements creates diagonal tension.

Unlike the dimensional pulls that have only one spatial tendency, a diagonal pull has three equal spatial tendencies (Dell, 1977). Each diagonal pull has vertical, horizontal, and sagittal tendencies. The relationship between two or more spatial pulls creates spatial tension. Therefore, in the *épaulement croisé* position, cited above, the diagonal tension is created from the low/left/forward pull where the twist begins in the upper torso to the high/right/back pull of the head position. In the épaulement effacé position, cited above, the diagonal tension is created from the low/right/forward pull to the high/left/backward pull (Figure 3).

The positions of the body are specific poses that relate to three aspects of classic line. The first aspect is the design formed by the arms, upper torso, and head within the *épaulement*. The second is the relationship of the *épaulement* to that of the legs within the dancer's kinesphere. The third is the relationship of the body within its kinesphere to the general space of the dancing area. The main concern in this study is the spatial organization of the épaulement.

Although the concepts of *croisé* and *effacé* are fundamental to the three schools, the positions of the body vary. There are 8 positions in the Cecchetti Method and 11 in the Russian and French schools. Some of these are the same; therefore, in total, there are 12 basic positions of the body from which numerous variations evolve.

The three positions that create dimensional tension are the same for each of the schools. However, in the Cecchetti Method, the arms are held slightly lower. These include *à la quatrième devant*, *à la quatrième derrière*, and *à la seconde*. They create flatlike poses since the complete stance (hips, shoulders, and head) is *en face*. In each of these poses, the

ÉPAULEMENT CROISÉ   ÉPAULEMENT EFFACÉ

Figure 3. Diagonal tension.

dancer faces downstage with the upper body upright and the arms *à la seconde* (Figure 4).

In the nine other positions of the body, the dancer stands on the *diagonale* at an oblique angle to the audience. (The term *diagonale* is used in ballet to identify a direction in the general dancing area, and should be distinguished from the Laban term "diagonal," which identifies a specific relationship within the dancer's kinesphere.) Therefore, the stance in these positions is facing either downstage left or downstage right.

The *croisé devant* position is the same in the three schools, except that the arm to the side is lower in the Cecchetti Method. In this pose, one arm is *en haut*, the other is *à la seconde*, and the head is rotated

À LA QUATRIEME DEVANT

À LA QUATRIEME DERRIERE

À LA SECONDE

Figure 4. *En face* positions of the body.

CROISÉ DEVANT

CROISÈ DERRIÈRE
RUSSIAN AND FRENCH SCHOOLS

CROISÉ DERRIÈRE
CECCHETTI METHOD

Figure 5. *Croisé* positions of the body.

Billie Lepczyk

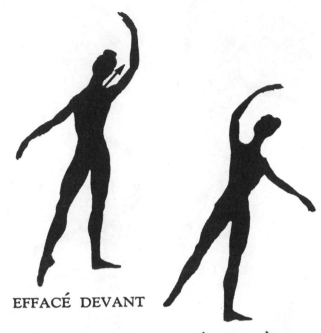

EFFACÉ DEVANT

EFFACÉ DERRIÈRE
RUSSIAN AND FRENCH SCHOOLS

Figure 6. *Effacé* positions of the body.

ÉCARTÉ
CECCHETTI METHOD

ÉCARTÉ DEVANT
RUSSIAN AND FRENCH SCHOOLS

ÉCARTÉ DERRIÈRE
RUSSIAN AND FRENCH SCHOOLS

Figure 7. *Ecarté* positions of the body.

slightly and tilted along with the upper torso towards the lower arm. There is diagonal tension in the upper torso and head, and dimensional tension in the arm position (Figure 5).

In the épaulement of the *croisé derrière* position in the Russian and French schools, diagonal tension is created from the base of the neck to the top of the head, and dimensional tension in the arm position. In this pose, the torso is held upright with the same arm *en haut* as the leg that is extended back. The other arm is *à la seconde,* and the head is rotated slightly and tilted toward the lower arm (Figure 5). In the Cecchetti Method, planal tensions are created in this pose.

The three dimensional planes include the vertical plane referred to as the "door" plane, the horizontal plane referred to as the "table" plane, and the sagittal plane referred to as the "wheel" plane (Dell, 1977). Each planal pull has two spatial tendencies.

In the *croisé derrière* position of the Cecchetti Method, the arm *en haut,* opposite the leg extended back, is in line with the torso, which is tilted slightly forward. Sagittal planal tension is created from the forward/high pull of the arm, through the torso to the backward/low pull of the extended leg. In addition, the upper torso and slightly rotated head are tilted slightly to the side over the other arm, which is held low *à la seconde.* This creates vertical planal tension from the high/side pull of the head to the low/side pull of the arm (Figure 5).

In the *effacé devant* position, which is similar among the schools, diagonal and sagittal planal tensions are evident. The head is rotated slightly and tilted, which creates diagonal tension. The arm *en haut* is in line with the torso, which is tilted and bent slightly backward, and the other arm is low *à la seconde* with the same leg extended forward. Sagittal planal tension is evident from the backward/high pull of the arm *en haut,* through the torso to the forward/low pull of the extended leg (Figure 6). In the Cecchetti Method, the upper torso is twisted along with the head rotation; therefore, the diagonal tension is more pronounced.

The *effacé derrière* position is taught in the Russian and French schools. The head is rotated slightly towards the arm *en haut* with the eyes looking into the palm of the hand, the torso tilts slightly forward, and the other arm is *à la seconde.* Sagittal planal tension is created from the forward/high pull of the head, through the torso, to the backward/ low pull of the extended leg (Figure 6).

Écarté means separated or thrown wide apart. In the *écarté* position of the Cecchetti Method, the upright torso, the arm *en haut,* and the other arm low *à la seconde* create dimensional tension. The head is slightly raised and rotated toward the arm *en haut* so that the eyes look into the palm of the hand. This creates a slight vertical planal pull (Figure 7).

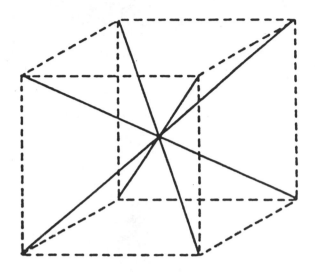

Figure 8. The crystalline form of the cube.

ÉPAULEMENT ÉPAULÉ

ÉPAULÉ

Figure 9. *Epaulé* position of the body.

However, in the other schools, vertical planal tension is pronounced, and both *écarté devant* and *écarté derrière* positions are taught.

In *écarté devant*, the eyes look to the arm *en haut*, and in *écarte derrière*, the eyes look to the arm low *à la seconde*. In both poses, the arm *en haut* is in line with the upper torso and slightly rotated head. The whole upper body is tilted to the side away from the leg extended to the side. Vertical planal tension is created through the high/side pull of the arm and torso, the low/same side pull of the other arm, and the low/opposite side pull of the extended leg (Figure 7).

Epaulé means shouldered, and this position is found in each of the schools. In addition to the *épaulé devant* position, the Russian and French schools include the *épaulé derrière* position, which is the same position but performed facing upstage right or left. The *épaulement* of the *épaulé* position creates cubic tension.

Within the framework of choreutics, the crystalline form of diagonal orientation is the cube. There are four diagonals, each with two spatial pulls. Within the reach zone of the upper body, the diagonals intersect at the center of the chest. When the eight pulls of the four diagonals are connected, the cube is established (Figure 8). In this study, the center of the cube coincides with the center of the chest.

In the *épaulé épaulement*, the upper torso is twisted in the direction of the back arm, which is in view of the audience and the head is tilted slightly and rotated in the opposite direction towards the audience (Figure 9).

When facing downstage left, diagonal tension is created from the low/left/backward pull of the waist across the chest to the high/right/forward pull of the right shoulder. There is also diagonal tension from the low/right/forward pull of the chest to the high/left/backward pull of the left shoulder. In addition, there is diagonal tension from the low/left/forward pull in the chest through the high/right/backward pull of the head. Therefore, there are six diagonal pulls in this pose. Three full diagonals pass through the center of the chest.

Cubic tension is created through the peripheral and central relationships among the diagonal pulls. There is pronounced cubic tension among the high/right/backward pull of the head, the high/left/backward pull of the left shoulder, the low/left/backward pull of the waist, and the high/right/forward pull of the right shoulder. Less cubic tension is created by the other diagonal pulls. There is also dimensional tension created through the arms, which are positioned back and forward in line with the stance. *Epaulé* also appears with the addition of a backward tilt in the upper torso. This increases the three-dimensionality of the form;

and therefore, the spatial tensions of the crystalline form of the cube are heightened.

SUMMARY

In summary, the spatial organization of the upper-body technique of classic ballet is classified according to the choreutic framework. Dimensional oriented positions include the arm positions and the body positions of *à la quatrième devant, à la quatrième derrière,* and *à la seconde.* These positions can also be viewed as oriented to the octahedron. Other octahedral orientation includes the pathways of the *ports de bras.*

Planal orientation includes five positions of the body. Although the *écarté* position of the Cecchetti Method is basically oriented to the dimensions, there is a slight vertical planal pull in the head position. The *écarté devant* and *écarté derrière* positions of the Russian and French schools create vertical planal tension. The *croisé derrière* position of the Cecchetti Method creates vertical and sagittal planal tension, and the *effacé derrière* position of the Russian and French schools creates sagittal tension.

Diagonal tension is created in the fundamental positions of *épaulement croisé* and *épaulement effacé.* Two positions of the body create diagonal and dimensional tensions. These include the *croisé devant* position, and the *croisé derrière* position of the Russian and French schools.

Diagonal and planal tension is created in the body position of *effacé devant.* The *épaulé* position creates cubic tension in the *épaulement* and dimensional tension in the arm position.

REFERENCES

Beaumont, C. W., & Idzikowski, S. (1975). *A Manual of the theory and practice of classical theatrical dancing (méthode Cecchetti).* New York: Dover. (Original work published by C. W. Beaumont, London, 1922).

Dell, C., Crow, A., & Bartenieff, I. (1977). *Space harmony* (2nd rev. ed.). New York: Dance Notation Bureau.

Grant, G. (1982). *Technical manual and dictionary of classical ballet* (3rd rev. ed.). New York: Dover.

Hammond, S. N. (1984). *Ballet Basics* (2nd ed.). Palo Alto, CA: Mayfield.

Kirstein, L., & Stuart, M. (1978). *The classic ballet.* New York: Alfred A. Knopf.

Laban, R. (1974). *The language of movement: A guidebook to choreutics* (L. Ullmann, Ed.). Boston: Plays. (Original work published by Macdonald and Evans, Great Britain, 1966, under the title *Choreutics.*)

Lawson, J. (1960). *Classical ballet, its style and technique.* London: Adam & Charles Black.

Vaganova, A. (1946). *Fundamentals of the classic dance* (Anatole Chujoy, Trans.). New York: Kamin Dance. (Original work published in Leningrad, 1934.)

10

A PRISMATIC APPROACH TO THE ANALYSIS OF STYLE IN DANCE

BETSEY GOODLING GIBBONS

The purpose of this study was to develop a theoretical framework and conceptual model for the definition of style in western theatrical dance that would account for the various components that contribute to the unique character of a dance event or performance. First, an examination of style in music, drama, and the visual arts, including a multidisciplinary review of literature, was used as the basis for identifying components that comprise, contribute to, and affect style. Second, information gained from this inquiry was synthesized and a framework for the study of style in dance was formulated. Third, the conceptual analysis resulted in the development of a comprehensive theoretical model for the definition and analysis of style in dance. The three-dimensional global model incorporated both taxonomic and generative views of style in art and was developed to view each dance performance as a unique gestalt that combines several aspects of style. The global model was concerned with the interactions between the stylistic features of the work, the genre with which it is associated, the performance process of the dancer(s) who give it utterance, the choreographer who created it, and the director who restages it. The horizontal dimension of the global model examined the qualitative features that contribute information concerning classification of the genres and works of art in the dance medium. The vertical dimension studied the three parallel artistic processes of choreographing, performing, and directing works in dance. Elements of style for genre were identified as schema, vocabulary, rules, and qualities. The elements of style for the work were identified as intent, vocabulary, structure, and qualities. Elements of style in artistic process were identified as disposition to act, schema, strategies, and training and temperament. The third dimension studied the changes over time that occur in processes and works.

Style is central to the understanding of art. Style analysis enables us to understand the work of art itself and the artist who created it, and enables us to understand the work in temporal and spatial relation to other works of art. The concept of style, by defining relationships, helps us to make order out of what might otherwise be a vast array of unrelated objects or events. However, whereas one may argue that style is the single most important aspect of aesthetic discourse in the arts, there have been few attempts to systematically study and define what constitutes style in dance.

What is meant by the term "style' is not always clear. At a dance critics' conference entitled "The Subject of Style" (Armelagos, 1984), style was called "a convenient label," "an inhibitor of creative energies meant to be overthrown by the avant-garde," "a goal only the pretentious strive for," and "what keeps sausages grinding out of the old dance mill" (p. 57). All of these portray style as something external to the work of art or to the artistic process. Style is not an evil external force. Rather, it is a constellation of qualitative features *embodied* by the dance work or by the artistic processes of the performer and/or the choreographer who have created that work. Style is to the process or product of art as "personality" is to people. While it may be jokingly said that a boring individual has no personality, personality is inherent in the person, as style is inherent in the work of art or the process that produced it. What is needed is an approach that recognizes style as the qualitative features arising out of the creative processes of the dance artists who contribute to the dance performance, and recognizes how these features are embodied in the genres and works of art.

In order to consider the formulation of aesthetic theory focusing on style analysis in dance, several aspects of dance warrant attention. First, the complexity of the dance product must be considered. What is the dance artifact? According to Maxine Sheets (1966), dance is an illusion: "The actual components of force which underlie the illusion of force are plastic, and as such, are transformed into qualities of movement as a revelation of force" (p. 57). Suzanne Langer (1953) wrote that "a dance is an apparition of active powers, a *dynamic image*. Everything a dancer actually does serves to create what we really see; but what we really see is a virtual entity" (p. 7). Thus, the artifact in dance is a temporal, virtual image.

Second, how is this image, the dance artifact, created? Dance is an artform whose works come into full being only through performance, by means of artists with diverse talents. The choreographer typically composes by creating directly with the uniquely skilled bodies of the performers, so that the dancers are often accomplices in the choreographic act.

Third, how is this image conveyed? The performer-mediated aspect of dance complicates the understanding of how the dance image functions. It is only through the dancer that the audience is able to observe the dance performance, and the audience sees the dance only through the dancer's skill in dynamics, phrasing, and focus. Armelagos and Sirridge (1977) have stated that "in the important symbolic functions of dance, . . . style is the crucial link between the dancer and the dance as perceived" (p. 20). Thus the dance image is conveyed through the body and sense of understanding of the unique performer.

Finally, though the audience sees the dance through the dancer's movement, the audience does not attend solely to the performer. The dance as a work of art does exist separately from the dancer. A dance role may be performed by various dancers, or a group work may be performed by different companies with diverse styles. One example that presents an interesting stylistic dilemma was the 1975 production of José Limon's *The Moor's Pavane*, danced by Rudolf Nureyev, Dame Margot Fonteyn, Karen Kain, and Paolo Bortoluzzi. Critic Anna Kisselgoff (1975) referred to this performance, a decidedly balletic interpretation of the modern dance classic, as a "travesty." She wrote that the performers, "totally misunderstanding the choreographer's intentions, . . . read inexcusable changes into the choreography" (p. 7). Even though the dancers were highly trained in one particular genre (ballet), they had no training in or understanding of the style of the choreographer (Limon), the style of the work, or the style of the genre (modern). This can drastically affect the outcome of a performance and the import that a dance work has in history. According to Deborah Jowitt (1985), an "off-base execution of a dance can write its obituary" (p. 132).

Even two performances of the same work by the same dancer will differ, from slightly to radically. As a dancer matures, often studying with different teachers or choreographers, her or his approach to dance will change. When Suzanne Farrell returned to the New York City Ballet after five years of performing with Maurice Béjart's Ballet of the XXth Century, dance critic Marica Siegel (1977) noted that "she looks very different from the pliant, vacantly beautiful dancer-creature she was before. Somehow this new firmly centered, risk-taking Farrell has shifted the [Don Quixote] ballet for me, just enough . . . so that I could look carefully at its weird theatricality" (p. 87).

These examples demonstrate the complex nature of style analysis in dance. It must be realized that any dance performance is a product comprising several different aspects of style. One may wish to analyze the particular style of a single performer, the overall style of a certain choreographer, the style of a particular work, the style embodied by a genre such as ballet or modern dance, or how any of these have changed over time. This, then, posits the *unique dance event* at the center of any discussion of style analysis. Rather than referring to the dance *performance*, which tactily tends to emphasize the *performer*, it is necessary to refer to the dance *event* as the point at which all of these come together: the style of the artistic processes of the choreographer and the dancer (and often, but not always, the reconstructor); the qualitative features of the work and the genre with which it is associated; and the point in time of the performance. Each performance in dance is an interactive event comprising several different aspects of style.

The net result of this interaction is a unique blend of the creative processes of the choreographer and the performer, the qualities of the dance composition, and the general movement style with which it was created. Existing models for the analysis of style in art have tended to focus on the end product as the sole consideration. However, when analyzing style in dance, neither the work of art nor the process of the artist can be seen as the final point. Rather, these are two of the interactive forces, each with a unique style, that contribute to the overall character of the dance event. In addition, it must be remembered that these parts constitute a unique whole. Analysis of the event is dependent not only upon identifying and analyzing each of these components separately, but also upon understanding how they interrelate. When trying to define aesthetic principles of dance, Edwin Denby (1965) found that any force in dancing involves numerous elements that appear contradictory but coexist in the actual event. It is impossible to see all of the elements of dance simultaneously in one performance; however, Denby has maintained that "you can't build a system out of consistently separating one element from the other" (McDonagh et al., 1969, p. 33).

The prismatic approach to style recognizes that style in dance is a multifaceted concept. Like a prism, which allows the scientist to study the various wavelengths constituting the phenomenon of which light, the prismatic approach allows the viewer to study the various styles that interact to produce the incandescent phenomenon of the unique dance event. A prismatic analysis is not necessarily to use the prism as a model per se, but rather is a way of *approaching* a phenomenon (see Figure 1). A dance event may be seen as a lambent glow. It can be observed and enjoyed as such, but in order to analyze this white-light phenomenon, it must be diffracted so that the component parts may each be displayed for study.

For such research, an appropriate method for study must be determined. Gombrich (1968) has pointed out two methods of analysis: statistical morphology or mathematical analysis, and connoisseurship or intuition. While intuition may not be infallible, mathematical analysis serves only to confirm informed intuitive recognition. According to Gombrich, "the intuitive grasp of underlying *Gestalten* that makes the connoisseur is still far ahead of the morphological analysis of styles in terms of enumerable features" (p. 360). In addition, Shapiro (1979) has stated that

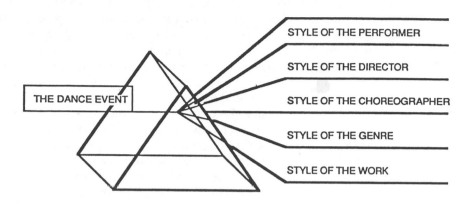

Figure 1. Prismatic approach to the analysis of style in dance.

"while some writers conceive of style as a kind of syntax or compositional pattern, which can be analyzed mathematically, in practice one has been unable to do without the vague language of qualities in describing styles" (p. 320).

This brings into focus the idea that for analysis of style in the arts, qualitative descriptions, while perhaps seen as "vague," are more relevant to the aesthetic experience of observing art than are quantitative measurements. Greater precision can be reached in dealing with qualities, and the intuitive grasp of underlying *Gestalten* is preferable to a statistical morphology analysis. This emphasis on qualitative description, and the need for a comprehensive, cohesive system for describing qualities in dance and movement will help to shape an aesthetic theory model for the analysis of style in dance.

The very nature of dance poses challenges for those attempting to formulate theory for the analysis of style in dance. Dance is ephemeral in nature, disappearing as it is created; dance uses the human body as instrument; and dance is primarily a performer-mediated artform. Furthermore, it must be recognized that in dance, the art "object" is the unique dance event. Each performance of a particular work, even by the same dancers, is a unique and different event. Style analysis for dance must recognize, even celebrate, the ephemeral, performer-mediated, ever-changing nature of this artform.

The framework represented by Figure 2 comprises three main components. The first component is concerned with the *classification of qualitative features*: what the general movement style has in common with other general movement styles, what qualities suggest its association with a particular genre, and what the dance work has in common with other works that may cause it to be grouped with them. The second component is concerned with *artistic process*: the choreographic process that produces the composition, the performance process that interprets the composition, and the reconstructive process that interprets the composition. The third component is concerned with changes that occur in any aspect over time. This may be used to study changes over time in the choreographic process of a single artist or the performance process of a single dancer, the changes made in the structure or qualities of a dance work over time, or the subtle changes that occur in a genre. This can also be used to study how performances of a single work are related to each other and how they may differ.

The Global Model (Figure 3) that was developed from this framework represents these three components of style as three dimensions. *The dance event* is the central point of the globe. *Classification of qualitative features* is the horizontal dimension, *artistic process* is the vertical dimension, and *change through time* is the sagittal dimension. Each of these components is then made up of several aspects.

THE HORIZONTAL DIMENSION: STYLISTIC FEATURES CONCERNING CLASSIFICATION

This aspect of style refers to the qualitative features of the genres and works in dance. Style analysis of genres and works does not imply the use of an established labeling process. Genres used as convenient labels would only serve to halt the process of gaining deeper understanding of the dance phenomenon as a whole. The information that arises from classification can be very useful in the analysis of style. Explanatory analysis allows for grouping works that have certain qualitative features

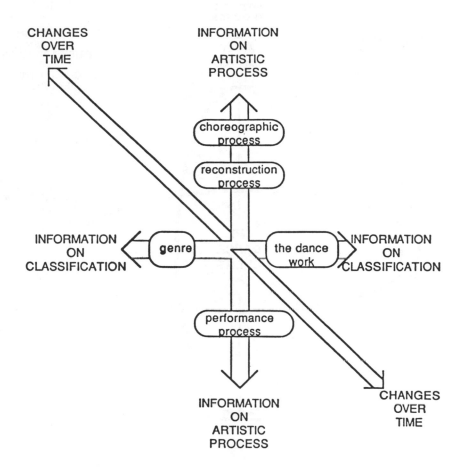

Figure 2. Framework for the analysis of style in dance.

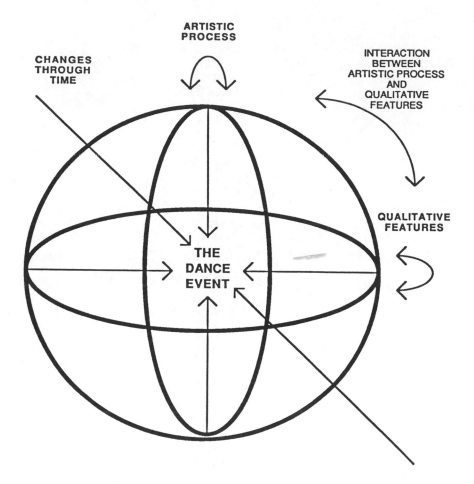

Figure 3. Global model for the analysis of style in dance.

in common. Classification may affect analysis because even though it reveals nothing, it does point to features that occur together and defines some repertory. It also tends to function heuristically by leading the observer to ask why the features characteristic of a class or group occur together. For example, to say that the works of Trisha Brown, Lucinda Childs, and Meredith Monk are classified as postmodern dance does not in itself give any information as to why they are grouped together. However, such a classification should lead one to inquire what features they share to cause such a grouping. To state that certain works by Merce Cunningham are considered modern dance and others are considered postmodern should lead one to inquire what features the former and the latter works have in common with others of the same classification.

Classification may also function heuristically in relation to history. When an earlier class or group of events is related to a later one, the earlier events can be understood not only by their own structure and process, and what led up to them, but also by what is believed to have followed or perhaps been caused by them. Thus a historical classification allows prospective and retrospective comprehension of temporal events. Some features of a class, genre or individual style are significant or relevant primarily in terms of what went before or came after. For example, in order to understand more fully the genre of postmodern dance, it is necessary to understand modern dance of the mid-20th century, its relationship with early modern dance, and the relationship of both of these with late Romantic ballet. In order to understand the qualitative features that distinguish works by Merce Cunningham, it is useful to study the qualitative features that distinguish works by Martha Graham and Margaret Jenkins, the former from whom Cunningham diverged, the latter who diverged from Cunningham. Taxonomy can thus be seen as a method for seeking information on relationships between genres or works, on stylistic aspects of works in specific and the artform in general. Classification or taxonomy is thus used here not as a dissecting tool for dividing the art form into neat, discrete categories, but rather as an analytical device for gaining a deeper understanding of the art form in order to unify it. Thus analysis and classification of stylistic features provides information on genres and individual dance works.

Genres

When one attempts to define style in genres, one finds that no single property or quality is sufficient in itself to define the genre. However, the combinations of properties for each genre provide a great deal of information on how that genre organizes the medium of dance and manifests itself. Ballet, modern dance, and jazz are genres that may encompass a number of distinct subgroupings, and may also "borrow" from each other or take on characteristics previously linked exclusively to another genre. This borrowing of characteristics does not necessarily result in a merging of genres. Genres are not made up of a single quality, but of a constellation of qualitative features, although some one quality may be discovered to be pervasive throughout and even essential to the genre.

Arriving at a qualitative definition of the major genres in western theatrical dance is a difficult task. As previously discussed, rigid definitions have no explanatory function, nor could they allow for the variety within the artform. However, identification of qualitative features allows examination of why works are grouped into certain classes, and also allows further examination of the creative processes of the artists who produce works in dance. Ballet has a relatively long history strongly grounded in oral tradition. However, subtle changes have been wrought unrecorded over the centuries. Modern, on the other hand, has had a shorter but more explosive history. Jazz, arising from the ethnic and folk dances of the African people, has been recognized as a theatrical form of dance only fairly recently.

The elements that constitute the style of a genre are *genre schema, rules, vocabulary*, and *qualities*. The Ring Model of Figure 4, incorporating these four elements, provides a multifaceted approach to the study of stylistic features of genres. Like the concentric rings found in the cross-section of a tree, each layer develops from an interactive relationship with the one before it: a particular way of organizing the artform gives rise to characteristic uses of the body, instructions for working with the medium, and dynamic qualities. Whereas the use of any single approach to definitions of genres provides only limited, superficial descriptions, the use of these four provides a more complete view.

Schema refers to how the genre as a whole organizes the artform. The schema for ballet is often referred to as a system, with a movement vocabulary, pedagogical framework, and choreographic canons. It is characterized by a sense of tradition and classicism, extroversion as exemplified by the use of outward rotation in the legs and openness in the torso and arms, and the view of dancers as disciplined instruments of precision, virtuosic, and elegant. The schema of modern dance has been referred to as a point of view, and has been characterized as existentialist in nature. Central to this schema is the individualistic spirit, will, and imagination. Discovery-oriented, training and choreography are viewed as a journey along which the individual develops a sense of coming to understand, rather than means to an end, with dancers considered freely creative and self-expressive individuals. The schema of jazz has been characterized as conceptualizing dance as highly skillful entertainment to be appreciated rather than analyzed, demanding physical technique of the dancer but little or no symbolic illusion. Central to the schema of jazz is the personal expression of the dancer through the purely physical and sensual aspects of movement.

Vocabulary includes characteristic use of the body. Ballet uses a codified vocabulary that grew out of the court entertainments of 17th-century France, with emphasis on geometry and the five basic positions of the feet from which all movements originate. The legs maintain outward rotation, the torso is characteristically held upright, with an emphasis on verticality. Modern dance vocabulary is seen as a protean continuum, developing and changing through the influence of individual choreographers and teachers. The torso and spine are used in a dynamic manner with the center of gravity of the body as the initiator of movement. Emphasis is on moving and falling off the vertical. Jazz dance vocabulary is characterized by the use of isolation of body parts, with movement initiated by the hips, pelvis, or shoulders. Knees are often bent, and movements often ripple sequentially from the center outward.

Rules refer to the tacit, traditional and/or codified instructions for working within the medium, what is chosen, and how it is applied. The ballet genre relies on its strong sense of tradition and oral history to "teach" the rules for creating, performing, and appreciating works. For the modern dance genre, whereas texts for choreography and training are becoming more numerous, the rebellious, independent spirit of the modern genre has tended to see rules as points of departure, to be broken rather than followed. Rules in jazz dance, with its ethnic and folk origins, have usually been informally handled, borrowed from other theatrical forms.

Qualities refer to the dynamics of movement and can be described and discussed using the movement analysis system developed by Rudolf Laban and his followers. Qualities, which are called Efforts, are divided into four basic components: space, time, weight, and flow. Each of these comprises a continuum between two extremes—sustained and sudden for time, fine and firm for weight, free and bound for flow, and direct and flexible for space. According to Laban, all human movement exhibits constellations of these factors that form certain identifiable textures of movement. The qualities characteristically associated with ballet include lightness or fine weight, extremes of sudden and sustained, with direct focus and spatial intent. Qualities usually associated with modern include strength or firmness, subtle shadings along the continuum of the time

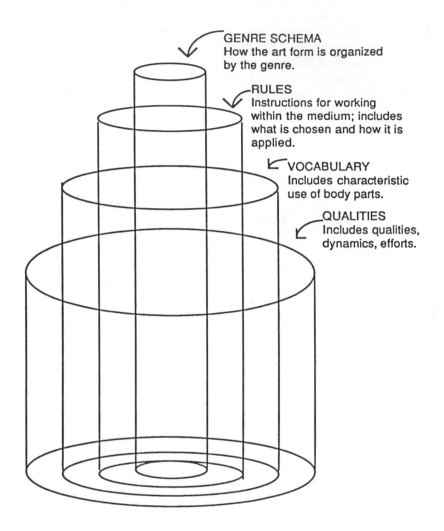

GENRE SCHEMA
How the art form is organized
by the genre.

RULES
Instructions for working
within the medium; includes
what is chosen and how it is
applied.

VOCABULARY
Includes characteristic
use of body parts.

QUALITIES
Includes qualities,
dynamics, efforts.

Figure 4. Elements which comprise the style of a genre.

element between sudden and sustained, and flexible spatial intent. Qualities often associated with jazz include strength and weightiness, rather
than lightness. Bound flow is often combined with sharp contrasts in the
time element between suddenness and sustainment.

Thus the *schema* of the genre refers to how the genre organizes the
art form; *vocabulary* refers to how body parts are used; *rules* refers to
instructions for working within the medium; and *qualities* refer to the
dynamics of movement.

Works

Four interactive elements can be identified as constituting a dance
work and thus constituting the distinctive style of a dance work: *intent,
structure, vocabulary*, and *qualities*. Figure 5 represents the Ring Model
for the style of a dance work. As with the previous ring model, each
layer develops from an interactive relationship with the ones before it.
From the original idea and the qualitative negotiation and transactions
of the choreographer with the medium, the dance develops an *intent*,
which may be seen as an overall schema for the dance's relationship
to the world and to its viewers. It often parallels the schema of the
choreographer of the work. Intent is ineffable, elusive, least translatable
into verbal discourse, but it is the spirit of the work. From this arises a
structure, vocabulary, and *qualities*, which embody the intention of the
dance.

One way of conceptualizing the *intent* of the work is as analogous
to, or a manifestation of, the schema of the artist. One approach to
intent in the work is that used by Suzanne Foster (1986), who used the
four tropes or principal figures of speech, *metaphor, metonymy, synecdoche*,
and *irony*, as an analytical tool for understanding the choreographer's
relationship to the body and to the dance. These tropes can also be seen
as forming the schema of the work as a result of the schema of the
choreographer. *Metaphor* contains an implied comparison in which a
word or phrase ordinarily and primarily used of one thing is applied to
another, such as the phrase, "all the world's a stage." In a dance in which
metaphor predominates, the choreographer translates worldly events
into movement, the dance functions as an analogy to the world, and the
dancer's body is an analogy to his or her sense of self. The works of
Doris Humphrey and José Limón often function as metaphors to present
ideas and illustrate conditions and universal traits of peoples and periods. In *metonymy*, the use of the name of one thing is substituted for
that of another associated with or suggested by it. The works of ballet
choreographer George Balanchine are examples of this trope. When

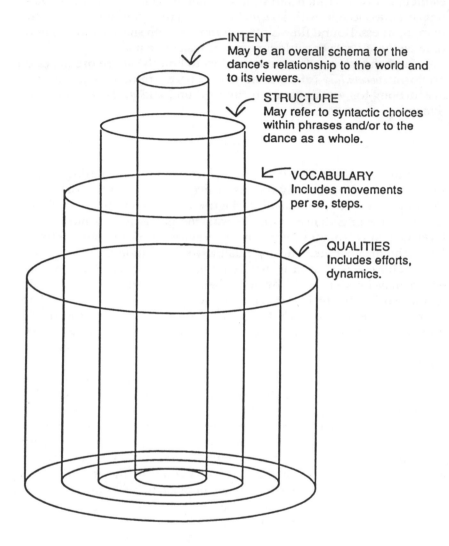

INTENT
May be an overall schema for the
dance's relationship to the world and
to its viewers.

STRUCTURE
May refer to syntactic choices
within phrases and/or to the
dance as a whole.

VOCABULARY
Includes movements
per se, steps.

QUALITIES
Includes efforts,
dynamics.

Figure 5. Elements which comprise the style of a dance work.

metonymy is dominant in a work, the world is made over in the image of the dance, which replaces and improves upon the world to which it refers, and the body substitutes for the subject, offering the best version of the subject. In *synecdoche*, a part is used for the whole. Through synecdoche, the work transforms the personal experience of the choreographer into a universal condition, and the dance becomes a special voice speaking to the world about essential things, with the body serving as a representative of the subject. *Irony* reflects a method of humorous or subtly sarcastic expression in which the intended meaning of the words used is the direct opposite of their usual sense. Irony is exemplified by the contemporary postexpressionist experimental dance of the latter half of the 20th century, especially that of Merce Cunningham. In this trope, the message will be one of several the viewer can choose. The dance is another of the many activities that make up the world, and the body is simply the subject, and yet it may be something else (Foster, 1986).

Structure refers to the overall form or framework, the "composition" of the work, the principles of syntactic arrangement that give an internal coherence to the dance. As inseparable as form is from content, it is obviously an important element in identifying and discussing the work in dance. It may be seen as the musical and literary compositional forms of Doris Humphrey (1959) or Louis Horst (1961), or the syntactic choices identified by Foster (1986) as *mimesis, pathos,* and *parataxis.* Different syntactic principles may operate simultaneously throughout a work on different levels, such as the level of a phrase, a section, or over the entire work. In this sense, choreographic strategies become the structure of the work of art.

Vocabulary refers to the steps or movements that are developed in order to convey the intent of the work. A distinctive movement vocabulary is essential to analysis of a dance work. Jack Anderson (1983) has identified Idealists and Materialists as two opposing views concerning the importance of vocabulary in the dance work. Typically, Idealists regard a dance as the incarnation in movement of ideas or effects. The Idealist may not mind that in different productions of the same dance steps are altered, provided that the changes express the same idea, produce the same effect, or illuminate the work's central concept. Materialists, on the other hand, regard a dance as a composition of specific steps or specific instructions for improvisation, from which ideas or effects may be derived. Murray Louis (1980) has identified use of the body, shape, space, time, and dynamics as factors that can be combined in any fashion to allow the choreographer a new and different vocabulary for each dance. Thus an identifiable vocabulary of movement is an essential part of a work.

Dynamic qualities are another crucial aspect of style in a dance. Dynamic qualities, or Efforts, are what give certain movements their unique texture in a dance. Each work of dance art created by the choreographer has distinct qualities that differentiate it from other works. Deborah Jowitt (1985), discussing Paul Taylor's works, remarked that Taylor uses the same "vocabulary of big winging, coiling steps" (p. 50) to make works such as the macabre *Big Bertha*, the satiric *From Sea to Shining Sea*, and the arial *Aureole* and *Esplanade*. In *Three Epitaphs* the dancers look weighty, even fatigued. *Aureole*, however, with its tender, seraphic character, uses weight quite differently; the movements appear spongy, buoyant, like sails in the wind. The same steps, given distinctively different qualities, will become different movement material. If the dynamics are changed, the style is changed, and the dance itself is altered. Qualities are the most prone to change through individual interpretation, and are the most prone to decay over time.

THE VERTICAL DIMENSION: ARTISTIC PROCESSES

The vertical dimension, *artistic processes*, refers to the work of the choreographer, the performer, and often, but not always, a reconstructor. The Ring Model of Figure 6 represents a model for these elements of artistic process. At the core is the *disposition to act*, central to all creative activity. From this arises an artist's personal *schema, strategies*, and *training and temperament.*

Disposition to act refers to the concept of formulating a problem. One of the central issues of artistic activity is the ability to interact with the medium, allowing the problem to develop through the process of art-making. The ability to seek, discover, formulate, and resolve problems in the medium constitutes the disposition to act. This is the key to the distinction between having a style and merely working in a style, the essential difference between the artist and the craftsman or technician. When this aspect of the artistic process is not well developed, the lack is apparent. Marcia Siegel (1977) has written, "Natalia Makarova, dancing in it [*Dark Elegies*] for the first time, seemed to me not to undertand it. She danced very well, but she was acting out grief, rather than feeling the solemnity of the movement as the others do" (p. 50). Of Martha Graham's company, she wrote, "there have been too few times when I thought everyone in the cast understood the dance in the same way and worked together to create one dance image" (1977, p. 216). When a performer has not developed the disposition to act, or does not apply it to a particular situation, this aspect of style is lacking, and the presentation of the dance work is incomplete. On the other hand, when this aspect of artistic process is particularly well developed, the dance event as a whole entity is complete. Siegel (1977) has written of the New York City Ballet, "There isn't another organization in the world that can show you dancing in such an advanced state of intelligence" (p. 73).

Schema refers to how an artist conceptualizes the artform. Each artist has a particular vision of the world, the artform, and the purpose of art, which helps to sculpt process. According to Cohen (1983), "For the dancer to execute the visible dimensions of the prescribed steps is not enough; that is only part of the style. The style lies also in the attitude toward the movement, which is also an attitude toward life" (p. 350). Each artist explores a conceptualization of dance movement, the dancing body, and a personal conviction about the purpose of art. "Conceptual-ization" does not imply that the artist necessarily verbalizes or has a verbal equivalent for the way that the medium is organized according to this personal framework. It may involve qualitative thinking, thinking in the medium: the painter may think in terms of line, hue, saturation of color; the musician in terms of tonal relationships and the timbres and durations of sounds; and the dancer in terms of the organic or geometric shapes of the body, the ineffable connotations of gestures, or the flow of movement. Maxine Sheets-Johnstone (1981) has referred to this in dance as "thinking in movement." She described the mental processes of a performer as not merely a symbolic way of designating things or thoughts, but the very presence of thought, providing individually or-dered information, stating that "to think in movement does not mean that the dancer is thinking *by means of* movement or that thoughts are *being transcribed into* movement. . . . In such thinking, movement is not a medium by which thoughts emerge but rather, the thoughts themselves" (p. 400). This qualitative thinking in the medium is as important to the choreographer's creation as it is to the reconstructor's interpretation and direction and to the performer's re-creation of the work in the dance event.

One way of looking at schema in dance can be to recognize the genres of modern dance, ballet, and jazz as general schemata in dance, from which individual artists may then form a personal schema. Jazz has often been characterized as highly skillful popular entertainment to be appreciated but not studied (Freisen, 1975; Giordano, 1975), dealing with the purely physical and sensual aspect of dance. Ballet has often been referred to as a "system," characterized by a sense of tradition, its relatively long and strong collective history, and a movement vocabulary, pedagogical system, and "rules" for choreography developed over centu-ries. George Balanchine was a choreographer who exemplified the ballet schema. According to Foster (1986), "Balanchine and his dancers see themselves as part of a tradition, centuries old, in which procedures for transmitting knowledge about dance are defined as rigorously as the scope and content of the knowledge itself" (p. 23). Cohen (1983) wrote that in the early days of the modern dance "a real dichotomy existed: the ballet dancers felt themselves disciplined instruments of precision; their counterparts considered themselves freely creative and self-expressive individuals. They moved differently, felt differently" (p. 350). Modern dance has been referred to as "a point of view" (Fraleigh, 1987; Martin, 1966), and is characterized by its individualistic spirit and individual discoveries, creativity, will, and imagination.

These genres exemplify but are not exclusively bound to these schemata. Performers or choreographers trained in any of the genres may conceptualize dance primarily as an individual point of view developed through individual discoveries, as a movement system embodying established ideals, or as purely physical entertainment. A dancer's conceptualization of the artform may not necessarily be a *result* of training in a particular genre; individuals also *seek* training that closely resembles a personal schema.

Strategies involve choices for acting upon what the artist has selected as material. The nature of these strategies will vary for the choreographer, the reconstructor, and the performer, and are determined by the aspects of the medium with which each artist interacts. For example, the choreographer interacts with the idea and the medium, so the strategies available to the choreographer are concerned with selecting or creating movement that will convey the idea. What the reconstructor interacts with is delimited to the dance work in the form of the score, and thus strategies will be concerned with interpretation of the score. The performer interacts with one role in the dance work, and will tend to be concerned with bringing a unique understanding to one role in relation to the whole dance.

Training and temperament refer to an interaction of the artist with the learning environment. Training in the form of technique class is more than simply exercising the body to increase speed, flexibility, and endurance; it also helps to shape how the dancer conceives the act of moving and motivates movement. For example, a *porte de bras* (arm movement) may be seen as a geometric shape, an arm framing the body, a spatial investigation, or a vehicle for a certain use of energy. Furthermore, the dancer will choose to study a style that "fits" his or her personal temperament. If a dancer's movement temperament is not fulfilled by a particular genre or style, the dancer will leave that style for another.

Thus we see that the aspect of *artistic processes* comprise several interacting elements. The personal sensibility of the artist, whether concerned with choreographing, performing, or reconstructing dances, reveals itself through a deliberate set of restrictions and choices. The *disposition to act* guides the artist to use a personal *schema*, employ *strategies* for working in the medium, and apply *training and temperament* to the creative process.

Interaction between Artistic Processes and Qualitative Features

In the framework presented, the horizontal dimension is concerned with classification of works and genres, and the vertical dimension with artistic processes. Qualitative features of the genre and of the dance work may be seen as forces that interact with the parallel artistic processes of choreography and performance in order to produce the unique dance event. Similar qualitative aspects may be identified in the genre and in the dance work, which then provide information on style in these aspects of the dance event, as well as providing information on choreographic style and performance style. Stylistic features are not merely *possessed* by dance works. Individually, the features of the works exemplify themselves; together they cohere to exemplify the artist. Style analysis of works by the same choreographer may provide insight into the evolution of the creative process and stages in the artistic life of the choreographer.

CHANGES THROUGH TIME

The third dimension of the framework for the analysis of style in dance is concerned with changes over time (see Figure 7). In order to develop a comprehensive model of style, it is necessary to understand what forces are active to bring about transmutations of style.

Rudolf Arnheim (1981) has stated that "most of the trouble with style arises in the time dimension" (p. 284). It is especially necessary, and especially difficult, to trace changes and study relationships through time in an ephemeral, performer-mediated art form such as dance. Analyzing changes through time and space helps scholars, researchers, critics, and students understand the interaction between artistic processes and sociocultural forces, and helps keep dance history from being simply a jumble of unrelated works. What is needed is a way of relating artistic activity and works of art that is active through time.

Rather than avoiding the issue of temporal forces in discussing works of art, Arnheim (1981) has suggested application of gestalt theory to provide the methodology for a dynamic approach to structure. This reflects a change from the atomistic conception of the world as an array of self-contained and discrete elements to that of a world of forces interacting in a field through the dimension of time. This conception of the world recognizes the simultaneous occurrence of a variety of events and allows for forming relationships among them.

This viewpoint also explains the interactive relationship between historical causality and the individual. Rather than seeing causality as the behavior of linear chains of events, attempting to separate the artist as a person from the artist as a creator, or negating cultural and historical conditions, gestalt formation provides "a unitary view of genetic and historical processes, in which cause and effect account without break for all their individual components" (Arnheim, 1981, p. 286). According to Suzanne Foster (1986), any given art event is simultaneously oriented in two directions. It refers to itself both as an artistic event and to the cultural and social circumstances of which it is a part. The ways in which dance can make reference to the world, and the images of the world evoked by dance as an artform, can be understood through analysis of choreographic style and the modes of interpretation that are active in society in certain historical periods. Thus it may be seen that changes in style over time are due to the interactive gestalt of the personality of the artist or artist-as-person, which is inseparable from the process of the ripening and maturation of the artist qua artist. Both of these are interactive with the cultural forces, historical epoch, and social setting in which the artist lives and works.

Delving further, the dance phenomenon comprises several interactive components. Changes in any one aspect give rise to modifications, from slight to radical, in the others. Changes in the artistic processes of the choreographers and performers who work with and contribute to the growth and development of a particular genre have an interactive effect on the qualitative featurs of the genre or the work. These changes also necessarily have an impact on other genres in the artform. In addition, works of art in the performance arts are not static, fixed objects, but depend upon the artistic processes of the reconstructors and performers who give them life. As such, they are prone to evolution through time as well. Thus it is necessary to maintain a holistic conceptualization of style in dance in order to understand how changes occur in any one area.

Evolution in Individual Artistic Process

Changes undoutedly take place in artistic process. Marcia Siegel (1977) commented on the stylistic differences between two works by Eliot Feld, *Intermezzo* (1969), and *Mazurka* (1975), and concluded, "Maybe the difference between these two ballets has something to do with the artist's process of growing up" (p. 64). The works of choreographers such as

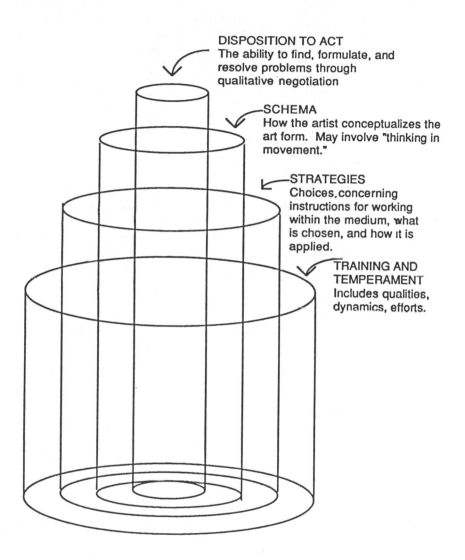

DISPOSITION TO ACT
The ability to find, formulate, and resolve problems through qualitative negotiation

SCHEMA
How the artist conceptualizes the art form. May involve "thinking in movement."

STRATEGIES
Choices concerning instructions for working within the medium, what is chosen, and how it is applied.

TRAINING AND TEMPERAMENT
Includes qualities, dynamics, efforts.

Figure 6. Elements which comprise the artistic process in dance.

Martha Graham and George Balanchine span some 60 years; as the artist matures, both personally as well as in the role of artist qua artist, alterations in the schema, disposition to act, temperament and training, and strategies will be inevitable. Furthermore, the choreography cannot be separated from the changing historical and social circumstances that surround each choreographer's career. Changes in cultural and historical forces have a strong interaction with the art-making process. One must recognize the fallacy of creating a duality between these two forces, and must give credit for their interaction. Art and society are mutually influencing forces in which the activity of artists changes and is changed by the culture.

Change in the style of an artist, traced through changes in the styles of works, is the manifestation of change in the artistic process over time due to evolution in how the artist conceptualizes the artform, which strategies are employed, or even changes in the disposition to act. Several critics noted a distinct transformation in the performance style of Suzanne Farrell following her work with Maurice Béjart and subsequent return to Balanchine's company. Balanchine himself has said, "When you are young you do the steps. When you are more experienced you dance the movement" (in Taylor, 1983, p. 88).

Change in the style of a choreographer who is also a performer may also be due to the inevitable effects of the aging process. For example, lightness was a trademark of the style of Merce Cunningham in a time when so many modern choreographers were exploring weight. This gradually gave way to a less aerial style that emphasized rapid changes of direction, retaining a certain leanness. Marcia Siegel (197) noted that "No more is he trying to remind us that he was once buoyant, fast, engaging. . . . This time it's the weightiness of age that he plays with—the sense of solidity and mass, of the earth not as something to resist or to celebrate but as something with which he is in intimate contact" (p. 238).

Evolution in Genres

Changes in any of these areas may bring about subtle transformations in other areas. The interaction of artistic process with genre will result in changes in the genre. For example, Michel Fokine and Vaslav Nijinsky were two choreographers who initiated major changes while working within the established ballet genre. While Nijinsky trained, performed, and choreographed within the ballet genre, many of his choreographic concerns were consonant with the expressionistic dance that was developing simultaneously, and was a forerunner to the modern dance. Fokine was influenced by the work of Isadora Duncan, and while his works reflect the ballet vocabulary, his schema, disposition to act, and strategies resulted in an expanded vocabulary, intent, and qualities.

Efficiency in training has resulted in stronger, more technically proficient performers. This has a distinct interaction with the choreographic process. For example, the evolution of vocabulary in ballet has tended toward a longer, leaner line that includes a more open angle of the leg in attitude, the increased height of the leg in arabesques to approach the "six o'clock" line, the over-90° dévélopé that was once considered vulgar, and a popular contemporary pas de chat in which the leading leg stretches and snaps out instead of remaining bent. Increasingly, dancers study a variety of dance forms, and transformations occur in the genres, artistic processes, and in the works that result.

The interaction between genres is another force that gives rise to transformations within genres. Intergenre exchanges have caused what Deborah Jowitt (1977) has called "cross-pollination." She has written that this has produced "a hybrid style that, typically, is showy, bright-colored, and intricately convoluted" (p. 64). This contemporary virtuosity provides new materials for choreographer, reconstructor, and performer to deal with. It must be recognized not as a kind of inevitable evolutionary "improvement," but as a force that will interact in numerous ineffable ways with the other forces. Just how it interacts must be considered in order to understand the full extent of temporal forces in dance and the impact on the dance event. Murray Louis (1980) has commened on the changes this new virtuosity in training has had on the artistic process of the performer. "Not only do dancers today look differently and dance differently, they think differently. When they are called upon to perform the squareness that generally characterized the structure of revived choreography, they don't know what to do with all their technique and consequently overact the role to release their untapped energy" (p. 111).

The scope of what was considered appropriate thematic material broadened considerably with the development of modern dance. This change began to be reflected in the contributions of ballet choreographers such as Anthony Tudor, whose works, such as *Dark Elegies* and *Pillar of Fire*, portray a greater depth of psychological insight.

Evolution in Works

Many factors may be involved in how dances as performance works are transfigured over the years. Changes are often made in classical ballet works due to considerations such as needing to lengthen, shorten, or excerpt the work to fit a program. Poetic license or even faulty memory on the part of a director who restages the work from memory alone are also factors. Sir Frederick Ashton offered two different opinions concerning changes that occur when works are "revived." On the one hand, he has said, "No, I don't trust these 'improvers.' It's like they want to improve *Lac des Cygnes* [*Swan Lake*] or *Sleeping Beauty*. Well, they don't improve them, not at all. They make them worse. . . . Petipa knew what he was doing" (Philip, 1987, p. 138). On the other hand, he has said, "*Nutcracker*. Now that's a ballet everybody fiddles with. It seems that *Nutcracker* is all right in just about any version you desire, provided the tree grows" (p. 138).

Changes in a work over time may occur due to changes in how the choreographer conceptualizes the work. According to Tobi Tobias (1979), "Balanchine treats even his landmark achievements as organic, evolving material, from time to time redesigning elements in them to reflect a given performer's gifts (or conceal his or her weaknesses), and to embody his own changing vision" (p. 20). Alterations may be made during restaging due to differences in the abilities of the dancers, who may be more or less technically proficient than the original cast, or trained in a distinctly different style. A dance work may change through modifications made during reconstruction from memory. Slight erosions often occur in the repertory of a company as the works are performed over and over. Arlene Croce (1977) referred to this as "the flattening out of certain details. . . . The dancers who now do the role aren't able to extract the right dance values from it, and so miss its spirit" (p. 57).

Changes in culture and society mean changes in audience expectations. Works are often "updated" to align them with changing audience taste and expectations. According to Vivi Flindt (personal communication, July 5, 1988), former first soloist with the Royal Danish Ballet, showy divertissements have been added to some Bournonville classics in order to increase appeal to modern audiences. Siegel (1977) remarked on this when she wrote, "Even in Denmark, where the technique and choreography of the great Romantic ballet master August Bournonville have been preserved as a national treasure, the subtle, delicate Bournonville style is gradually eroding as the gaudier effects of contemporary ballet win audience approval" (p. 7). Toby Tobias (1985) has written that the common practice of "modernizing" classic works has usually meant minimizing the mime, introducing additional anachronistic dancing, and often weighting the fairytale libretto," exquisitely suggestive in itself—with Freudian motivations" (p. 46).

The sense of tradition on which ballet is based is kept through revivals. The rebellious modern choreographers of the early pioneering days were more concerned with creating new works for the new dance than with preservation of previous works. However, a time for reflection and conservation has arrived. Modern dance is becoming more concerned with preserving historical landmark works and styles. Furthermore, Murray Louis (1980) has stated, "Perhaps [modern dance] should consider what ballet has concluded; since the training of the dancer has changed over the years and audiences have grown more sophisticated, perhaps it would be wise to update revivals, rather than recreate" (pp. 113–114).

SUMMARY

An approach that is prismatic in nature sees the dance event comprising several aspects that interact to produce a unique temporal phenomenon. Thus, rather than approaching style as a force external to the processes by which dance events are created, the prismatic approach enables the observer to approach style in dance as a multifaceted concept. This enables the observer to identify, study, and analyze the components of style.

Analysis of a multifaceted phenomenon involves two levels: identifying and examining the component parts, and understanding how they function as a gestalt. The ring models identify component parts that constitute the genre, the work, and the artistic processes of the choreographer, the director, and the performer as individuals who contribute to the event. The global model explains how these elements interact to produce the incandescent force of the dance event, and the changeability of all these aspects over time.

Theories, models, and the language they employ are the basic tools with which scholars, historians, students, and artists work to broaden and deepen understanding of the artform, art works, and the artists who produce them. A theoretical framework as a way of looking at dance and a method of organizing what is seen and experienced is necessary for discussions on a scholarly level. The transitoriness of dance, far from hindering serious and sustained reflection, can provide challenging opportunities for discussion and development of aesthetic theory.

REFERENCES

Anderson, J. (1983). Idealists, materialists, and the thirty-two fouettes. In R. Copeland and M. Cohen (Eds.), *What is dance* (pp. 410–419). New York: Oxford University Press.

Armelagos, A. (1984). Dance critics converence: The subject of style. A conference report. *Dance Research Journal, 16*(1), pp. 57–59.

Armelagos, A., & Sirridge, M. (1978). The identity crisis in dance. *The Journal of Aesthetics and Art Criticism, 39*, 129–140.

Armelagos, A., & Sirridge, M. (1984). Personal style and performance preroga-
tives. In M. Sheets-Johnstone (Ed.), *Illuminating dance: Philosophical explorations*
(pp. 85–100). Lewisburg, PA: Bucknell University Press.

Arnheim, R. (1981). Style as a gestalt problem. *The Journal of Aesthetics and Art
Criticism, 39,* 281–289.

Cohen, S. J. (1983). Problems of definition. In R. Copeland & M. Cohen (Eds.),
What is dance (pp. 339–354). New York: Oxford University Press.

Croce, A. (1977), *Afterimages.* New York: Alfred A. Knopf.

Denby, E. (1968). *Looking at the dance.* New York: Horizon Press.

Foster, L. (1986). *Reading dancing: Bodies and subjects in contemporary American
dance.* Berkeley: University of California Press.

Fraleigh, S. (1987). *Dance and the lived body.* Pittsburg: University of Pittsburg
Press.

Friesen, J. (1975). Perceiving dance. *The Journal of Aesthetic Education, 9,* 97–108.

Giordano, G. (1975). *Anthology of American jazz dance.* Evanston, IL: Orion Publishing House.

Gombrich, E. H. (1968). Style. In D. Sills (Ed.), *International encyclopedia of the
social sciences,* vol. 15 (pp. 352–361). New York: Macmillan and Free Press.

Horst, L., & Russel, C. (1961). *Modern dance forms.* New York: Dance Horizons,
Inc.

Humphrey, D. (1959). *The art of making dances.* New York: Grove Press.

Jowitt, D. (1977). *Dance beat.* New York: Marcel Dekker, Inc.

Jowitt, D. (1985). *The dance in mind.* Boston: David R. Godine.

Kisselgoff, A. (1975, August 24). When ballet dancers stumble into modern
dance. *The New York Times,* section 2, pp. 1, 7.

Langer, S. (1953). *Feeling and form.* New York: Charles Scribner's Sons.

Louis, M. (1980). *Inside dance.* New York: St. Martin's Press.

Martin, J. (1966). *Modern dance.* New York: Dance Horizons.

McDonagh, D., Croce, A., & Dorris, G. (1969). A conversation with Edwin Denby: Part 2. *Ballet Review, 2*(6), 33.

Philp. R. (1987). Revivals. *Dance Magazine, 61*(6), 136–149.

Schapiro, M. (1979). Style. In M. Rader (Ed.), *A modern book of esthetics* (pp.
317–327). New York: Holt, Rinehart and Winston.

Sheets, M. (1966). *The phenomenology of dance.* Madison, WI: University of Wisconsin Press.

Sheets-Johnstone, M. (1981). Thinking in movement. *The Journal of Aesthetics and
Art Coriticism, 39,* 399–407.

Siegel, M. (1977). *Watching the dance go by.* Boston: Houghton Mifflin Company.

Sirridge, M., & Armelagos, A. (1977). The in's and out's of dance: Expression
as an aspect of style. *The Journal of Aesthetics and Art Criticism, 36,* 15–24.

Taylor, B. (1983). Dancing Balanchine. *Dance Magazine, 57*(7), 84–89.

Tobias, T. (1979, January 21). She knows Balanchine ballets by heart. *The New
York Times,* section 2, pp. 1, 20.

Tobias, T. (1985). Pennsylvania Ballet's La Sylphide. *Dance Magazine, 59*(4),
46–49.

11

TIMING IN WEST AFRICAN DANCE PERFORMANCE: THE INFLUENCE OF EXTRAMUSICAL FACTORS ON RHYTHM

Robert W. Nicholls

Musical timing in West African dance music is marked by stylistic peculiarities including offbeat timing, cross rhythms, polymeter, asymmetric progressions, and free meter. However, an exclusive focus on musical products in isolation from their cultural setting is unlikely to provide an adequate understanding of West African rhythm, for certain organizational principles and aesthetic judgments are common to the African perception of time at the level of both sociocultural macrorhythms and musical microrhythms. Because expertise in music requires social learning as well as the ability to translate drum texts and interpret dance movements, the influence of such extramusical factors as world view, language, and dance also need to be considered. Participation in music and dance in effect demonstrates the extent of an individual's enculturation. Stylistic peculiarities in West African drum patterns can be attributed to: the specific context they reflect; their function as a psychoacoustic device aimed at certain behavioral outcomes; the reproduction of surrogate speech patterns; aesthetic demand for rhythmic abstraction; spontaneous audible responses to inaudible dance movements; and their reflection of transitory social input within a "live" event.

In studies of art in Africa, dance studies have been somewhat of a poor relation to studies in visual and audial arts, yet dance is coextensive with many visual arts and much music, and, unlike them, lives at once in both time and space. During dance festivals, visual arts and music are understood in relation to ongoing dance activities. Dance has been Africa's superlative art form, fulfilling a greater variety of functions than is associated with dance in Western traditions. Many of these have been documented (Gorer, 1972; Hanna, 1987; Harper, 1976; Kwakwa, 1979; Nicholls, 1985; Nketia, 1963). Africa uses dance in a variety of contexts, and often the moods evoked are unfamiliar to Westerners, because in the West dance is most often used simply for recreation and entertainment. During a wake in Igede, for example, dance expresses grief and pays homage to the deceased. The Azande and the Fon use dance as a means of divination, while dance acts as healer during Ndembu curative rituals.

Monographs on rhythm as an organizing principle in the performing arts are rare. More often rhythm features as a subtheme in a larger work devoted to another topic. This essay examines the extent to which the West African expression of musical time would appear to be influenced by extramusical factors and suggests that a people's world view can be embodied in the movements of dance and translated into musical form. The role of dance in determining rhythm in West African music is discussed in terms that are meaningful to dancers, musicologists, dance ethnologists, and scholars in African art alike. For evidence, the author draws on his own study of the expressive culture of the Igede of Nigeria's Benue state and other studies of music and dance in West Africa. The drumming of Ghana has received more scholarly attention than other areas, principally due to the definitive study of the Akan by Nketia but also through the studies of the Ewe by Locke, and the Ewe and Dagomba by Chernoff. Other examples from equatorial Africa are appropriate since the Igede, like their neighbors the Ibo, possess many cultural traits in common with ethnic groups to their south with whom they share the equatorial forest.

Although dance is common to all societies, West African music and dance is characterized by a rhythmic complexity that is unparalleled elsewhere. Rhythm, not synonymous with drum beating, is an aesthetic organization of phenomena or events (in this case dance gestures/locomotion and musical sounds) structured in time and/or space. For Chernoff, "an African has had a more comprehensive education in rhythm" (1979, p. 53). Through musical form and dance choreography, Africans have developed mechanisms for internalizing complex configurations of musical time. For the Western musicologist, many of the sounded beats in African music seem arbitrary or irregular, and the underlying cycle that the beats manifest, difficult to determine. That much African music contains not only polyrhythms but multiple meters has been recognized by Herskovits, who comments:

> Our relatively simple system of time signatures, with fixed measures, is less than satisfactory when, for example, a piece on the xylophone must be set down that has a 4/4 beat in the left hand and a 5/4 in the right, making a "measure" that is more than we are trained to carry as a unit. (1947, p. 437)

The complexity of timing in African music often seemingly defies notation by conventional methods. There is accordingly a dearth of adequate transcriptions of African music.

The degree to which rhythmic timing in African music is influenced by extramusical factors is debatable, and conflicting arguments appear in the literature. Approaching this question from a strictly musicological perspective, Koetting writes:

> I believe that the key to understanding the African perception of musical time is not linked to non-musical thought patterns, social structures, world view, or anything outside music. In trying to account for African timing in music, we will not be helped by delving more deeply into the *why* of music making—that myriad of phenomena that surrounds and informs a performance of music. (1986, p. 61)

Without mentioning dance, Koetting lists language, calendrical cycles, social structures, and world view as extraneous factors that "ultimately cannot account for timing in music" (p. 62). For Koetting, an understanding of rhythm can best be obtained by a single-minded analysis of musical products. He does, however, advise caution on subjective approaches to analysis and argues that we too often spend time "spinning out theories about what *we* hear and what *we* see in our transcriptions, and we spend too little time digging beneath the surface to discover what the African carriers of the tradition conceptualize and hear" (p. 58).

Stone, in her analysis of Koetting's article, reinforces the notion that the discussion about African rhythm pivots around the distinction between text and context or "musical" and "extramusical." She suggests that Koetting's discomfort "may stem from the tendency of anthropologically oriented scholars to consider elements of context that are of a far broader scale and scope than the musicologically oriented" (1986, p. 54). Stone poses the question that is at the heart of this debate: "What do we need to study in order to grasp music and its rhythm? Is it enough to do a close reading of an extended transcription" (p. 56).

My essay proposes that an exclusive focus on musical sound in isolation, not only from dance but also from pertinent sociocultural factors such as language and world view, may not only prevent an adequate understanding of the African perception of musical time but also hinder the development of a framework of analysis. Bebey outlines the limitations of a narrow approach when he says: "The real disappointment of a foreigner arises when he tries vainly to grasp a melody, chord, or movement, without seeing the music in its entirety" (1975, p. 134). Nketia suggests that extramusical factors can be legitimate determinants of musical form in Africa:

> Although the formal organization of vocal and instrumental sound is guided principally by musical considerations, details of structure are influenced by extrinsic factors as well. Form may be influenced not only by the roles assumes by various members of a performing group or by the context of a performance, but also by the nature of the movements and expression with which music is integrated. (1974, p. 177)

Similarly Kauffman, in his study of African rhythm, writes: "The nature of physical movements that accompany music (dance and instrumental technique), language rhythm, and the social structures of a society are probably very time determining" (1980, pp. 400–401). Kauffman talks of an "African sense of time," and he states: "an all encompassing view of rhythm includes the possibility of looking at the influence of a culture's time sense upon all aspects of its musical time" (p. 400). He uses the term *macrorhythm* to describe "a culture's time sense and its formal structure," with *microrhythm* being "the perceptual present (what one can feel in a moment) such as meter, rhythmic configurations, and the relationship of parts" (p. 401).

Within my essay the term *sociocultural macrorhythm* describes the way time is organized at the communal level, especially as it relates to the timing of ritual festivals. *World view* is, by its nature, a broad term, which approximates the corpus of knowledge and beliefs that inform social behavior. This includes factual information, productive skills, metaphysical beliefs, attitudes, and organizing principles, and is reflected in a people's perception of themselves and their history, the social structure, economic behavior, and cultural expressions. Language and dance are expressions of the world view and thus receive dual treatment within these pages. In addition to examining language and dance separately as direct determinants of musical rhythm, it will also examine the extent to which each of them embodies the world view and becomes a medium by which it is translated into timing in music. Language, like music and dance, is a form of communication, and the existence of speech surrogates performed on "talking" instruments in many West African communities blurs the distinction between speech and music. Talking drums have often been used to choreograph and coordinate the movements of dancers.

Dance can hardly be considered an extramusical factor since, in Africa, it shares a "structural interdependence" with music (Nketia, 1974, p. 215). For Chernoff, "African music with few exceptions, is to be regarded as music for the dance, although the 'dance' involved may be entirely a mental one" (1979, p. 49). It is generally true in West Africa that each dance has not only distinctive gestures and locomotion but also a characteristic rhythm and that "the name of a dance is also the name of a rhythm" (p. 120). Among the Igede most music and dance activity is structured within a framework of music and dance associations. Although the Igede word *eje* refers to a song text, Ramung says:

> There is in Igede no general term for "music" as separate from dance. The Igede language has a word for dancing, *ewoh*, but the term *ayilo* denotes a complex of song, instrumental music and choreographic movements. Each music and dance association is formed around such an *ayilo* complex and the combination of elements from these three fields of expression (song, instrumental music and dance) will distinguish one type of music from another. (1973)

Hanna, in her discussion of the Ibo term *nkwa*, which similarly includes "dance, song, and drum accompaniment," states, "an analogous situation in Western societies would exist if the concept 'opera' could not be broken down into its song, accompaniment, and dance components" (1965, p. 48).

Chernoff maintains that in Ghana, "one who 'hears' the music 'understands' it with a dance" (1979, p. 143), whereas Keil suggests that for the Tiv (neighbors to the Igede), dance makes songs "jucier" (1979). The Igede's view might describe dance as the "icing on the cake," for the music for a solo dance (*ewoh-okpokpo*), even including the recurring vocal refrain, is, in effect, a "rhythm section" and the ensemble music is enhanced not by a lead intrument or vocalist, but by a *dancer*. This support is Thompson's view that "multiple meter essentially uses dancers as further voices in a polymetric choir" (1966, p. 98). The paradox of the symbiotic relationship of dance and music in Igede was brought home to me when I asked one informant whether he considered a drum passage that I had recorded was a good one. He replied that he was not able to say, as he could not see the dancer! It might seem equally pointless to attempt to appraise a dance performance without hearing the music (on silent film for example). Through the medium of dance the dimension of sound that exists in time erupts into three-dimensional space. As Chernoff states, "dancing gives the rhythms a visible and physical form" (1979, p. 143).

WORLD VIEW: AN AFRICAN SENSE OF TIME

In order to explore the connection between timing in music and the larger rhythms of West African life, traditional perceptions are examined in the light of certain questions. What organizing principles can be identified that are common to both the macrorhythms of sociocultural life and the microrhythms of musical timing? By what means does the world view with its cultural time sense exert influence on the microrhythms of music? In examining rhythm in African music, some writers (e.g., Agawu, 1986) have found it useful to differentiate between two dimensions—horizontal and vertical, or in Nketia's (1974) terms, "linear" and "multilinear." The horizontal or linear dimension relates to the forward momentum of rhythm as it moves through time, while the vertical dimension encompasses the multilinear stratification of an integrated rhythmic structure.

Horizontal Dimension

It is sometimes suggested that the traditional African concept of time is qualitatively different from the linear model held by the Western world. In the latter, according to Chernoff, "we tend to think of 'time' as a single objective phenomenon, moving quite steadily (as our philosophical heritage tells us) toward some distant moment" (1979, p. 85). It has been suggested that the African has a cyclical rather than a linear concept of time. For example, Locke argues that dance drumming among the Eʋe (Ewe) of Ghana "has a circular or spiral, not linear, rhythmic character" (1982, p. 218). Bebey discusses the relationship between musical form and sociocultural processes and suggests that music mirrors human cycles:

> African music has a cyclical quality, for it symbolizes the actual lifecycle of Man. And because it is cyclical, one must never forget that it is made up of "micro-cycles" of particles of sound which are released into the air in the extremely short musical phrase. (1974, p. 117)

Rhythm is a means of perceiving elapsing time. Often conceived as fleeting, time is an illusive entity. The perceptual present—the omnipresent moment of "now"—ushers each individual through the phases of physical existence. In the literature the time sense of lineage-based segmentary societies is sometimes represented as circular, with "now" in the center, and past and present radiating from this point. In Igede, this is supported by the association of the ancestors with the dawn, which represents both the beginning and constant renewal, and by a belief in reincarnation that depicts life as a continuous cycle routinely interrupted by death. Certain rites are performed before burial in order to insure successful rebirth. Major tribes in Nigeria such as the Yoruba and Ibo share this belief in reincarnation, and so do some areas of the Muslim northern regions. In the village of Zango in Nigeria's Kaduna state, I was introduced to a 7- or 8-year-old boy with the Hausa name of Baba Sabo, which is translated as "New Father." He was thought to be the reincarnation of a great grandfather. Le Moel (1981) suggests that adults among the Bobo accord importance to children's imitation of adult ritual because of their cyclical sense of time: in a sense these children are the parents' own ancestors.

In addition to ancestral cycles and the cycles of reincarnation, other cycles inform the traditional sense of time. Some of these are astronomical. For the Ngas of Nigeria's Jos Plateau, the moon is believed to regulate the rhythm of all life. At the turn of the year an astronomer-priest symbolically shoots the moon with a spear and engenders the new year. Ritual ceremonies also correspond to agricultural processes such as sowing, harvesting, or the arrival of the rains. Other ceremonies relate to the human life cycle and the passage of an individual from one stage of existence to another—naming ceremonies at birth, initiations, marriages, title-installations, and funerals. In addition to these predictable celebrations that recur with regularity, further ceremonies, such as curative and preventative rites, exorcisms, and divination rituals, may be called for at irregular intervals. The same is true of celerations of occupational successes, in hunting or fishing, bush clearing, house building, and, in the past, battle victories. The commemoration of these events reinforce the continuity of traditional cycles and inform the community's sense of time.

The circle as an organizing principle is readily apparent in African dance. Among most African groups, the dance ring is a consistent feature of communal ceremonies, and circle dances possibly depict the cyclical perception of time. By joining the dance ring, the individual participants partake of the life force invested in the community by the ancestors. Hanna points out that circle dances in Africa often rotate in a counterclockwise direction, "because clockwise movement is believed to be the path of the dead" (1987, p. 94). She states: "In the sphere of specific movement, the circle appears as a metaphor for safety, solidarity, stability, and the never ending cyclical characteristics of agricultural societies and the process of reincarnation" (p. 94). Among the Igede, the circle dance (*ewoh ologba*—literally, "line dance") is a prominent feature of funerals and other ceremonies. Before a member of the Ogirinye warrior society is buried, the members, dance seven times around the corpse, symbolically creating a bond between the living and the dead. The assertion that Africans have a cyclical sense of time is not to suggest that they do not also have a linear sense of time. They know that today is followed by tomorrow and that the dry season is followed by the rains. In stressing cyclical principles in the organization of time, the difference is one of emphasis.

The cyclical character of West African music at the microrhythmic level is readily apparent, both in the repeated call-and-response of the vocal (and instrumental) refrains and in repetitive drum patterns. The definition of a cycle as a "regularly recurring succession of events or phenomena" can also describe rhythm. In the horizontal dimension, rhythm consists of an organization of periodic events (e.g., drum beats) in a repeated pattern. A state of balance exists, but not rest—motion is intrinsic to the concept of rhythm. While the parts exhibit the contrast arising from the novelty of their detail, the whole never loses the unity of the controlling pattern. An unvarying repetition destroys rhythm as surely as does a conglomeration of differences. A metronome provides a pulse but not a rhythm. However, the linear structure of most African music is marked by a regularly recurring pulse. Described by musicologists as a "density referent," the pulse provides a metric reference against which other ensemble instruments can organize their varied contributions. The pulse might be provided by metrically symmetrical drumbeats, handclaps, or other percussive sounds. Gongs provide pulse accompaniment in many Igede arrangements. Sometimes a pulse is not sounded but is simply felt.

The pulse is overlayed by more complex rhythms that may shift and change within the linear progression of a music piece. In complex rhythmic configurations, such as "hemiola," the pulse might be reduced to the smallest common denominator, referred to musically as the "fastest pulse." In discussing the rhythmic overlays, such as drums play over the pulse, Nketia differentiates between regular, symmetrical "divisive" rhythms, and irregular "additive" rhythms:

> Divisive rhythms are those that articulate the regular divisions of the time span, rhythms that follow the scheme of pulse structure in the groupings of notes. They may follow the duple, triple, or hemiola schemes. (1974, p. 128)

In contrast, "additive" rhythms may be asymmetrical:

> While divisive rhythms follow the internal divisions of the time span, additive rhythms do not. The durational values of some notes may extend beyond the regular divisions within the time span. (p. 129)

Thus a distinction can be made between "strict time" and "free meter." Strict time has metrical symmetry, whereas free meter lacks rhythmic regularity.

Vertical Dimension

In contrast to the Western world's perception of time as one-dimensional, an African time sense emphasizes that more than one thing is happening at any given time and each event is governed by its own time continuum. This pluralism is apparent in the world view and in the music. The Igede are traditionally monotheistic in the sense that they conceive of a supreme creator God (*Ohe Oluhye*), but polytheistic to the extent that in the intangible world of the spirit, various canalizations of spiritual power, such as the spirit of the earth (*Ohe-Eji*), ancestors (*alegwu*), guardian dieties (*akpang*), and other forces, intercede in a human's relationship with the divine. In common with other African groups, the Igede also traditionally believe that an individual has multiple souls. This resolves the paradox wherein, at death, the individual both joins the ancestors and is *also* reincarnated. In addition to the subjective self, there is a reincarnated ancestor and a destiny soul. The Akan symbolize the three souls that constitute an individual by the colors red, white, and black (Bartle, 1980, p. 8). Dieterlen found that in Mali the Dogon understand the human personality to be made up of many parts that not only come from various exterior sources but also remain in some sort of relation to those sources (1973). According to the Gourma of Burkina Faso, a human being comprises six separate existences, with different purposes and possibilities that operate according to its own time continuum (Swanson, 1980, p. 71). Such pluralistic concepts may give rise to the idea of cycles within cycles that defines rhythm in the vertical dimension.

The perception of multiple selves interacting with a crowded stage of dieties, and other pluralistic notions, possibly contributes to the multilinear organization of West African music, polychronic choral forms, and polyrhythms, which are essentially multipart or group products. Turnbull (1983) maintains that because the mass of sound emerges as more than the sum of individual parts, the polyphonic choral technique of the Mbuti of Zaire reflects the intensive cooperative patterns of their mode of production. Chernoff observes:

> African affinity for polymetric musical forms indicate that, in the most fundamental sense, the African sensibility is profoundly pluralistic. . . . There is a clear parallel, certainly, between the aesthetic conception of multiple rhythms in music and the religious conception of multiple forces in the world. (1979, pp. 155–156)

Kauffman contrasts the Western emphasis on the development of themes with the African emphasis on accumulating new material in relationship to the initial patterns: "The mono-chronometry of Western music is apparent in the concept of a conductor's beat to which all rhythms may be oriented" (1980, p. 402). In West African music multichronometry is manifested in the stratification of rhythmic layers, wherein interlocking percussive patterns reinforce the pulse. Each component rhythmic pattern has a determinate duration and recurs periodically according to the metric rules of its particular cycle. The power of the music emanates from the dynamic way the component microrhythms highlight and compliment each other. The depth of the strata in a multipart rhythm is often related to the number of percussion instruments involved. Kauffman (1980, p. 411) provides an example of a rhythmic mosaic produced in the Ewe dance, *Sohu*, that has 11 percussion instruments and as many rhythmic lines. Sowande (1966) has found 24 different hierarchically arranged rhythm parts in a Yoruba ensemble.

Due to the African polychronic time sense, music can exploit the potential for both cross rhythms and multimeter. A cross rhythm occurs where rhythms based on different schemes of pulse structure are juxtaposed. An archetypal cross rhythm that is widely cited is created by crossing "two against three" (Olum Oludhe, personal communication, 1972). One performer (or one hand) plays two regular beats against another's three.

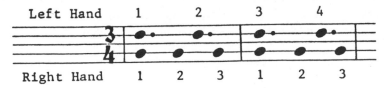

Nketia describes this simple but effective cross rhythm as the "vertical interplay of duple and triple rhythms (as opposed to hemiola, where the interplay is linear)" (1974, p. 135). Although a single rhythm emerges as a gestalt of the vertical interplay of the two rhythms, within their separate schemes the duple and triple pulses are moving through time at different speeds. According to Koetting (1986, p. 59), the single line may be described as a predominant two with a three syncopated against it, or as a predominant three with a two syncopated against it. A cross rhythm is differentiated from polymeter in that, depending on the metric stance of the listener, a cross rhythm is heard as a single meter. This is not the case with polymeter, which involves the simultaneous use of two or more meters. Relative to his transcription of Agbadza, an Ewe social dance, Wilson states:

> A composite polymetric rhythm is set up because the basic accents of the fixed rhythmic group and the variable rhythmic group are not coincident except at the terminal point of the bell pattern, which is precisely what makes the end of the pattern a perceptible focal point. The polymeter is thus the result of the simultaneous occurrence of several rhythmic strata, each with an independent meter. (1974, p. 12)

Although poly or multimeter usually describes drum passages, this stylistic device can also be observed in the independent pace of songs and drum rhythms. For example, in discussing the music of Akan religious associations, Nketia says that "recitatives bearing no relation to the drum pieces may be sung by the chorus as the drummers outline particular dance rhythms for the priests" (1963, p. 99).

The sense of pluralism is manifested during ritual festivals by the dynamic interaction of multiple elements within circumscribed time and space. "Musical performances are generally multidimensional in character, for it is customary to integrate music with other arts, with dance and drama, as well as with various forms of visual display, such as masks" (Nketia, 1974, p. 244). Each of the elements, explicit and implicit, interact and reinforce each other.

From Macrorhythm to Microrhythm

The timing for traditional ritual festivals among West African ethnic groups is determined by the world view and coincide with calendrical and life-cycle events and other activities. The organization of time at the macrorhythmic level is analogous to a musical progression. "Events" within musical rhythm equate to drum beats or other percussive sounds, while "events" at the macrorhythmic level equate to ritual festivals or other communal occasions celebrated with music and dance. At the macrorhythmic level the regularly recurring events that mark calendrical cycles might be likened to the *pulse* of sociocultural life. Group initiations and individual title installations, births, deaths, and marriages and other events that occur with relative frequency but at unspecified intervals might be equated to the more intricate *divisive rhythms* that overlay the pulse of sociocultural life. Those sporadically occurring ceremonies associated with healing or divination and occupational successes may be compared to the *additive rhythms* that overlay the other rhythms without necessarily complying with the metric divisions.

Not only do sociocultural macrorhythms determine the timing *of* ritual festivals, they also determine timing *in* ritual festivals, that is, the rhythm of a festival and the sequence of component events are determined by its larger sociocultural purposes. Thus, an individual festival is a microrhythm to the sociocultural macrorhythm of cultural life, and is in turn a macrorhythm to its component events. As such, a festival and its unfolding is governed by the rules of its own timespan. Religious ceremonies often take the form of plays that go on for several days. Although an Akan puberty festival may last five or seven days, the musical activities rarely go beyond the first couple of days (Nketia, 1963, p. 56).

At the level of the music there is some justification for noting the relationship between the formal structure of the music and the smaller temporal units:

> In its larger dimensions time is divided into segments that display pat-
> terning much in the same way as is found at the microrhythmic level.
> These longer patterns determine the formal structure of music at the
> macrorhythmic level. (Kauffman, 1980, p. 403)

The aggregate of component sequences, then, comprise the macrorhythms of music and dance. Individual dances often form part of a
series within a larger dance suite. The *akom* is a suite of dances performed by an Akan priest that "follow a particular order and each of
the dances has a particular meaning" (Kwakwa, 1979, p. 14). In Igede,
Oge is a set of girls' dances that accompany songs that relate a story.
Individual dance compositions often have opening and closing formats
and a series of dance sequences to be accomplished. A dancer may be
prepared emotionally at the beginning of a performance by preparatory
songs. The Adzogbo dances of the Ewe are introduced by a chanted text
that is reproduced by a talking drum before the commencement of a
dance in which the dancers' movements are synchronized with the drum
texts. In Igede, musical finales are often synchronized with dramatic
terminal gestures of the dance.

In a discussion of vocal refrains, Kauffman further points out that
"the formal structure of call and response can have some relationship
to the more minute rhythmic relationship of parts" (1980, p. 400). As
with other ethnic groups, most Igede dance music utilizes a call-and-
response vocal format. During circle dances the participants dance
slowly around repeating a chorus initiated by the ensemble singers. The
textual meaning of a refrain is often secondary to its function as a rhythmic superstructure and although repeated continuously they are seldom
developed further. The repeated ostinato provides the larger/slower
cycles in which the smaller/faster cycles of the percussive patterns are
embraced. This supports Chernoff's observation that "in effect, African
music is *both slow and fast*" (1979, p. 112). The dancers that enter the
arena are more likely to coordinate their movements with the rapidly
delivered percussive patterns than with the slower cycles of the ostinato.
By contrast, the dancers in the circle will coordinate their movements
with the refrain they are singing.

DANCE: CONTEXT AND FORM

That the arts are the medium by which the world view is made
salient to African communities is confirmed by Davidson: "In a deep

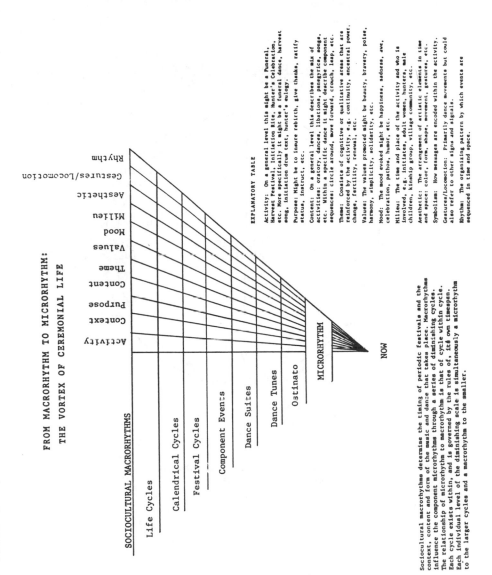

FROM MACRORHYTHM TO MICRORHYTHM:
THE VORTEX OF CEREMONIAL LIFE

SOCIOCULTURAL MACRORHYTHMS

Life Cycles

Calendrical Cycles

Festival Cycles

Component Events

Dance Suites

Dance Tunes

Ostinato

MICRORHYTHM

NOW

Activity
Context
Purpose
Content
Theme
Values
Mood
Milieu
Aesthetic
Gestures/Locomotion
Rhythm

EXPLANATORY TABLE

Activity: On a general level this might be a Funeral, Harvest Festival, Initiation Rite, Hunter's Celebration, etc. More specifically it might be a funeral dance, harvest song, initiation drum text, hunter's eulogy.

Purpose: Might be to insure rebirth, give thanks, ratify status, instruct, etc.

Content: On a general level this describes the mix of activities: oratory, dances, libations, panegyrics, songs, etc. Within a specific dance it might describe component sequences: circle around, move forward, crouch, leap, etc.

Theme: Consists of cognitive or qualitative areas that are reinforced by the activity, e.g. continuity, ancestral power, change, fertility, renewal, etc.

Values: The values promoted might be beauty, bravery, poise, harmony, simplicity, solidarity, etc.

Mood: The mood evoked might be happiness, sadness, awe, celebration, pathos, humor, etc.

Milieu: The time and place of the activity and who is involved, e.g. initiates, adult women, hunters, male children, kinship group, village community, etc.

Aesthetic: The arrangement of artistic elements in time and space: color, form, shape, movement, gestures, etc.

Symbolism: How messages are encoded within the activity.

Gestures/Locomotion: Primarily dance movements but could also refer to other signs and signals.

Rhythm: The organizing pattern by which events are sequenced in time and space.

Sociocultural macrorhythms determine the timing of periodic festivals and the context, content and form of the music and dance that takes place. Macrorhythms influence the component microrhythms through a series of diminishing cycles. The relationship of microrhythm to macrorhythm is that of cycle within cycle. Each cycle exists within, and is governed by the rules of, its own timespan. Each individual level of the diminishing scale is simultaneously a microrhythm to the larger cycles and a macrorhythm to the smaller.

Figure 1.

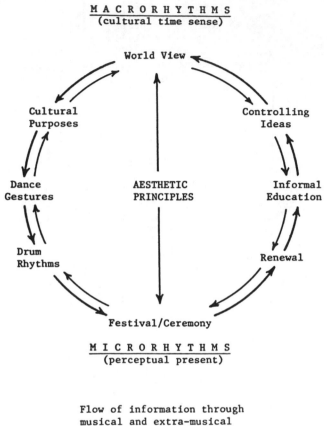

Flow of information through
musical and extra-musical
domains

Figure 2

sense the arts of non-literate Africa composed its holy books and testaments" (1969, p. 163). Riesman notes a change in the way African art and rituals are studied:

> The more recent studies have approached these aspects of culture as if they were a mode of communication. Rituals, then, are not recorded to be a collection of artifacts that can be exhibited in a museum, but are viewed as way a group of people have of sending a message. (1986, p. 82)

It is frequently argued that there is no "art for art's sake" in Africa. Although this is an overgeneralization, it emphasizes the extreme functionality of African art. According to Hanna, "In traditional Black African cultures . . . dance is less an 'art' than a 'craft' " (1965, p.49). Kwakwa feels that an understanding of this functional orientation is essential in distinguishing the fundamental difference between African dance and Western dance (1979, p. 25). In any functional art, including African music and dance, the form of the art product is subordinated to its adaption to a particular purpose, and cannot be properly understood without reference to this purpose. As a functional craft, the movements and gestures of a dance expresses sociocultural realities. For example, in many African communities, members of professional organizations—hunters', farmers', and fisherman's guilds—perform specific dances that express local modes of production. In northern Nigeria such dances often include mimetic reenactments or occupational gestures:

> The implicit use of occupational gestures may be clearly seen in the repetitive gathering-scattering arm gestures and patting movements of the hands in the Icough dance of the Tiv women . . . in Yelwa town, where many of the dances of the Hausa and Nupe women are based on mimetic re-enactments of the working movements of the men of their community. The Makera dance illustrates the hammering of the blacksmiths, the Nama Hausa mimes the action of the meat sellers, and the Rawan Gwandon Kifi illustrates the work of the fishermen in casting nets and using spears and fish traps. (Harper, 1976, pp. 157–158).

An Igede funeral ceremony contains fundamental values relating to kinship, ancestors, tradition, and the Igede perception of life and death. In common with other West African oral traditions, Igede ideology is not simply theoretical or contemplative, but lives within the activities by which it is expressed. Through music and dance, the *medium* in effect becomes the *message*. Through the music and dance performed, and other activities within a ritual festival, the general rule is applied to the specific instance. The sequence and character of the events that constitute the festival are determined by purposes relative to the larger world view. In other words, the *why* of a festival—in terms of its sociocultural context—determines the *what*—in terms of the form of the activities that take place. African dance, as an avenue of expression closely related to the themes and purposes of a particular occasion, is, in effect, *context determined*.

That a society's world view determines both the timing for a ritual festival and also its intrinsic character is exemplified by a fertility ceremony from southeast Ivory Coast that commemorates the seasonal arrival of the rains. Within a dance circle comprising the whole village, various dances that express the themes of the occasion are performed by dance groups of different ages and sexes. These include a performance by four little girls who "danced almost squatting on the ground, holding their tiny aprons in one hand, and scattering imaginary seeds with the other," and a "pantomime of the copulation of various beasts and birds" by "strangely dressed old men" (Gorer, 1972, p. 38). In this ceremony every action is not only relevant to larger agricultural cycles, but, in that the ceremony ceases with the first drops of rain, it is specific to about two hours in the year.

Life-cycle ceremonies may similarly involve forms of music and dance that are specific to a particular event. The distinctive music of the Ogirinye warrior ensemble of Igede is only heard publicly at the funeral of an Ogirinye association member, at which time Ogirinye members take turns to honor the deceased by performing solo dances. The arrival of the Ogirinye masquerade is pure theater. He does not dance but simply runs at full speed through the meeting ground to the burial place. His speed represents that of a great warrior, who is so fast that he can hardly be seen, and by extension, so too death, which also appears unexpectedly among the living (Nicholls, 1984, p. 73). These behaviors are specific to a cycle that is measured by the frequency of death among Ogirinye members.

Music and dance also serve to convey the mood of an occasion. Zhem is a dance of the Dagomba that projects the institution of chieftaincy. It is played when a new Ya-Naa (paramount chief) is installed and also when a chief dies. Chernoff describes Zhem as portraying "both death and happiness" (1979, p. 83). In his discussion of Akan funerals, Nketia states that "the drums that are played in other contexts with mirth and jollity must in the context of the funeral be played in the excited mood of bereavement" (1963, p. 64). The distinction between serious and light-hearted rhythms has been explored by Locke:

> Most southern Eʋe (Ewe) dance drumming uses 6/8 or 12/8 meter. Eʋe musicians usually consider music of this type to be serious and poignant and, in contrast, music with a binary division of the main beats to be gay and lighthearted. An explanation for this may be that within Eʋe tradition rhythmic structures of much *greater complexity* are found in ternary music. (1982, p. 224; my emphasis)

Because West African dances are integrated into specific social situations, the same dances are performed on each appropriate occasion. Therefore, in addition to being context determined, they can also be described as *event specific*. As an educational device, dance often communicates socially valuable information during initiation ceremonies. The form of dances performed at Dangme puberty festivals are determined by the purpose of the ceremony, whereby, through dance, adult women convey to the girl some of the functions of womanhood:

> Dangme girls of Ghana . . . are taught the Otofo dance which is said to symbolize the utmost in femininity—the simple and delicate foot patterns; the gentle thread of the feet on the ground; the deliberately controlled swing of the arms along curved paths; the slight tilt of the neck to the side and the slightly downward cast of the eyes—are said to teach the girls how a woman should walk and behave. (Kwakwa, 1979, p. 4)

According to Johnston, during girls' initiation rites among the Tsonga of southern Mozambique, the "novices perform a series of mimes, such as imitating the crocodile . . . (whereby) . . . initiates file past the drummer officiant while imitating the crocodile and singing the crocodile song." Johnston points out that "both the songs and the drumming are *mime-specific*" (1974, p. 61; my emphasis).

In some cases the purpose of the dance is directed to goals external to the performance. In Igede, as elsewhere in West Africa, warrior groups would dance during warrior initiations, battle victories, and prior to battle, and skilled dancers would wear the mask and costume of the *okomu* (masquerade). Nketia states that Akan warriors ensembles require "high spirited music and a lot of messages of incitement, encouragement and direction" (1963, p. 110). He describes the drumming as "stirring." The stirring effect is achieved by "peculiarities of style such as the *unpronounced or seeming lack of metrical symmetry* in some of the drum combinations, and the *independent pace of drums and songs*" (p. 110, my emphasis). Many Akan refer to the drums of warrior associations as bad drums, "because of their peculiar emotional quality . . . their incitement to destructive as well as constructive action" (p. 110).

In his discussion of Tsonga girls' initiation rites, Johnston suggests that the trance state and visions that characterize the rites is induced by "fast rhythmic drumming at basic brain wave frequencies" (1974, p. 60) and "energetic dancing which causes a flow of adrenaline and a drop in blood sugar content" (p. 61). He states: "It is interesting that the speed of the drumming appears to be that best suited for tapping and slightly altering human basic brain wave frequencies which are in the order of 8-to-15 cycles per second" (p. 61). Further to this, Johnston suggests that the polyrhythmic structure of Tsonga drumming, with several drum patterns performed at the same time, "may represent an intuitive attempt to tap the wide range of brain wave frequencies possessed by different individuals within a group (individuals are not alike in this respect), thus ensnaring the entire assembly in one psychophysiological net" (p. 62).

In addition to warrior dances, other examples of the use of stylistic peculiarities in dance rhythms to induce social outcomes beyond the context of the dance performance exist. Dance is a regular feature in curative rituals such as Afruja in Igede. Such rituals, termed "drums of affliction" among the Ndembu of Zambia, are described by Turner (1968). The origins of the Adzogbo dance of the Ewe was as a divination dance through which "the war leaders could foretell the course of an upcoming battle by interpreting the possessed boys' movements" (Locke & Agbeli, 1981, p. 26). The Azande of southern Sudan use divination dances in an attempt to discover why hunters repeatedly fail.

LANGUAGE AND MUSIC: SPEECH SURROGATES

The influence of language on musical form in Africa is far reaching. Such traditional use of language as poems, epics, incantations, proverbs, and wise sayings are often musically constructed. Euba argues that "literature is almost inseparable from music in the Nigerian tradition" (1976, p. 20), and Kauffman says, "Speech is probably one of the major determinants of all African music making" (1980, p. 402). In Africa, songs are treated as though they were speech utterances, and the tones and rhythms of spoken language are respected. Distortions of words to fit a tune that is commonplace in Western musical styles is unusual in the tone-language areas of West Africa. In Igede, this is readily apparent in the songs of Imwo and Ogbete women's associations, which orchestrate gossip and express social criticism and whose renditions are often spontaneous (Nicholls, 1985, p. 113). According to Nketia the influence of speech on music is twofold, influencing both the melody line and the rhythmic structure: "As many African languages are tone languages, there is a tendency to follow both the intonation contour of speech in melodies, and the rhythms of speech in song rhythms" (Nketia, 1974, p. 244). Nketia argues that in music, lexical units may be organized as freely as they are in speech and "need not be organized on the basis of a uniform metrical scheme" (p. 182). Where rhythmic patterns are determined by speech rhythm, regular metric divisions may be ignored and a "lack of a uniform meter will be noticed at the boundaries of the regular divisions of the time span. . . . In other words, what appears in songs as additive rhythm may in fact be a speech rhythm" (p. 182). Language rhythms, then, are musically determinative, and further to this, stylistic peculiarities in rhythm such as metric irregularities are often the result of speech influences in music.

Speech Mode of Drumming

In addition to the direct influence of speech patterns on music the intrinsic connection between language and music in Africa is further compounded by the existence of speech-reproducing instruments that can converse with dancers and direct the choreography. Many African languages are essentially bitonal—each syllable of a word has either a high tone or a low tone and serves to distinguish meaning in much the same way as do vowels and consonants. As a result, the possibility of representing speech on two-toned instruments arises. Africans have produced the most highly developed speech surrogates known anywhere in the world.

The slit drum that is used by the Igede and the Ibo is an all-wooden drum made from a hollowed log that produces two tones when beaten with sticks. The Akan traditionally use a pair of large membrane drums—each with its own tone—for functions of signaling. Not all drums are limited to two tones. Locke and Agbeli relate that the language of the Eʋe (Ewe) has three tones and these "must be rendered on the single membrane of the leading drum" (1981, p. 25). The hourglass tension drum used by the Yoruba, Hausa, Wolof, and Dagomba is multitoned. By subtle variations of pressure this drum can directly mimic speech with all its nuances, including slurred notes and onomatopoeias. Although drums are the best known talking instruments, they are part of a broad spectrum of instruments that can reproduce speech, as Locke and Agbeli confirm: "Chordophones, aerophones, membranophones, and idiophones are all used in this manner" (1981, p. 25). The Igede have three types of two-toned signal horns derived from use in battle. Made from buffalo or antelope horn, they signaled commands and sounded retreats and reassemblies much in the manner of the military bugle.

The use of surrogate speech probably originated in the need for message relay in warfare and other emergency situations. Many communities installed a large drum in the village square to warn of invasions or report bush fires and missing persons. They came to be used to announce life-cycle events—births, initiations, marriages and deaths. The Igede slit drum, for example, plays a major role during funerals. When a notable individual dies, the drummer will beat out the news using the drum names of his compatriots to call them to the compound. Other groups such as the Lokele of Zaire used the slit drum to announce recreational events—wrestling matches, fishing trips, hunting expeditions, and communal dances. Nketia differentiates between four uses of texts in the speech mode of drumming among the Akan: (a) "texts of greetings, warnings, congratulations, various emergency calls, and announcements" (1963, p. 46); (b) "texts of invocations to spirits, the spirit of the wood of the drum, the components of the drum, certain creatures, dieties and ancestor drummers" (p. 43); (c) "texts of proverbs which are usually incorporated into other texts" (p. 47); and (d) "texts . . . in the nature of panegyrics or eulogies" (p. 44).

Dance Mode of Drumming

In addition to its function of disseminating linguistic information, the drum is also used in the more familiar context of providing rhythmic music for dancing. Nketia differentiates between "drumming as a form of linguistic communication, and drumming for music" (p. 111). Within these two major forms, he further distinguishes three separate modes of drumming: the speech mode, the signal mode, and the dance mode. For Nketia, the speech mode is characterized by "a steady flow of beats, often lacking regularity of phrasing, but distributed with a two-tone framework" (p. 25). The dance mode tends to have a strict rhythm and increased tonal variation. The signal mode "includes all forms of drumming which may be interpreted as 'signals' " (p. 17). In this mode the drummer uses the speech propensity of the drums but contains the texts within short repetitive phrases. In his discussion of Nketia's classification, Agawu points out that "each mode of drumming has a verbal-rhythmic basis which becomes less explicit as we go down the hierarchy from speech through signal to dance, the whole describing a continuum from 'free' to 'strict' rhythm" (1986, p. 78). Thus free meter and rhythmic irregularity within West African music often correlates with surrogate speech performed on a talking instrument. In some dance music, such as the Adzogbo of the Ewe, the modes of drumming are combined: "Unlike many African drums which 'talk' in free rhythm, the leading drum in Adzogbo 'speaks' while playing complex patterns in strict rhythm that accompany the dance; in this respect we might accurately term it a 'singing' drum" (Locke & Agbeli, 1981, p. 26).

In his consideration of the verbal basis of drumming, Nketia distinguishes between speech texts and burden texts. Burden texts are verbal guides that mirror the score of the music, "the verbal 'correlates' in terms of which the drum sounds may be reproduced or interpreted"

(1963, p. 32). As such, burden texts constitute a form of oral notation that helped preserve unwritten scores of drum pieces from generation to generation. Relative to drums performing in the dance mode, Agawu points out that due to "the need to provide a steady metrical framework for the dance . . . the speech of (supporting drums) is necessarily stylized and repetitive, and therefore of limited associative meaning" (1986, p. 78). This situation, however, in no way limits the rendition of the master drummer:

> So long as there is a musical ground, the master drummer can break away from the fragmentary texts of a dance piece. He is at liberty to make incursions into the repertory of the speech mode of drumming and change his style from the strict form of the dance to that of the speech mode of drumming in order to give directions to drummers, greet or praise dancers, convey a message of sympathy, or quote a suitable proverb. . . . (Nketia, 1963, p. 49)

Burden texts, like dance gestures and locomotion, are closely related to the themes and purposes of a specific social occasion and are often only heard within this context:

> In general, serious burden texts have reference to the social function of signal and dance drumming, the participants, or the occasion of use. The burden text of the *adowa* dance (old style) includes a reference to death and burial, for the *adowa* is played mostly at funerals: Termites will feed on you (*Nkanda bedi wo nam*) says the master drum. . . . The tribunal drums of the Akan court enjoin councillors and all to "ponder over something" (*susu biribi*). . . . The dance drums of the court refer to the chief that lays other chiefs low (*ohene kyere ahene*). (p. 42)

In addition to burden texts that consist of recognizable words, a specialized form of speech known as "vocables" exists that is constructed of nonsense syllables. Vocables are a means of communicating drum rhythms by verbal means: "Each type of beat can be mimicked by an onomatopoeic syllable which has no meaning except in reference to drumming" (Chernoff, 1979, p. 78). Nonsense syllables are a means of teaching drum rhythms for dancing. Chernoff reports that "Freeman Donkor used nonsense syllables extensively when he was teaching me to play Atsimewu. I would learn to say the rhythm before I learned to beat it" (p. 78). The vocables for the "half-turning" dance sequence of the Agbekor dance are "*Tonten, gazegi, tenten, gadega gedegi, gagedegi, kre, kre, kre, gagedegi gedega.*" The drum language, which has an identical syllabic structure, runs "*Tso tso avawovi, mitso ne mia bla alidzi, kple dzidodo; tso, tso, tso, avagbedzi nya de dzo* ('Stand up, warriors! You stand up and gird your waists. With courage, stand up, stand up, stand up! Hear of the battlefield; something has happened')" (p. 85).

The Drum as Choreographer

Through their capacity to store and communicate practical and eso-teric knowledge, group history, and proverbs, and even make im-promptu comments, drum texts are able to disseminate sociocultural information on appropriate occasions, and are thus, like dance, an em-bodiment of the world view. In addition, a master drum is often awarded special status. According to Uka, the Ibo *ikoro* slit drum "was used as a spirit, an authoritative voice of its community" (1976). In Igede, a chicken is sacrificed on the slit drum on the night preceding its use in a funeral. Symbolically, the drum is the voice of the ancestors, and this offering is said to improve the sonority. The slit drum and signal horns will interject statements derived from the battlefield during "music of war" (*ayilo nya ewu*) performed at the funeral. Using their drum names, the slit drum will rally, cajole, and praise the dancers, and urge the masquerade to express the qualities of a great warrior: fearlessness, determination, and vigor. A description of an Akan hunter's festival that celebrates the killing of an elephant provides some idea of the way drum phrases are integrated with songs, dance, and pantomime in the traditional context. The hunter is formally welcomed to the festival site, then:

> He goes around shaking hands while drummers and singers call to him with his own strong names and praise appelations and such traditional epithets of hunters as: . . . *okum-anini*—slaughterer of males, the brave one; . . . *toto-atuo*—shooter of gun; . . . *mmoa kunu*—Lord of animals; *mmerewa mpena*—one loved by old women; *aka-mnena-agu*—despoiler of elephants, etc. The hunter is of course very busy, joining in the singing, alluding to his experiences in the lead of chorus refrains, and dancing with a gun in his hand, making symbolic gestures, impersonating ani-mals, and so on. (Nketia, 1963, pp. 86–87)

The potential of a talking instrument for vocalization and its ability to converse with dancers makes it an active participant in performances. An example is provided by a lively repartee recorded among the Fang of Gabon:

XYLOPHONE: Hey there, girls!

DANCERS: Yes!

XYLOPHONE: Where are you from?

DANCERS: We are from Endoumsang, from Nseme Nzimi's family. You can tell from his eyes that he is sad and would be capable of dying from hunger right next to a pile of sugar cane.

XYLOPHONE: Aha?

DANCERS: Aha!
XYLOPHONE: A poor country. . . ?
DANCERS: Is one where a man must rely on his flocks to live.
XYLOPHONE: The sin of adultery. . . ?
DANCERS: You forgive your brother if he steals from you, don't you?
XYLOPHONE: Cocoa leaves. . . ?
DANCERS: I made a mat from some this evening.
XYLOPHONE: An evil place. . . ?
DANCERS: Is where you meet the man you love.
XYLOPHONE: Spinsters' letters. . . ?
DANCERS: Never mention men.
XYLOPHONE: Aha?
DANCERS: Aha! (Pepper, Side A, sequence 4)

As one might anticipate, the ability of an instrument to communicate with dancers is exploited musically among many African ethnic groups, and talking instruments are used to choreograph and synchronize the movements of dancers. The ability of an instrument to deliver directions related to movements is evinced by a game of "hide and seek" described by Carrington. The *sese* is a two stringed lute of the Bolombo people. Two-toned speech texts are worked into familiar *sese* tunes, giving the seeker instructions as to how to find the hidden object. Carrington provides a sample of some of the instructions:

if the seeker has overstepped the mark: yaku la mbisa
  L H L H L
  come back

if the seeker has not gone far enough: omaci ko la felo
  L L H L L L L
  you leave it in front

or: yaku ko la felo
  L H L L L L
  come on in front

if the seeker is on the spot: olenjeke, olenjeke
  H H H L H H H L
  don't forget, don't forget

(L = Low note, H = High note)   (Carrington, 1949, pp. 79–80)

Within an Ibo dance performance "a melo-rhythm (talking) instrument is equally required to direct the ensemble, the dancers, as well as communicate with the audience" (Nzewi, 1983, p. 12). Within the dance the master drum will orchestrate a dancer's entry and exit points and provide other cues: "Melo-rhythm instruments would tell the dancer what position to take, to stand by, when to start an improvisation, how to realize his improvisations; it would give him the rhythms and tell him when to stop" (p. 12). The dancer has to be mentally and physically alert to match his movements to the drummed instructions. Nketia provides an example of drummed choreography:

> In the great *fontomfrom* dance the master drum may drum directions to the dancer: "Move outwards, move towards us; take it easy; do it gracefully," and so on. . . . When at an appropriate moment the dancer stretches his hands sideways, jumps up and crosses his legs in the landing, the master drummer begins the piece proper followed by the rest for the crossing of the legs is the sign that the dancer is ready to dance vigorously. From this point the dancer must follow the drummer closely for the cue to end the dance, in a posture or appropriate gesture carefully timed to the end beats. (Nketia, 1963, p. 160)

Not all of the drum's comments are complimentary to the dancer, for "master drummers . . . get impatient with dancers who keep on ignoring the music and may make rude remarks to them on the drum (e.g., I am seeing foul things) or may play less vigorously or ignore the movements of the dancer" (p. 162).

The extent of formal drummed choreography varies according to the ethnic group. It is notable among the Ewe where the lead drummer acts as a master of ceremonies. According to Locke the two principle functions of the Ewe leading drum are to "(1) play the traditional phrases of a dance music and (2) play rhythm patterns that provide choreographic signals for the dancers" (1982, p. 219). Agbekor of the Ewe is highly standardized dance in which the drummer must change his patterns continuously because they are correlated to each element of the choreography: "In Agbekor, the drum patterns are specifically related to the dance steps, and consequently the master drummer's beating is standardized to the language which calls and describes the dance steps" (Chernoff, 1979, p. 84). The dancers stylize their movements in keeping with the form and meaning of the dance: "Several dancers try to describe the situations of war: 'Get down and be ready' or 'Go forward slowly; stop and watch right and left, and go forward again' or 'If I get you, I'll cut your neck' " (p. 86).

Although the drummer is responsible for relaying signals to the dancers and coordinating their performance, Agbekor demonstrates that dance movements determine drum rhythms because drum patterns are ultimately created to meet the requirements of dance sequences.

According to Chernoff, the "master drummer can watch the lead dancer for cues" (1979, p. 118). Chernoff recalls, "when Freeman Donkor, for instance, would forget the sequence of the Agbekor drumming patterns he was teaching me, he would dance the steps and then, having remembered the proper rhythm he would return to the drum" (p. 143).

In addition to the drum other percussive instruments are also used to signal dance movements to the dancers. The gong delineates the footwork of the *atilogwu* dance of the Ibo (Nzewi, 1971), while "in the case of the Ijaw *eseni* dance, the movements are fixed to the rhythmic line of a song rather than the accompanying percussion, and are repeated with every repetition of the song" (Nketia, 1974, p. 212). In the Ogbete dance of the Igede, blasts on a tin whistle provide the signal to stop singing and start dancing vigorously. In the Vai Sande society of Liberia, the gourd-rattle (*sasaa*) player directs the sequences "using various rhythmic patterns on the *sasaa* to signal the dancers to proceed to different segments of the drama" (Monts, 1984, p. 54). Choreographed in this manner, the *yagbe* dance is performed by the whole troupe:

> The rhythm of the *yagbe* is built around an eight-beat pattern divided into six beats and two beats. During the first six beats the dancers, arranged in line formation, alternate left and right movements in a stationary position, then move forward on the last two beats. (Monts, 1984, p. 54)

Due to the structural interdependence of music and dance in West Africa, it is unrealistic to definitively isolate rhythm as a musical concept as separate from dance. Both team dances and solo dances generate levels of performance wherein dance movements inform drum rhythms. At this level, the music expresses in sound the timing and character of the dance, as is shown by Mont's description of the choreographed team dance of the Vai Sande society:

> Not all dancers are bound to a fixed rhythmic accompaniment. The improvisatory skills nurtured during training are displayed in a wide range of dazzling executions by individual girls. During these sequences *the instrumentalists improvise rhythmic patterns according to the dance movement.* (1984, p. 54; my emphasis)

Thus musical sound becomes a by-product of bodily movement. Drummers also develop personal styles of drumming to match the characteristic movements of an individual dancer, as the example of the Takai dance of the Dagomba serves to illustrate. In Takai the drummers stand within a circle of dancers. The lead drummer sometimes follows a dancer around the circle, beating to him to inspire his dance. A statement of the Dagomba drummer Ibrahim Abdulai shows that the drummer may take his cues from the movements of the dancers:

He watches their feet and how they take their feet for the dance. He watches the movement of the body and the feet, and as the dancer takes his steps in the dance, he will drum according to it. . . . We have individual dancers and they have individual styles of dancing and we know how to play with each man. (Chernoff, 1979, p. 110)

During solo dances in Igede, a dialogue is created between the dancers and the drummers, and it is the degree of synchrony that exists between movement and music that denotes a remarkable performance. A dancer "converses" with the music, and in dancing to "hidden rhythms," may well add additional rhythms that cut across the rhythm of the drums. As Nzewi points out, "in solo dance improvisation . . . the process of comprehension and interpretation in dance and music are simultaneous and often spontaneous" (1983, p. 12). Within this synthesis it is meaningless to make a distinction between the dance and the music, for they both manifest the same reality in a fusion of sound and action.

RHYTHMIC SOPHISTICATION

The Africans' aesthetic preferences and rhythmic sophistication has created certain stylistic demands that music and dance must fulfill. Through music making and choreography, Africans have developed "an aesthetic perspective quite different from ours" (Chernoff, 1979, p. 87). Dance rhythms possess aesthetic qualities, and whether the drums are communicating linguistically or not, it is the structural organization of rhythm and the precision in timing that dancers coordinate their movements to. For the drummer rhythmic sophistication entails, first, the ability to disect and control miniscule elements of time (the "fastest" pulse of Igede music is often over 200 beats a minute) and produce complex and precise rhythmic configurations; second, it entails the ability to reduce things to their vital essences in thought and image. This latter sensibility results in rhythmic abstraction. In order to meet the aesthetic demands of their audience, innovative artists work at the margins of their discipline. African performers can be expected to stretch the border of what is perceived as language or music; free meter or strict rhythm; gestures, locomotion, or dance.

Some of the stylistic peculiarities created to meet the demands of African rhythmic tastes have been discussed above, namely cyclic configurations, divisive and additive rhythms, multichronometry, free meter, cross rhythms, and polymeter. Other stylistic devices that provide a dynamic propulsion to the rhythm include, "playing forward to the beat," "offbeat timing," and the "silent downbeat." In Western traditions, musical refrains start on the main beat. Chernoff points out that in

African music the situation is often reversed and the main beat comes not at the beginning of a phrase but at the end. He states:

> Part of the power and the drive of African music comes from the way that African musicians play *forward* toward the beat. . . . An African musician is not so much moving along with a pulsation as he is *pushing* the beat to make it more dynamic. (1979, p. 56)

This device is sometimes encountered in jazz or blues. Stereotypically, in 4/4 time a phrase will consist of a triplet played on the last beat of the bar coupled with an emphasis on the first beat of the following bar. Overlapping ostinatos appear with regularity in Igede choral music and is exemplified by a tune of the Onyantu association in which the lead singer "presents a phrase to the small choir and continues singing on the last syllable against their repetitive answer" (Ranung, 1973). By unifying the overlapping syllables with the first beat of the bar, such overlapping ostinatos are "playing forward to the beat," for the response of the chorus becomes an avenue of approach that emphasizes the statement of the lead singer.

Locke discusses the principle of *offbeat timing* in African music and states, "it is useful to identify specifically the important offbeat positions within each main beat" (1982, p. 277). A familiar example of a rhythm that accents the offbeat is provided by the Tango. In addition to accenting every beat of the bar in 4/4 time, the Tango accents the halfbeat between the last beat of the bar and the first beat of the following bar, that is, 1, 2, 3, 4, *and* 1, 2, 3, 4, *and* 1, and so on. Chernoff notes, "generally in African musical idioms most of the notes seem to fall on what we would call the 'offbeat' . . . the musicians play 'around' the beat" (1979, p. 48). This is notably true of the Igede; rather than play a single note on the beat, a drummer will instead play a succession of notes around the beat. This creates a fragmented, crumbling, rhythmic quality. Consistent offbeat timing, as is found in West African music, provides a contrasting stream of accents that pull against the main beat, creating a dynamism and relentless forward momentum.

Agawu has noted the existence of a device "commonly found in West African music and frequently encountered in jazz and blues: *the silent downbeat*" (1986, p. 71; my emphasis). For Agawu, it is not that nothing is happening in the downbeats, but rather that something is silence. He states: "The silent downbeat, then, creates tension by propelling the music towards and beyond the nominal downbeat. . . . Its suppression places into relief the cyclical patterns that originate and terminate elsewhere in the measure" (p. 72). Chernoff also addresses the strength of articulation that derives from the rhetorical use of silence: "In the conflict of rhythms, it is the space between the notes from which

RESPONSORIAL PATTERNS

(INSERT MUSICAL NOTATION NO. 2)

the dynamic tension comes, and it is the silence which constitutes the musical form as much as does the sound" (1979, p. 113). He argues that an African drummer concerns himself as much with the notes he does not play as with the accents he delivers.

By weaving silences into the music, space is provided for the creative imagination of the performer or spectator. For Chernoff, "we begin to 'understand' African music by being able to maintain, in our minds or our bodies, an additional rhythm to the ones we hear" (p. 50). According to this hypothesis, African rhythm operates according to the same principles as an impressionist painting, wherein the spectator/participant assembles a coherent whole from an assortment of juxtaposed colors/beats. Chernoff states, "in the best dancing, the dancer, like the drummer . . . tunes his ears to hidden rhythms, and he dances to the gaps in the music" (p. 114). In dancing to the "gaps" in a drumming arrangement that is stressing offbeats, there is a likelihood for the timing of a dancer's movements to fall on the main beat. This proves to be the case with the Ijege masquerade of the Igede. In a recording I made, the leg-rattles of the dancer can be heard distinctly in the spaces between the drum beats. The dancer's steps are regulated with the main beat of the music.

The multiple rhythmic layers of African music and the spaces between the accented rhythms all offer a dancer "a range of dynamic points at which changes in position or changes in the flow of timing of body movements may be effected" (Nketia, 1974, p. 211). Locke discusses a "dynamic principle of aural illusion" that functions in southern Eʋe (Ewe) dance drumming 'wherein a pattern may be heard differently depending on the metric vantage point of the listener" (1982, p. 223). The polychronic orientation of an African dance performance means that an accomplished dancer can move different parts of the body independently in response to different parts of the music. "While the feet are moving regularly in duple beats, the body may be tilting sideways in similar or shorter durational units, with hands or arms perhaps moving at a different pace" (Nketia, 1974, p. 209). In some dances specific parts of the body may be accented. Among the Ibo, "To dance with a particular part of the body only is a noteworthy feature—with the chest (called *Edere* or *Ogbu na Ngu*) in Afikpo, the arm in Ohafia, the hips in Ubakala" (Ireole, 1975). Further examples are provided by Nketia:

> In the *nyindogu* dance of the Dagomba of Ghana, primarily the muscles of the belly are employed. . . . There are also dances such as those of the Kalabari of Nigeria, in which the hips are used in a subtle way, dances with intricate footwork, such as the *seyalo* dance of the Nguu of Tanzania . . . and dances with exaggerated leg gestures and raised knees, such as the *yongo* dance of the Builsa and the Kassena-Nankani. (1974, p. 209)

Fast foot-stamping dances are popular in Igede, while among other Nigerian groups, notably the Western Ibo, contortions of the body are common and the whole torso can be temporarily airborne. In Igede, acrobatic feats are found most commonly in Ito district.

DANCE AND RENEWAL

The perception that African arts serve as a repository for tribal knowledge implies that, in one sense, the macrorhythms of the world view and the microrhythms of music and dance are one and the same. The views of various scholars lend weight to the hypothesis that in Africa, music and dance activity are appraised by the same aesthetic criteria that are applied to the larger world view. Hardin (1986) discovered that among the Kono of eastern Sierra Leone, aesthetic criteria are directly related to the principles people use to organize their lives in general. Relative to dance, Hanna maintains that "what we perceive as aesthetic factors are intermingled and designed for practical application in the economic, political, social, and religious spheres of life" (1965, p. 49). According to Chernoff, "the values which inform the African musical sensibility embody the philosophical and ethical traditions of African culture" (1979, p. 154). Chernoff emphasizes that relationships between people are comparable to relationships in music. In discussing Chernoff's theories, Riesman states: "What is exciting about this analysis is that we see playing the music as participating in a relation, and that relation expresses in music the qualities of feeling that Africans value in the conduct of social life itself" (1986, p. 110). It would appear that in Africa, musical values and social values are interchangeable.

Because the underlying theme of most West African festivals is transition, they accordingly take place within transitory time—a period between stages. All that matters is concentrated in time and space and orchestrated with music and dance. Considering the coincidence of transformation rites and music and dance throughout West Africa, it is pertinent to enquire, What is intrinsic in music and dance that makes it relevant to periods of renewal? Bebey says that among the Fali in northern Cameroon, "two drums beaten with bare hands at the moment of death symbolize the everlastingness of man, who is ever born anew, even if our eyes see his body pass away" (1974, p. 119). In Igede and among other West African ethnic groups also, drum beating accompanies death, both during the wake and the funeral. Rhythm manifests elapsing time and, according to Bebey, has an orientation that simultaneously encompasses what is, what was, and what what is coming. He states: "Rhythm beats out the time for both present and future. For while song fixes action in the past, rhythm through the alchemy of movement, thrusts man towards the future" (p. 120). Rhythm is relevant to periods of change due to inherent qualities of consummation and expectation, and through recurrent cycles of closure and awakening provides human affairs with a future orientation.

Dance similarly contains features that make it appropriate to occasions of renewal. According to Hanna, "Dance metaphorically enacts and communicates status transformation in rites of passage, death ceremonies, curative and preventative rites" (1987, p. 121). Dance helps a people perpetuate themselves by providing continuity to their cultural identity. That continuity is dependent on periodic renewal was well understood in traditional Africa. Hanna states: "Nigeria's Ubakala dance often reflects past, present, and future—the dancer, a reincarnated ancestor, will die and probably be reborn. Thus dance represents the continuity of the lineage" (p. 29). Referring to the funeral dances of the Dogon of Mali, Hanna reports, "death creates disorder; but through the dance, humans metaphorically restore order to the disordered world" (p. 113). The overt purpose of an Igede funeral ceremony is to transform the deceased into an ancestor. The masquerades, as emissaries from the ancestors, dance to signify the acceptance of the deceased's soul in the ancestral realm. Thus, the change in status receives divine ratification. The funeral, although commemorating a death, is a celebration of life. It honors the achievements of the deceased in his lifetime and affirms the continuation of the community in the midst of trauma.

Every festival or ritual ceremony unfolds according to its own rhythm, and although the component events are established by custom, there is nothing predetermined about the outcomes, for "A ritual is a living thing, not just a routine following predetermined lines mechanically, but the final symbolic form is dependent on the character of the interaction between human actors of roles. For the role he or she occupies is always a representative one." (Turner, 1968). An Igede funeral ceremony is protected by various rites and medicines, and any untoward occurrence that jars the rhythm of the occasion is taken very seriously. If a masquerade falls during his dance, it is the equivalent of a curse, and remedial measures are taken. A he-goat is sacrificed and the miscreant dancer is required to eat the neck parts to symbolically strengthen his own neck for the wearing of the mask. Fortunately, this happens very rarely.

Festivals are communal events, and everyone present contributes to the expressive quality of the occasion. Contexts are provided that dramatize social relationships and stimulate motor behavior. Negativity that has arisen in the community can be expressed and discharged. Because dance is a medium of communication, it can embody concerns of the moment:

> Through the dance, individuals and social groups can show their reactions to attitudes of hostility or cooperation and friendship held by others towards them. They can offer respect to their superiors, or appreciation and gratitude to well-wishers and benefactors. They can react to the presence of rivals . . . or express their beliefs through the choice of appropriate dance vocabulary or symbolic gestures. (Nketia, 1974, pp. 207–208)

In Igede, dance serves social, aesthetic, and competitive instincts. During a solo dance a male dancer enters the arena by the authority of a cloth tied around his waist. He might end his performance by throwing this cloth at the feet of a rival, a challenge destined to bring bad luck to the recipient, unless resolved within a dance performance. In this spontaneous situation the drum rhythms that are played become a composite of other activities that manifest the celebration of a particular festival. As Chernoff points out, "The drummer must integrate the social situation into his music, and *the situation itself can make the music different*" (1979, p. 67; my emphasis). Because rituals are living things, the final symbolic form is reflected in the dances performed and the rhythms that are played.

Although traditional practices can be expected to have a basic conservatism, change or innovation is not stifled when it appears as a logical extension of established usage. Being of the dawn, the Igede ancestors represent both past and future and are as concerned with creative and regenerative aspects as they are with continuity and conservation. The periodic recurrence of ritual festivals provide a community with opportunities to modify established sociocultural practices: "When society perceives a change to which there is a general tendency among the people, the change can be refined to become that of the gods" (Ade Ogun, 1967). By this means, dance festivals can become active agents of change or harbingers of modernity. An example of dance applied to the change process comes from Burkina Faso, whereby: "The Dodo is a ritual of change which shows people how to change, thereby serving as an important setting for learning in the society. . . . It is clear that the masquerade is a series of symbolic communications about the nature of being young, African and modern" (Hinckley, 1985). As Leventhal and Schwartz discussed at the 1982 "Dance and the Child" conference in Stockholm, a basic tenet of dance therapy is that "a change in movement expression will result in a personality or behavioral change" (Hanna, 1983, p. 224). By means of participatory and informal education technique, dance in West Africa communicates acceptable modes of behavior, both in terms of general messages gleaned from the world view and particular messages that are specific to the interpretation of a particular performance. New aesthetic judgments may be derived from the latter, which may involve impromptu interpretations thought to be inspired by the ancestors.

CONCLUSION

This essay has groped toward a modicum of understanding in an area that still retains much mystery: the phenomenon of rhythm and the role it plays in West African dance performances. Musical timing in West African music is marked by stylistic peculiarities, including cyclic configurations, divisive and additive rhythms, polymeter, cross rhythms, offbeat timing, free meter, and asymmetric progressions. A major debate centers on the complexity of timing in African music. If simple meter were the norm, it is less likely that the influence of extramusical factors would be questioned. Evidence has been marshaled to refute Koetting's (1986) contention that extramusical factors are irrelevant to a study of timing in African music, for such factors as world view, dance, and language seem to influence musical timing. Stylistic peculiarities in West African rhythm can be attributed to various factors:

1. Both dance patterns and drum rhythms are context determined and event specific, and reflect the sociocultural purposes of the occasion in which they are performed.
2. Some dance rhythms, including those used for war dances, divination, and curative rites, deliberately employ a lack of metrical symmetry and other stylistic peculiarities as a psychoacoustic device to induce specific behavioral outcomes external to the dance.
3. Free meter and additive rhythms often reflect the influence of speech on music. Asymmetric patterns occur when a drum is producing surrogate speech.
4. African rhythmic preferences demand complex configurations of musical timing. These can include the independent pace of songs and drum rhythms, music that is both slow and fast, cross rhythms and polymeter, offbeat timing, and a general dynamic momentum.
5. At certain levels of a dance performance drummers may spontaneously improvise arbitrary rhythms to reflect dance gestures and locomotion, and thus provide audible responses to inaudible movements that appear in the dance.
6. As a composite of other activities in a ritual festival, drum rhythms may provide audible responses or commentary to social input and transitory occurrences.

Considering these factors, an exclusive focus on musical products in isolation from the cultural setting from which they were derived is unlikely to provide an adequate understanding of the West African perception of musical time.

In attempting to discern how the perception of time at the level of sociocultural macrorhythms might have an impact on the microrhythms of musical time, I propose that the world view and music and dance are understood according to common aesthetic criteria. In a sense, music is a microcosm of the world view. Thus, the organization of time at the level of sociocultural macrorhythms is analogous to a musical progression and vice versa. As vehicles of public education, music and dance transmit skills, information, and attitudes, and through the movements of dance and the rhythm of the drums, the world view is translated into musical timing.

In West Africa, dance is coextensive with music and is a major determinant of musical form. It communicates sociocultural information, and as a functional craft, its form reflects the sociocultural purposes it fulfills. During festivals that demarcate individual or social renewal, dance conveys messages about order and organization, standards of conduct, coordination, moderation, poise and harmony, cultural integration, respect, and being up to date. Dance movements determine drum rhythms, for percussive patterns are created to meet the spatial requirements of the dance. Additionally, drummers will improvise rhythm patterns in response to a dancer's movements.

Language is also musically determinative. Songs are treated as if they were speech utterances, and the intonation contour and rhythms of speech are followed in music. Surrogate speech performed on drums and other musical instruments disseminate sociocultural information and can also play a role in choreography. Within burden texts performed on talking instruments, speech provides a verbal score for the strict rhythms of dance music, while drums sometimes "talk" in free rhythm during dance performances.

Through the medium of language, dance, and world view, extramusical factors have an impact on the microrhythms of musical sound, and conversely, judgments derived from dance inform the larger sociocultural context. According to such variables as purpose, social attitudes, creative input, communal kharma, the dynamics of participation, aesthetic factors, and so on, on the dance, variations in expression can influence the final sociocultural statement and affect the community's view of the world. Within a traditional ritual festival the general rule is applied to the specific instance, and the outcomes of the specific instance can lead to a modification of the general rule. Thus, sociocultural macrorhythms and musical microrhythms can mutually influence each other.

I attribute the multipart structure of music to the influence of facets of the world view such as multitheistic religious beliefs or a cooperative mode of production. Kauffman, however, sees physical movements as the predominant influence on music, and proclaims that "the multi-movement possibilities of the body obviously determine a multi-rhythmic musical structure" (1980, p. 402). In his opinion "the rhythm of physical movement . . . (is a) . . . major determinant of the African time sense" (p. 402). He cites not only dance but states that "the physical behavior appropriate to the playing of musical instruments is also rhythmically determinative" (p. 402). He points out that the "interlocking of hands" is common not only to drum playing but also to many other African instruments such as the xylophone, mbira, and kora. He additionally points out that: "Work songs . . . certainly have built-in rhythms that determine the basic rhythm and songs" (p. 402). These are areas that deserve to be researched further.

Although dance shares a structural interdependence with music and clearly determines musical form, with language and social processes the causal relationship between the alleged determinants and musical timing is less obvious. Often an element of translation exists. Demonstrating that extramusical factors are *translated* into musical timing falls short of showing that musical form is directly determined by them. Whether in fact musical timing is inherent in a burden text or syllabic cipher, or whether it is applied to them, requires a familiarity with the conventions that possibly only an indigenous tone-language speaker trained in music could provide. However, conceptual abstractions, whether musical notation, nonsense syllables, or speech texts, all involve translation, for the rules of the cipher have to be learned. When, in Igede, I was confronted by a six-year-old who could beat out complex rhythms on a tin-can, I conceived that acquiring rhythmic skills is comparable to learning a language and that similar cognitive aptitudes are employed. Children are socialized informally into language and can learn more than one with relative ease. At a later stage learning a language, or mastering a rhythm, can be achieved only by much intellectual effort. The similarity between learning a language and learning a rhythm is worth pursuing.

In discussing the African perception of time, Stone refers to "inner time." She suggests that inner time "exists for participants within the stream of consciousness and does *not* contain homogenous units of measure" (1984, p. 20). This implies that timing in music is informed by a metric orientation shared by the performers, rather than musically prescribed time lines. Such a notion would seem to suggest that Africans have a metric orientation that is qualitatively different from others, and that is the result of intuition rather than learning. To depict musical timing emerging spontaneously on the basis of intuition alone creates a metaphysics that precludes scientific study. Because mastery of skills creates an immediacy of response that circumvents rational control, a discipline can be transcended, but only after the skills have been learned. Mastery of timing and seemingly spontaneous reflexes are displayed by any skilled team working on a common task.

I have shown that to participate fully in traditional West African dance it is necessary that the performers are initiated into various cultural conventions. This involves learning not only in music and dance but social learning also. In addition to the ability to translate drum texts and interpret dance gestures and locomotion, working knowledge of the world view, cultural calender, social structure, esoteric lore, and socialization processes are also necessary. Mastery of these diverse areas might then yield the rhythmic sophistication to perform adequately. Participation in a dance performance in effect demonstrates the extent of an individual's enculturation.

That aesthetics are derived from the world view is true of all societies but especially of traditional West Africa, where sacred and secular, art and philosophy, have not yet been compartmentalized. Rather than "what can the world view and sociocultural life tell us of musical form?", the question might be rephrased—"what can musical form tell us about sociocultural factors and world view?" In real terms, whether it is easier to learn about a people's philosophy through a study of their art, or to learn about their art through a study of their philosophy, is a moot point. Both a precise analysis of musical form and an understanding of the traditional context are important, and an examination of either emphasizes just how important the other is. However, because social changes in Africa are leading to the demise of many traditional customs, an agenda of cultural conservation is needed (Nicholls, 1987).

This essay has attempted to emphasize the role of dance in determining timing in African music. It is recognized that dance is conterminous with music and visual arts. An interdisciplinary approach has been adopted whereby dance has been discussed primarily in musicological terms. Such an approach is fruitful, for in most cases an examination of dance as separate from music (or music without dance) will provide an incomplete picture. Additionally, the written word and photographs do not provide a facsimile of a live performance. Cinematography could be an important medium for documenting traditional West African dances, but has yet to emerge as a vehicle for serious scholarly study. Implicit in this essay are implications for further research demonstrating the connection between extramusical factors and musical performance and the interrelationship of dance, music, and the visual arts. Ideally, a set of criteria should be established to examine African performance as an integrated experience.

REFERENCES

Ade Ogun, A. (1967, December). *Nigeria Magazine.* Ministry of Information, Lagos, Nigeria.

Agawu, V. Kofi. (1986). "Gi Dunu," "Nyekpadudu," and the study of West African rhythm. *Ethnomusicology, 30*(1), 64–83.

Bartle, Philip F. W. (1980). *The universe has three souls: A few notes on learning Akan culture.* Leiden: Afrika Studiecentrum.

Bebey, Francis. (1974, Fall). The vibrant intensity of traditional African music. *The black perspective in music, 3*(4), pp. 117–121.

Bebey, Francis. (1975). *African music: A peoples art.* New York: L. Hill.

Carrington, John F. (1949). *The talking drums of Africa.* London: Carey Kingsgate.

Chernoff, John Miller. (1979). *African rhythm and African sensibility.* Chicago: University of Chicago Press.

Davidson, Basil. (1969). *The African genius.* Boston: Little, Brown and Co.

Dieterlen, Germaine. (1973). L'image du corps et les composantes de la personne chez les Dogon, in Colloques internationaux du centre national de la recherche scientifique, no. 544: *La notion de personne en Afrique noire.* Paris: Editions du Centre National de la Recherche Scientifique, pp. 205–229.

Euba, Akin. (1976). Music. In Saburi O. Biobaku (Ed.), *The living culture of Nigeria.* Lagos: Thomas Nelson. *The living culture of Nigeria* (Saburi O. Biobaku, Ed.). Lagos: Thomas Nelson.

Gorer, Geoffrey. (1972). The functions of different dance forms in primitive African communities. In Franziska Boas (Ed.), *The function of dance in human society.* New York: Dance Horizons.

Hanna, Judith Lynne. (1965). African dance as education. *Impulse 1965: Dance and Education Now,* pp. 48–56.

Hanna, Judith Lynne. (1983, April). Dance and the child. *Current Anthropology.*

Hanna, Judith Lynne. (1987). *To dance is human: A theory of nonverbal communication.* Chicago: University of Chicago Press.

Hardin, Kris. (1986, April 4). Aesthetics, "Arts," and the cultural whole. Paper presented at the Seventh Triennial Symposium on African Art, Museum of Cultural History, University of California, Los Angeles.

Harper, Peggy. (1976). Dance in Nigeria. In Judy van Zile (Ed.), *Dance in Africa, Asia and the Pacific: Selected readings.* MSS Information Corporation.

Herskovits, Melville J. (1947). *Man and his works.* New York: Alfred A. Knopf.

Hinckley, Priscilla B. (1985, March 5). Creating contemporary ritual: A Voltaic children's masquerade. Visual and Performing Arts Seminar, African Studies Center, Boston University.

Ireole, Iheukwumere. (1975, September 7). Dancing and Ibo musical instruments. *Sunday Renaissance* (newspaper). Nigeria.

Johnston, Thomas F. (1974). A Tsonga initiation. *African Arts, 7*(4), 60–62.

Kauffman, Robert. (1980). African rhythm: A reassessment. *Ethnomusicology, 24*(3), 393–415.

Keil, Charles. (1979). *Tiv song.* Chicago: University of Chicago Press.

Koetting, James. (1986). What do we know about African rhythm? *Ethnomusicology, 30*(1), 58–63. (Edited posthumously by Roderic Knight.)

Kwakwa, Patience Abena. (1979). Traditional African dance forms: Context, role and meaning. Seminar paper, Centre for Nigerian Cultural Studies, Ahmadu Bello University, Zaria, Nigeria.

Le Moel, Guy. (1981). Les activities religieuses des jeunes enfants chez les Bobo. *Journal des Africanistes, 51*(1–2), 235–250.

Locke, David. (1982). Principles of offbeat timing and cross-rhythm in southern Ewe dance drumming. *Ethnomusicology, 26*(2), 217–246.

Locke, David, & Agbeli, Godwin. (1981). Drum language in Adzogbo. *The Black Perspective in Music, 9*(1), 25–50.

Monts, Lester P. (1984). Dance in the Vai Sande society. *African Arts, 17*(4), 53–59.

Nicholls, Robert W. (1984). Igede funeral masquerades. *African Arts, 17*(3), 70–76.

Nicholls, Robert W. (1985). Music and dance guilds in Igede. In Irene V. Jackson (Ed.), *More than drumming: Essays on African and Afro-Latin American music and musicians* (pp. 91–117). Westport, CT: Greenwood Press.

Nicholls, Robert W. (1987). Igede in the twentieth century. *The World & I, 2*(7), 517–531.

Nketia, J. H. Kwabena. (1963). *Drumming in Akan communities in Ghana*. London: Thomas Nelson.

Nketia, J. H. Kwabena. (1974). *The music of Africa*. New York: W. W. Norton.

Nzewi, Meki. (1971). The rhythm of dance in Igbo music. *The Conch, 3*(2), 104–108.

Nzewi, Meki. (1983). Philological derivation of melo-rhythm improvisation. *African Musicology, 1*(1), Institute of African Studies, University of Nairobi, 1–13.

Pepper, Herbert. (n.d.). *Anthologie de la vie Africaine*. Long-playing record album. Ducretet-Thomson 320C-126.

Ranung, Bjorn. (1973). *Music of dawn and day: Music and dance associations of the Igede of Nigeria*. Long-playing record album with liner notes. Helsinki: Love Records.

Riesman, Paul. (1986). The person and the life cycle in African social life and thought. *African Studies Review, 29*(2), 71–137.

Sowande, Fela. (1966). Nigerian music and musicians: Then and now. *Composer, 19*, 25–34.

Stone, Ruth M. (1984). In search of time in African music. (This manuscript served as a basis for a panel discussion and is cited by Koetting, 1986. It will be published in *Music Theory Spectrum*, forthcoming).

Stone, Ruth M. (1986). Commentary: The value of local ideas in understanding West African rhythm. *Ethnomusicology, 30*(1), 54–57.

Swanson, Richard. (1980). Development interventions and self-realization among the Gourma. In David Brokensha et al. (Eds.), *Indigenous knowledge systems and development* (pp. 67–91). Lanham, MD: University Press of America.

Thompson, Robert Farris. (1966, Fall). An aesthetic of the cool: West African dance. *African Forum, 2*(2), 85–102.

Turnbull, Colin M. (1983). *The Mbuti pygmies: Change and adaption*. New York: Holt, Rinehart, and Winston.

Turner, V. W. (1968). *The drums of affliction: A study of religious processes among the Ndemu of Zambia*. London: Clarendon Press.

Uka, N. (1976). The ikoro and its cultural significance. *Ikoro: Bulletin of the Institute of African Studies, 3*(1). University of Nigeria at Nsukka.

Wilson, Olly. (1974, Spring). The significance of the relationship between Afro-American music and West African music. *The Black perspective in music, 3*(2), pp. 3–22.

12

THE SOCIAL ROLE OF ALASKAN
ATHABASCAN POTLATCH DANCING

Thomas F. Johnston

This is a statewide social study of dance among the Upper Tanana, the Tanana, the Atna, the Kutchin, the Tanaina, and the Lower Koyukon Athabascan Indians of interior Alaska. Fieldwork consisted of 10 annual month-long visits, 1973–1983, funded by the National Endowment for the Humanities. Preparation of this and other papers was facilitated by sabbatical leave from the University of Alaska.

Traditional Athabascan dance forms and practices in Alaska are strongest among the Upper Tanana, where there was relatively late contact, and weakest among the Kutchin, where they were replaced by acculturated Scottish jigs and reels brought in by Hudson's Bay Company traders. The Tanaina were somewhat oppressed by the Russian adventurers, and later strongly influenced by proximity to Anchorage; their dance has waned. The Lower Koyukon observe the religiously important week-long Feast for the Dead hi'o Stick Dance, generally held annually.

The formal potlatch is the main social context for Athabascan traditional dance. With feasting, gift-giving, and communal dancing, the potlatch functions to honor the deceased, to validate the fulfillment of social obligations, to augment individual and group status, to redistribute wealth, to feed the aged, and to mark community events. Dance being a prime potlatch component, it shares in these functions.

Contemporary Athabascan dance teams in Alaska are a viable form of recreational cooperative enterprise, and function as extended family and social networks. Membership offers modest economic rewards, a spectrum of gratifying expressive roles, and a creative outlet.

PRIOR DANCE RESEARCH

Several monographs on the Alaskan Athabascan Indians devote limited space to descriptions of traditional dance. These include Osgood (1936, 1937, 1958), McKennan (1959, 1965), Olson (1968), Guédon

(1974), and Clark (1974). In addition, there is Loyens's article "The Koyukon Feast for the Dead" (1964), Marchiori's dissertation "Stick Dance" (1981), Mishler's dissertation "Gwich'in Athabascan music and dance" (1981), and Pearce's thesis "Musical characteristics of Tanana Athabascan dance songs" (1985). The present study is intended as an initial survey of the several Athabascan dance styles in Alaska, and as a means of increasing current understanding of Athabascan aesthetic values and artistic values.

THE SIGNIFICANCE OF STUDYING DANCE

Traditional dance is but a small part of the Athabascan cultural whole, but it fills certain essential social roles and contributes to the ongoing culture in a special way. Radcliffe-Brown points out that "The function of a particular social usage is the contribution it makes to the total social life as the functioning of the total system. Such a view implies that the social system . . . has a certain kind of unity, which we may speak of as a functional unity. We may define it as a condition in which all parts of the social system work together with a sufficient degree of harmony or internal consistency, i.e., without producing persistent conflicts which can neither be resolved nor regulated" (Radcliffe-Brown, 1952, p. 181).

Athabascan traditional dance, particularly within the context of the formal potlatch, is one of the many social mechanisms with which the Athabascans cope with the problems and dilemmas of society that all men face everywhere. Kluckhohn notes that "Ceremonials tend to portray a symbolic resolution of the conflicts which external environment, historic experience, and selective distribution of personality types have caused to be characteristic of a society" (1968, p. 167).

In their folklore, in their songtexts, and in their ceremonies, the Athabascan appear to be particularly concerned with death. Athabascan subsistence is hazardous; there are many drownings on the great rivers of the interior, and rural health care is in its infancy. Turner points out that in order to make logical assumptions concerning a society's ceremonies it is necessary "to understand ritual and symbolic behavior in terms of the redefinition of statuses demanded by the death of individuals and the ongoing processes" (1965, p. 114).

Kimball likewise observes that "the function of ritual behavior is to restore the equilibrium where changes in social interaction occurred" (1960, p. xiii). These observations on the social function of ritual, taken from classic anthropology, do not of course refer specifically to the Athabascan; they refer to the need of all societies to muster integrative and cohesive forces in the service of maintaining social relations, including relations with the dead.

Koyukon Athabascan dancer Poldine Carlo, in her writings on the Stick Dance, affirms that "The Stick Dance is a very serious celebration that we the people of Nulato and Kaltag strongly believe in . . . we believed that during the potlatch the dead for whom it was given would all be happy and be participating with us" (1978, pp. 62–68; change of tense is Carlo's).

Soon after first white contact, dance traditions began to wilt under the well-intentioned but unfortunate abuse of missionaries and others. Poldine Carlo relates how "Years ago our Catholic priests started preaching to our Native people that the Stick Dance was the devil's work" (1978, p. 69). Furthermore, in recent times with the onset of rapid social change many musicoreligious beliefs of the Athabascans have waned. One of the purposes of this study is to identify surviving traditional dance traits, and to assess the degree of change in Athabascan form and function.

Dance may be said to consist of multichanneled, culturally patterned communication, learned through social experience. Dance is a prime enculturative mechanism, for many of the basic assumptions and orientations of a society, including its prescriptions and proscriptions, are locked into the dance mode of communication. In each of the various Athabascan groups in Alaska, the hand movements are sex specific, and are standard expressive motor symbols possessing subtle, acquired meaning that is learned by most members of the society. They are related to and based upon cultural attitudes toward posture, toward social dominance-submission hierarchies, and toward other social and religious factors I will touch upon.

Affect in Athabascan traditional dance results from selective perception, where the extraction of information results from sensory stimulation on the basis of memory, emotions, and cognitive structures. At time of performing, each Athabascan dancer is an incumbent of a special social role, and has intent to mirror, pass on, or transform in some dimension a unit of past experience. Dance encodes messages through cognitive-sensori-affective-motor patterns and devices, in time, space, and effort. It operates under cultural prescriptions, often using adjunct channels featuring music, song, and costuming (Hanna, 1979, p. 24). The audience participates actively, decodes the messages, and provides the catalytic environment necessary to further the goals of the sociomusical event.

In Athabascan dance, meaning is encapsulated conjunctively in the event and in the discursive sequences of unfolding movement configurations. Athabascan traditional dance movements project culture-specific shapes with attendant body images, which through the eye of the beholder stimulate recollected and unconscious perceptions and experiences. For example, in the Athabascan seasonal potlatch called Nuchalawoyya, the new spring with its profound ecological changes is celebrated, and the intrinsic meaning of dance within this context derives from time and place of the dance. At the Athabascan Feast for the dead, objects are made to dance; the gifts are wrapped in rolls of calico and danced around the decorated spruce pole, which is a way of offering them beyond the everyday world. Meaning here derives from superordinary symbolic action.

The centerpiece of the Stick Dance ceremony is but a spruce pole, but the act of dancing around it transforms it into an earth-sky axis representing the living and the dead, a syncretic assembly of spirits. The dance pole, stripped of its bark by women and erected by the hunter, is given magicosymbolic colors, danced around the village, and broken up. The broken pieces of today become the resumption and continuation of a hoped-for apprehension-free life tomorrow (Marchiori, 1981, p. 113). Meaning here derives from dance encirclement and from place—the pole is thrown into the river from which the Athabascan receive their continued means of subsistence.

At the Stick House, honored guests receive the favorite food of the deceased; through this food, the dancing, and the ritual dressing, they mystically acquire the identity of the deceased, acting out the Athabascan traditional concept of reincarnation. Meaning here derives from shared knowledge of Athabascan religious beliefs and awareness of the situational ethos. In studying Athabascan traditional dance, one partially opens a window into Athabascan cognitive and aesthetic processes, and while so doing, it is possible to learn something about one's self.

THE ATHABASCAN LANGUAGE

Athabascan dance in Alaska is accompanied by extremely rhythmic dance songs in one or other of several Alaskan Athabascan languages. The twenty-two Koyukon dance songs documented in a book coauthored by the present writer, for instance, are in Koyukon (Johnston & Solomon, 1978). Some in Craig Mishler's study of Kutchin music are in Gwich'in (1981). Some in Pearce's study of Minto music are in Tanana (1985). Some in James Kari's study of Athabascan dancer Chief Shem Pete are in Tanaina (1987).

The 10,000 Athabascan Indians of Alaska are dispersed over a vast area of the interior, reaching from near the mouth of the Yukon River in the west to the Canadian border in the east. From north to south they range from the Arctic Circle at Fort Yukon to Tyonek on Cook Inlet on the southern coast, these latter being the only coastal Athabascan and the only group with a maritime culture. It is not surprising, therefore, that they do not constitute one homogeneous social group, but several, distinguished by several mutually unintelligible languages.

Ingalik is spoken at Anvik and Shageluk. Holikachuk is spoken at Grayling. Koyukon is spoken at Kaltag, Nulato, Hughes, Huslia, Allaket, Koyukuk, Ruby, Galena, Tanana, and Stevens Villages. Tanana is spoken at Ninto and Nenana. Tanacross is spoken at Tanacross, Han is spoken at Eagle, and Eyak is a lost language.

Tananina, or Dena'ina as linguists prefer it be known, is spoken in five dialects. Upper Inlet dialect is spoken at Tyonek, Alexander Creek, Susitna, Kroto Creek, Montana Creek, Knik, and Eklutna. Outer Inlet dialect is spoken at Kenai, Seldovia, Kustatan, and Polly Creek. Iliamna dialect is spoken at Pedro Bay and Old Iliamna. Inland dialect is spoken at Nondalton, Lime Village, and Stony River (Kari, 1987, p. 12).

Of the 190,000 American and Canadian Indians who speak some branch of the Athabascan family of languages, approximately 165,000 are Apaches and Navajos of the American Southwest; about 22,000 speakers live in Canada. Krauss considers that interior Alaska is the original homeland of all Athabascans, who expanded into Canada and the Southwest over the last 2,500 years (1975). Of the various Athabascan groups living in Alaska, only three still speak the language to any great degree. These are the Upper Kuskokwim speakers at Nicolai, the Upper Tanana speakers at Tetlin and Northway, and the Gwich'in speakers at Arctic Village and Venetie. It is noteworthy that the distribution of cultural persistence in dance does not match the distribution of cultural persistence in the language; Arctic Village and Venetie no longer perform traditional dance, but have adopted imported reels and jigs. Dance survival is related to lateness of white contact, remoteness from urban centers, continued traditional subsistence hunting, and a configuration of other cultural factors such as close-knit family ties, the perceptual cultural filter, and the absence of persuasive acculturative alternatives in the specific area.

ATHABASCAN SUBSISTENCE

The food quest is strongly linked with Athabascan dancing, for it is at the Athabascan musical potlatch that the hunt and other cooperative subsistence ventures are endowed with an aura of spiritual validation. Furthermore, communal dancing among the Athabascan traditionally occurs in conjunction with feasting, and successful feasting depends on a plentiful supply of fresh meat.

In the Koyukon region, salmon fishing, caribou hunting, and moose hunting are important, these subsistence sources being supplemented by bear, rabbit, duck, geese, ptarmigan, and the gathering of wild berries. There are no salmon in the Upper Tanana region to the west. For this region Guédon gives a hunting calender (1974, p. 41). Subsistence sources there include pike, whitefish, caribou, moose, sheep, rabbit, beaver and muskrat, ptarmigan and grouse, waterfowl, eggs, and berries. Fur trapping is conducted December through April.

In the Kutchin area to the north, salmon fishing is conducted July to October, the king salmon coming first and lasting about a month. Animals hunted are much the same as for the Upper Tanana. Animals trapped for fur include fox, otter, mink, marten, muskrat, ermine, and wolverine. Osgood gives Kutchin names of the months; they are named after the game available in that month (1936, p. 98).

In the Tanaina region to the south, five kinds of salmon are caught in May and June: humpbacks, silvers, reds, kings, and chums. Hooligan are dip-netted in late April, which is called "geese month." In the mountain regions of the Susitna River there are sheep, said to make the best of any dried meat. Bears and caribou are hunted in some parts of Tanaina territory, and porcupines and rabbits are everywhere numerous. Moose are hunted in season. Women and children gather varieties of berries. The Tanaina are the only Athabascan who regularly hunted whales. This was done in stream mouths May–August, where small white beluga were found. There has recently been a renewal of Tanaina beluga hunting (Kari, 1987, p. 61).

Large quantities of fresh meat are mandatory at the Athabascan social potlatch, the hosting and feasting activities of which help to feed the weak and the elderly, and constitute a partial redistribution of wealth and an underpinning for the dancing and other forms of sociability which occur. Sullivan notes of the Lower Koyukon that "Before the Natives start out for their winter fish camps, the old people remind them that the *hi'o* Stick Dance is to be held at mid-winter and urge them to work hard to provide enough food for the festivities" (Sullivan, 1942, p. 125). For the same Athabascan group, Marchiori points out the same combining of dancing and feasting in contemporary time (1981, pp. 52–63). Guédon notes of the contemporary Upper Tanana that "Dancing and feasting go on for several days . . . an important potlatch is likely to take precedence over all other activities. It is at the last afternoon or evening that the hosts distribute all the gifts they have amassed for this occasion" (1974, p. 224).

Subsistence hunting and traditional dance are, for the Alaskan Athabascan, necessary not only for enhancing life with food variety and recreation, but as a deeply felt symbol of their group identity. Dance form and dance song content reflect life-style: "Song forms and performances are themselves models of social behavior that reflect strategies of adaptation to human and natural environments" (Szwed, 1970, p. 220).

The hunt in precontact times was carried out in family bands. While the father reared his children for another matriline and mother's brother reciprocated, the small bands who hunted and fished for some 8 months of the year did not in fact include the maternal uncle. When the father went away from the camp to hunt caribou and sheep, he was accompanied only by prepubertal and older sons who were strong enough to be of physical service. Hippler points out that when the Indians who now live at Fish Lake, Highway Point, and Caribou Springs were together in their permanent houses at Old Village, the men and older boys lived in the men's house, apart from their mothers, sisters, and younger brothers, and cooked for themselves. Old Fish Lake informants say the men also used to do their own cooking while camping (1974, p. 351). Modern technology has somewhat reduced the hardships endured by Athabascan hunters in former times, and also caused changes in the division of labor. These changes have shifted economic power to the younger generation, which has in turn affected potlatch function and the role of traditional dance. It is unlikely that the vast numbers of teenagers participating in contemporary potlatch dancing fully comprehend the spiritual and religious significance of the event. That is not to say Athabascan traditional dance has lost its meaning; meanings change, and yesterday's social needs give way to today's perhaps even more compelling cultural imperative: the search for psychosocial roots.

Before the combustion engine, before electricity, before the rifle and the steel saw, the Alaskan Athabascan harvested their sparse environment and provided for their families in the face of one of the harshest climates in the world. Athabascan potlatch dancing, with its connotations of tradition and of community integration, reminds them of this. As Marchiori points out, "the Athabascan Stick Dance is the web that confers cohesion on a social fabric undergoing a profound transformation, with its mechanisms of reciprocity, expressed in the distribution of gifts and the offering of food, and with its power to loosen social stresses through singing and dancing" (1981, p. 107).

As powerful industrial corporations seek new ways to exploit mineral resources in Athabascan ancient hunting grounds, potlatch dancers, in the organized group movement and emotional intensity of their traditional dance, sense a degree of reassurance of community stability. Under such circumstances Athabascan dance becomes a confrontation with perceived stressors through physical and cognitive structuring in which the filtered outcomes are favorable.

EARLY CONTACT AND THE EROSION OF DANCE TRADITIONS

The early historical accounts of Athabascan dance, though frequently ethnocentric and inaccurate, provide some idea of precontact dance style and a comparison base from which to estimate stylistic change over time. Therefore it is relevant to note the early encounters. The Cook expedition spent a week in Cook Inlet in 1778; Russian forts were built at Kasilof and Kenai in the 1780s and 1790s (Kari, 1987, p. 169. In 1793 the first group of Russian Orthodox missionaries arrived in Alaska. In 1799, Czar Paul I gave the Russian-American Company a monopoly over hunting and mining rights in what were in fact Athabascan traditional hunting territories. In the winter of 1839, Malakhov established a tentative trading post among the Lower Koyukon at Nulato, and in 1843, Lt. Zagoskin, whose Alaskan travels are now famous, reached Nulato, writing, "In many villages we were greeted with dancing . . . dancing and singing are part and parcel of their religious beliefs; they never begin anything without dancing (Zagoskin, 1842–44, ed. Michael, 1957, p. 248).

In the late 1800s Whymper noted the same of the Lower Koyukon: "The guests sang in chorus and danced unceasingly around a pole painted in lively colors, and decorated with bead necklaces, magnificent wolf skins, and marten pelts. They danced on until morning, stopping their joyful merrymaking only to eat and drink" (1871, p. 251). This last is significant, for it closely resembles the present-day week-long Nulato Stick Dance in its use of a decorated dance pole.

In 1846, Alexander Murray joined the Hudson's Bay Company as a senior clerk and wintered at Fort McPherson in 1846–47. The following summer he crossed over the divide and floated down the Porcupine to establish Fort Yukon among the Kutchin Athabascan in Alaska, writing an excellent journal (1910). Historical descriptions of Athabascan dance are most useful when they provide a substantial degree of detail concerning social context, function, and dance movements. In 1847, Murray reported that a young Kutchin chief held a dance in which 37 men and some women and children "danced a variety of figures accompanied always with songs, and continued at it for nearly two hours . . . they always danced in a circle, the only difference being in their step, gestures, and songs, of which latter they have a great variety" (1910, p. 49).

In 1861, Smithsonian collector Bernard Ross wrote a letter (never published but cited by Mishler, 1981, p. 29): "The band containing about fifteen persons formed in a circle round a man placed in the center (I now speak of the Dead Dance) who, in similitude of woe was crouched on the ground shrouded in a blanket." Ross further noted that there occurred "a rotary movement of the circle of performers."

In the early 1930s Cornelius Osgood noted of the Tanaina of Cook Inlet that "they perform their dances in a circle, often around the fire, sometimes to the accompaniment of drums and sometimes without them" (1937, p. 119). This formation of a circle is still characteristic of certain Athabascan groups today, and rotation of the circle occasionally is seen.

We have mentioned early descriptions of circle dances. Line dances also existed and still exist among certain groups. Strachan Jones, in a Smithsonian report for 1866, reported a "war dance" among the Kutchin, in which "the men get into a line on one side and the women on the other; the men then run at the women . . ." (1872, p. 326). The significance of this is that the Atna of Copper River to the south perform a war dance in which opposing lines threaten each other across an imaginary river, advancing and retreating to the "water." This dance diffused to the Yakutat Tlingit still further south, where it is performed today. However, the Atna and the Tlingit do not divide the lines by sex. The contemporary Upper Tanana at Northway perform a line dance in which the men and women separate, and in which opposing lines of dancers hop toward each other, pass through the oncoming line, execute an about-turn, and repeat the process. The line dance in question is not known among the contemporary Kutchin, although they do perform imported line dances. No contemporary Athabascan line of dancers "runs" at an oncoming line, and the likelihood is that the dance witnessed by Jones simply waned.

In his "The Chandalar Kutchin," Robert McKennan reports that his Kutchin informants state that many of their dances came from the Han Athabascan in Canada (1965, p. 48). The term Chandalar derives from the French *gens de large*, meaning "people of the expanses," or nomads. Dance diffusion is to be expected among a people whose vast territories are linked by great rivers. The Tanana River, the Yukon River, and others have long provided a convenient means of transportation from east to west; there was also dogsled travel. Today there is the snowmobile and the commuter plane. Intervillage potlatching dancing is much enjoyed, so that dance diffusion continues.

The last Athabascan group to experience white contact were the Upper Tanana of Northway and Tetlin. Lt. Allen visited and described this group in 1885 (Allen, 1900). The lateness of this contact and the geographical inaccessibility of the Upper Tanana may account for the remarkable persistence of their traditions, particularly dance within the context of the social potlatch.

In the early 1920s, Michael Mason observed a Crow Dance at Fort Yukon. In this dance, one participant lay flat on his back with his arms spread to represent fish fins. A woman wrapped in a large shawl stepped forward imitating a crow by waddling and croaking; she pretended to peck out the man's eyes and eat the "fish." Sometimes there were several crows who squabbled over the "fish." Another participant in a white sheet then pretended to be a white fish-eagle, chasing the crow away. The dance-play ended with the "fish" coming to life and the flight of the "eagle" (Mason, 1924, p. 70). This dance has recently been revived at Fort Yukon by teacher Katherine Peters, who has read the ethnographic literature and has interested Kutchin teenagers in traditional dance forms.

In the Tanana Athabascan community of Nenana in 1974, Athabascan dancers Paul George and Winnie Charlie and others performed and explained several traditional circle dances for the present writer. These included the Porcupine Dance, the Seagull Dance, the Grouse Dance, the Squirrel Dance, and the Rabbit Dance. In each of these a participant entered the circle and performed a degree of mime. Although similar in concept to the dance witnessed by Mason, none featured a crow. At Fort Yukon in 1973, Craig Mishler recorded several Kutchin traditional songs, among which was a Crow Song sung by Natalie Eric, and another by Myra Robert; this song may have accompanied the ancient dance.

The crow occupies a prominent position in Athabascan folklore. In her "The Atna of Copper River: the World of Men and Animals," Frederica de Laguna reports that "Little Old Crow set the Sun and Moon in the sky and established the Salmon runs . . . the shaman dreams of the creatures of mythology, of Little Old Crow, the Creator . . . thus he obtains his power to imitate them" (1969, pp. 18–19). McKennan gives several Kutchin Raven myths (1965, pp. 90–98). In the spring of 1987 the present writer witnessed a Raven Dance by these Atna of Copper River, when the Chitina Dancers performed at the Native Arts Festival. In the dance, a man attending his first potlatch watches the raven eat. He instructs his fellow hunters to eat their food in like manner. While two or three mime this, a clockwise circle of dancers holds hands and the drummer dances around the inside of the circle counterclockwise.

The Crow Dance among Athabascans past and present may be a reflection of folklore content. Additionally, bearing in mind the prominent role of shamanistic dance, it may be a reflection of the shamans' miming behavior during ritual. Athabascan animal and bird spirits possess aerial fluidity capable of transformations, and are feared. Mime is a means of coming to terms with the spirits and neutralizing this fear. Mime and dance constitute alternative methods of understanding predicament, and of glossing negative and positive experience.

Russian colonization and Hudson's Bay Company trading had goals diametrically opposed to the self-preservation goals of Athabascan traditional society. Early observers reported traditional dance as a quaint curio rather than as a valuable cultural asset to be protected and supported. As modern technology undermined the need for ancient subsistence skills, and as missionaries and teachers subtly implied that the Athabascan language and culture were inferior, ancient heritages such as dance came to be disdained by the new generations. In a world of wage labor and cash economy, federal Social Security and urban migration, many Athabascan saw no meaningful use for traditional dance. It was only with the advent of postwar nativism, land claims, and equal opportunity that Alaskan natives began to regain their ethnic pride and positive self-image. The traditional culture began to be seen as worthy of respect; this included dance. The performance of ancient dances then came to be symbolic of Athabascan Indian "nationhood," of longstanding but ungranted territorial rights, and of the cultural uniqueness of Athabascan childrearing, kinship, social customs, subsistence practices, and mythology.

THE POTLATCH

Apart from the Lower Koyukon Feast for the Dead, the formal social potlatch is the most important contemporary Athabascan ceremonial occasion, and in most potlatches dance occupies a prominent role. In the early 1930s Osgood reported that "The Kachemak Bay Tanaina have potlatches of two kinds, the Big Potlatch and the Little Potlatch. The former is more important, and the giving of it is primarily to honor a person who has died" (1937, p. 149). Osgood goes on to say that "Upon arrival of the opposite moiety, they are entertained by feasting and dancing. The host wears his potlatch costume and at intervals sings potlatch songs in memory of the deceased. The combination of feasting, dancing, and singing lasts for a number of days" (1937, p. 155).

Koyukon Athabascan dancer and writer Poldine Carlo, in her book "Nulato: An Indian Life on the Yukon," writes "Potlatches last for three or four days. Each evening there is singing and washtub dancing" (1978, p. 59). In 1927, Wendell Endicott observed a potlatch at Healy Lake in the Upper Tanana region, and reported that it involved hundreds of blankets as gifts, also rifles, and huge stores of moose meat (1928, p. 104). Athabascan gift-giving is a source of new social links frequently reinforced by the chain of reciprocal gift-giving. Marchiori points out that these are not the cold calculations of a mercantile society, but are imbued with affectiveness. Absence of the counter-gift is seen as a breach of the social pact. Gift-giving is a social response to communal psychological needs, and embodies an intrinsic, ritual symmetry. Some societies possess but a single term for buying or selling, lending or borrowing.

As an Athabascan hunter ages, he develops increasingly ramified relationships through his maturing offspring. At the same time, gift exchanges involve a growing number of persons who live in other communities and are related to him either matrilineally or affinally. He becomes the recipient of an expanding number of gifts through other potlatches. Having progressively more villagers to whom he is obliged to donate gifts and more from whom to borrow, his social status and power gradually increase. Sponsoring communal performances of traditional dance in his village is an intrinsic component of the status-acquiring process and a visible and audible means of demonstrating influence.

Among contemporary Athabascans, the most important form of potlatch is the memorial potlatch given for a revered elder. For example, in 1959 Shem Pete gave a potlatch in Tyonek in memory of Chief Simeon Chickalusian of the Water Clan, known as Tulchina. He composed a song and a dance for the occasion; the present writer made a transcription of the song (in Kari, 1987, p. 59). The Susitna River chief's dance regalia—necklaces, dance-shirt, rattles, and headdress—were passed on to Simeon by Big Chilligan in 1930. Simeon gave this dancewear to Shem Pete in 1957, signifying that Shem is now the traditional chief of the Upper Inlet Tanaina (Kari, 1987, p. 58). In 1977 a funeral potlatch was given for Tanaina chief Mike Alex. When 93-year-old Chief Henry of Huslia died on July 8, 1976, a great potlatch was given for him; he was a celebrated dancer and storyteller.

In 1974 the present writer attended and tape-recorded the funeral potlatch of Chief Dementieff at Nenana. The community hall was crowded with earnest, intense dancers who performed the night long, and the dances were interspersed with the singing of memorial songs, during the performance of which many of the elders wept.

A funeral potlatch is held soon after the notification of death of a relative; the memorial potlatch is held a year or so later, and is yet another stage in the progress of the spirit toward the spirit world. A potlatch requires much preparation and collecting of goods and food. The rural Athabascan are not wealthy, and must make a considerable sacrifice in order to provide the wherewithal for feeding and gifting large numbers of guests. Often this represents years of personal frugality. This is one reason for delaying the memorial potlatch. Another reason is that the immortal spirit requires time to become accustomed to the different diet of the spirit world. Additionally, if the pallbearing and body-dressing debts were immediately paid, the larger, much-antici-pated memorial potlatch would lose its reason for being, and the social bonds in question would be loosened.

Death is of course a rite of passage, an existential transfer from the everyday world to the spirit world. Among the Athabascan, the first spirit—the vindictive spirit—leaves the body at time of death; it is the second spirit that lives on. It is noteworthy that among the southern Athabascan of the American Southwest there is a ghost-chasing cere-mony, during which the vindictive spirit is chased from the village (Marchiori, 1981, p. 74).

Whereas the southern Athabascan have to chase the first spirit, the northern Athabascan have to coax the second spirit. It must be assisted on its multiphase journey, but cautiously, for it experiences loneliness and is looking for a companion with which to travel. Informant Paul Mountain, a Stick Dancer from Nulato, emphasizes this in a tape-re-corded account (Mountain, 1987). If a dead child's eyes remain open, they are glancing around for another child to go as playmate; one must put grease on the hands of the deceased, to make them slippery. One must exercise discretion over when and where to weep around a dead child, for the bereaved's tears adhere to the departing soul, will be visible to the guardians of the spirit world where sorrow is forbidden, and may prevent the dead child's soul from entering.

Athabascan name-avoidance taboos facilitate symbolic separation of the affection bonds, so that normal life for the bereaved may continue. Partly for this same reason, the dressing of the body is entrusted to a less-involved person.

In 19 Nulato potlatch songs (Johnston & Solomon, 1978) the texts overwhelmingly comprise idealization of the dead. This glorifying of the admired qualities of deceased loved ones helps to forestall private misgivings and qualms concerning possible personal negligence and faults which, in the imagination of the bereaved, may have caused the death of the loved one. Village life is hard enough; communal singing of the memorial song and communal dance at the memorial potlatch help to spread this subconscious guilt, diluting it and reducing its para-lyzing effect.

In the early 1970s Guédon observed several formal potlatches among the Upper Tanana, at Tetlin. She writes: "Fringed and beaded skin vests are regarded as highly valuable and are very much admired. Many people wear a special costume for dancing; in most cases the hosts, their close relatives and friends, the drummers and best dancers all dress in colorful dance dresses. During the mourning the dance dress is part of the ceremonialism and serves to identify the host party. The guests put on their dance dress a bit later and only after the first mourning is done" (1974, p. 209).

For many weeks prior to the event, dance composers and song composers rehearse the local village dance troupe in new presentations. This is necessary more for the songs than the dances: the latter rarely involve complex choreography. Dance costumes are made by experienced individuals in the community who specialize in the fine needlework and beadwork involved. "Tetlin, Northway, and Tanacross villages each have a community hall, a large log cabin where people gather for feasting and dancing," writes Guédon (1974, p. 212). Endicott reported that for the 1927 great potlatch of Chief Healy, a special log cabin was built (1928, p. 98).

Three persons figure prominently in the potlatch exchange of goods and hospitality, writes Guédon; these are (1) the giver or host, (2) the person for whom the potlatch is given, and (3) the guest or person *to* whom it is given (1974, p. 215).

There is one large meal of fresh meat per day as long as the potlatch lasts. At Chief Dementieff's funeral potlatch at Nenana in 1974, the present writer noted that long strips of butcher paper in rows on the floor helped define seating for the majority, while really important personages sat together near the entrance. The hosts generally refrain from eating, but sit and visit with the guests.

The formal potlatch (an informal potlatch is known as a Gather Up) is found in most Athabascan communities of more than 20 persons throughout Alaska, but to a greater or lesser degree. It is most common among the Upper Tanana and the Tanana in the east, and among the Lower Koyukon in the west. It is least common among the Kutchin in the north and the Tanaina in the south. The style of dancing and the musical accompaniment vary considerably, not according to language group but according to geographical region. This is because of (1) the vastness of the region in question—1,000 miles in breadth, (2) more than one language group along the same large river may share a dance style, and (3) differential loss of the heritage due to acculturation (the Kutchin) or oppression by the Russians (Tanaina). Contributing to Tanaina dance loss was the opposition of priests of the Russian Orthodox Church, and the extensive highway construction spreading out northward from the large city of Anchorage.

The Athabascan, in conversation, tend to mark the years and decades of their recent past by referring to the occurrence of important potlatches. They will travel great distances in subzero weather to attend. To some extent, but not to the same extent as with the Tlingit Indians of the southwest panhandle, Athabascan adults regard the successful giving of potlatches as promotions in rank and status. There has been a rise and fall in attitudes toward the potlatch as an institution, on the part of Alaskan native organizations. For example, in 1944 the mayor of Hoonah, Harry Douglas, pushed through a municipal ordinance making the potlatch illegal within the city limits. Despite such antipathy, the potlatch prevailed as an important social institution among both the Athabascan and the Tlingit.

Olson reports of Minto that "The social significance of the potlatch can be seen from the fact that it has continued over the years. In the fall of 1967 there was a great potlatch at Minto with visitors from as far away as Tanacross. In March of 1968 two funerals—one at Minto, one at Nenana—were observed with potlatches that attracted people from Tanana, Minto, Nenana, and Fairbanks (1968, p. 144).

Minto and Nenana each had a large memorial potlatch in 1983. Pearce's informant, Paul George of Nenana, states that "Song, dance, potlatching gathering, and memorial potlatch all go together, and they all mean dance" (Pearce, 1985, p. 9). Pearce points out that the Athabascan villages troupes are all named Dancers, not Singers: Nenana Dancers, Minto Dancers, and so on. Additionally, Pearce gives a useful calendar of Athabascan dance (1985, p. 26), which lists (among others) such events as the Minto Spring Carnival in April, the Minto Denaakanaaga Elders' Conference in June, and the Tanana Nuchalawoyya in June.

Among the Tanana Athabascan there are three main types of potlatches: (1) holiday potlatches, (2) funeral potlatches, and (3) memorial potlatches. The Tanana potlatches feature four main social roles for individuals: (1) orator, (2) singer, (3) dancer, and (4) server (Pearce, 1985, p. 219). Behind these performance roles, however, lie the protracted efforts of the hunters who provided the meat, the sewing experts who provided the costumes, and the personal little sacrifices of the relatives and other villagers who provided gifts. The mounting of a potlatch is a community endeavor and a microcosm of Athabascan life, for it brings together subsistence, religion, social interaction, and the arts.

At the end of a memorial potlatch comes the Dance for a Gift; Pearce writes that it is performed to thank all guests who brought gifts (1985, p. 196). Among the Athabascan, dance possesses inherent, transferable valuable benefitting both giver (the dancer) and recipient (honoree). Its value is not transient or of the moment; all that the potlatch dance symbolizes is contained within the essence of the dance, and this essence is carried home by the honorees when they leave the ceremony, as part of their aesthetic and social experience.

THE POTLATCH SONGS

Athabascan song categories vary regionally according to group. Guédon, for the Upper Tanana to the east, reports three types of songs at the potlatch: (1) the potlatch song, (2) the sorry songs, and (3) the dance songs (1974, p. 219). She adds much detail from Northway and Tetlin. Pearce, for the Tanana, reports the same categories, adding much detail from Minto (1985, p. 14). The potlatch song comes first each evening and is also known as the Lucky Song, for if the expected reciprocity occurs it will bring back the money and the meat. However, it may be preceded by the Entrance Song, sung as guests enter.

The sorry songs are mementos of the deceased, composed either for or by said deceased. In the potlatch memorial song composed by Shem Pete for Tanaina Chief Simeon Chickalusian in 1959, the song words extoll admired qualities: "The reputation of your hunting luck is over this whole wide world, the reputation of your wealth is over this whole wide world (music transcribed by Johnston, in Kari, 1987, p. 59).

Sorry songs focus on a distinct, special range of topics: (1) extolling the sex-specific subsistence skills of those who have passed on, (2) death by drowning, accident, or ill-health, and (3) notable events and incidents in community history. The composer of a memorial song derives his or her inspiration from nature while out on the river or up in the mountains; it might be given to the composer, verbally, by the spirit of a bear encountered. Combined with this supernatural aid is the composer's personal relationship with the deceased and the knowledge of his or her life history. Significant events in that person's life may be woven into the memorial song. Later, descendants may add subsequent stanzas incorporating additional family history, so that the song becomes a family record. A memorial song composed by Andrew Paul for Mrs. Dayton in 1922 goes "She left us without her leadership, like orphans." A memorial song composed by Old Toby for his mother in 1902 goes "She used to go out in cold weather to pick berries." A memorial song composed by Chief Henry for George Attla, Sr., in 1968 goes "Might as well make a merry farewell for his good hunting life . . . when will we hear words like his again?" A memorial song composed by Austin Joe of Koyukuk for Andrew Pilot goes "Good luck with the meat-giving animals, good luck with the fur-bearing animals. Remember how he shared his goods? Good fortune surrounded him everywhere he went. He shared it. He had a good old time, sharing it." A memorial song composed by John Dayton for James Demoski in 1923 goes "Remember the great things he shared with us . . . down there we depended on him" (all songs in Johnston & Solomon, 1978). The respected virtues of the deceased are thought, with appropriate propitiation, to be reborn in infants, and these songs constitute a permanent reminder—a tally list—of the remembered qualities.

Among the Athabascan the performance song style of memorial songs resembles highly emotional sobbing. The songs are sad and slow, accompanied by breaking of the voice and weeping, and generally not accompanied by drumming. A form of dance occurs at this time, where a half-circle moves slowly clockwise. The most distinctive feature of sorry songs all the way from the Canadian border in the east to the Lower Yukon in the west, is the hand movement of the women. They clasp large cleaned pelts as a group, holding the top edge as if shaking a rug, and move them up and down rhythmically as if dipping them into some giant washtub. This is well illustrated in an excellent color videotape published by Alaskan ethnographer Curt Madison, "Songs in Minto Life" (1986). The same movement, using scarves stretched between the hands of each dancer, is shown in a rare old photograph taken by Father Julius Jette; it is in the archives of Gonzaga University Library, Spokane (shown in Carlo, 1978, p. 60). The photograph was taken on the banks of the Yukon at Ruby, which lies 50 miles east of Nulato and 100 miles west of Minto. Scarves are common today.

The third song category mentioned by Guédon (1974, p. 219) and by Pearce (1985, p. 14), and plentifully recorded by the present writer, consists of the dance songs, the ones that most concern me here. The most common scale type is the pentatonic without semitones, the most common range is about one octave, and the most common melodic interval is the descending major second. A common melodic motif is that of the descending major triad G-E-C, and there is a distinctive ending pattern noted by Pearce, characterized by a low repeated note approached from above, and in which the drumming and singing get louder and faster (1985, p. 174).

The accompanying drum rhythm consists of unvarying quarter-notes in a continuous, even pulse, the melody providing clues as to where the beginning of each measure lies. Measures consist of uneven groupings of these quarter-notes, in additive combinations such as 4 + 4 + 2 + 6, and so on. The above general features apply for song style among the Upper Tanana, the Tanana, the Atna, and the Lower Koyukon. The Kutchin now use mainly acculturated music.

The Tanaina to the south are a little different. Traditional dance songs are heard occasionally in six main communities: Eklutna (population 30), Nondalton (184), Lime Village (25), Tyonek (232), Stony River (74), and Pedro Bay (20). There are not many surviving knowledgeable elders involved in music; in recent years there were Lily Stump of Tyonek, Pete Kalifornski of Kenai, Shem Pete of Tyonek, and certain others.

The last two are still active in traditional dance and music, and have encouraged others—young and old—to take a renewed interest. In 1974 the present writer taped numerous Tanaina songs at Tyonek on Cook Inlet; Shem Pete moved there and revived the traditional potlatch in 1979.

Tanaina dance songs are fast, usually between 100 and 150 quarter-note pulses per minute, and usually unaccompanied by drumming. Scale use is complex; songs are structured in sections and each section may use a different pentatonic scale, with liberal addition of grace-notes. Song-word elision frequently occurs, and internal vowel change within the text is common—there is virtually a sung pronunciation that stands apart from the spoken pronunciation.

In Tanaina dance songs there is a distinctive use of percussive vocal accents, resulting in a highly effective emotional delivery. This is commonly manifested by the use of "Scottish snap" phrasing, thus:
Percussive vocal accents are also featured at the ends of musical phrases and at song-endings, manifested by a fiercely executed short terminal cut-off on the second beat of a two-beat terminal measure, thus:
. Songs thus end on an offbeat rather than a downbeat, and remind one of French use of terminal schwa in song and poetry, where in speech there would be a silent "e."

With regard to the preservation of Athabascan traditional songs, Oral History and Traditions at the University of Alaska Library is cooperating with the Alaska Native Language Center in cataloguing and indexing 1,200 tapes collected since 1960, but dating back to 1900. These include recordings provided by Athabascan dancers Walter Charlie of Glenallen, Chief Andrew Isaac of Dot Lake, and the aforementioned Chief Shem Pete. Additionally, an original wax cylinder made in Anvik, on the Yukon below Kaltag, in 1925 has come to light at the Smithsonian, and the Federal Cylinder Project is sending a copy of it to Anvik (Pearce, 1986, p. 1). The Federal Cylinder Project is a cooperative effort between the American Folklife Center in the Library of Congress, the Bureau of Indian Affairs, and the Smithsonian. The Anvik recording contains eight songs sung by James Fox, who died in 1927. They are, with composition dates, "The Water Spirit" (1880), "The Fox" (1881), "The Crane" (1882), "The Owl" (1883), "The Woodpecker" (1884), "The Jay" (1885), "The Porcupine" (1886), and "The Crow" (1887). These are probably the earliest recordings of Alaskan Athabascan Songs.

THE DANCE MOVEMENTS AND THE DANCE COSTUMES

In Athabascan dance the dancers sing and dance at the same time. Everyone present participates in this, and there is no separate "choir" as in Eskimo dance, or separate drumming team. The dance leader is the sole drummer, and he possesses more freedom of floor movement than the others. Most dance teams do not consider it necessary to make a formal entrance and exit, as is customary among the Tlingit Indians to the southeast. The dance is initiated by the drummer, who often gives an emphatic nod of the head as he commences beating, singing, and dancing simultaneously. His first movement often consists of one step forward in a deliberate manner, to get the other dancers off to an energetic start. The dance commences at a high energy level and remains that way until its end, with a slight crescendo and accelerando at the conclusion. Its length is determined by the drummer, and consists of numerous repetitions of the short bipartite dance song; each dance is much longer than an Eskimo mimetic dance. The primary immediate goal of the dance and the drumming appears to be what might be referred to as hypnotic drive. Rhythmic auditory driving at the all-night potlatch involves nearly all participants in an intense emotional experience.

As Kealiinohomoku points out, "where dance is consonant with religion, as among Native American societies, dance behavior is an agent for transforming religious ideas to religious emotions" (1981, p. 137). Athabascan potlatches are the main social context for honoring the dead and thereby maintaining good relations with the spirit world. Even a holiday potlatch, unconnected with a funeral, will feature the singing of memorial songs and evince overtones of a religious occasion. This is because the Athabascan do not separate religious ideas from secular ideas—they are inextricably interwoven, and dance expresses this interweaving. "For the Native Americans, dance is perhaps *the* major vehicle over other forms of public worship, for the expression of religious ideas. The correlation of dance with religion among Native Americans is a distinguishing feature of Native American cultures" (Kealiinohomoku, 1981, p. 142). Athabascan dance movements, therefore, symbolize shared beliefs concerning the numerous supernatural beings of the Athabascan spirit world.

First to be discussed are the most characteristic and most common Athabascan dance movements, those of men dancers and of women dancers in communities along an east-west axis reaching from Tetlin and Northway in the east, through Tanacross, Minto, Nenana, and Tanana in the center, to Ruby, Kaltag, and Nulato in the west. Along this almost straight line, only the major villages are named here; there are numerous small communities in the Alaskan interior that fit the dance description that follows. These tradition-oriented Athabascan communities are linked by vast waterways, which provide excellent fishing and also convenient transportation. Traditional fish camps are often set up far from home. There is much intervillage visitation east-west and west-east, and this has resulted, with certain exceptions, in a degree of dance stylistic unity.

The exceptions are that the Lower Koyukon do not feature much dance in which the miming of animal and bird behavior occurs within a closed circle of dancers, and that the eastern groups feature use of the *ganhok* feathered dance staff of office, held and flourished by a dance officer. The eastern groups feature use of the drum, and line dances; the western group does not. The western group features, at special times, imitation of Eskimo dancing, use of Eskimo song style and drumming style, and of the Yupik *apallircuun* feathered dance wand. Costumes tend to vary regionally, with the most colorful being found among the Upper Tanana.

The most widely employed Athabascan women's dance movement is that referred to by Nulato dancer Poldine Carlo as the washtub movement (1978, p. 59), a generic term for the motion women utilize in each of several dance situations possessing different social functions, for example, the holiday potlatch, the funeral potlatch, the memorial potlatch, the gather-up, the Stick Dance, and the urban exhibition dance.

In the washtub movement the trunk is inclined slightly forward and sways from side to side, spending about one second on each side before swaying back in the opposite direction, that is, usually two drumbeats on each side. The two arms are raised in front at chest height, about 12 inches from the body, and move up and down holding a chiffon scarf stretched between them. This is in simulation of the earlier practice of holding and stretching large valuable furs, which today are not always available, or which are quickly sold. The chiffon scarves are also more convenient to carry on the small commuter planes. Bright colors are preferred for the scarves, and the two arms tend to roll the stretched chiffon from side to side as the trunk sways. The movement may have derived its name from its resemblance to former methods of washing clothes, states informant Walter Northway. One Athabascan dancer, who wrote a brief article on washtub dancing, illustrated the article with a drawing of an upturned washtub being beaten. However, the present writer has not witnessed this method of dance accompaniment. The usual drum is a well-made, moosehide frame-drum with thongs around the rear, beaten with a distinctive beater in the shape of a minim note (half-note).

This women's dance movement does not mime clothes-washing; the dance is not about dipping apparel in soapy water. It is simply a motion that the women consider appropriate in that particular social context, and that is culturally consonant with Athabascan attitudes concerning female posture. If considered in the light of the former custom of suspending furs or skins from the hands, the cultural and aesthetic origin of the movement is quite clear. Such skins must be held at the top, must be gripped with the fingers closed, are displayed because of animistic beliefs, and are "brought to life" by being moved up and down, so that the presence of the animal spirits is both visible and tangible.

Athabascan dance movements rarely mime subsistence activities directly, as in Eskimo dance, and once the dance commences there is little variance from the sex-specific common motion. The exception is the circle dance with an actor in the center; this will be described later. The function of most Athabascan dance is the communication of emotions and of abstract concepts. It takes a particular form among the Athabascan because of culture-specific expectations deriving from deep-rooted psychobiological phenomena—are Athabascan women submissive, and was it customary to carry an infant? McKennan writes that "the child faces the rear and the cradle is carried by means of a breast strap" (1965, p. 41). As many anthropologists note, our understanding of ritual processes as social phenomena is incomplete unless articulated with an understanding of ritual behavior as a psychobiological phenomenon.

The head of the woman dancer is tilted slightly downward, not from strong cultural prescriptions regarding the gaze of the eyes, as is the case with Eskimo women. It constitutes an alternative posture mode, projects a superordinary image, and imbues the dance with intensity. The feet are together or slightly apart, but never spread far apart, and body weight may shift from left foot to right foot as the trunk sways. The knees flex slightly, but not to the extent seen in Eskimo dance, and not always together in unison. As the weight shifts to one foot, the heel of the other may rise, but both feet remain on the ground.

The women are generally grouped separately from the men, and together with the men form a half-circle. They may glance at each other as if experiencing pleasurable sensations, and periodically change their forward-inclined posture to one in which the hands are raised higher and the gaze is skyward; this is not executed in unison but occurs "as the spirits move." The women wear decorative beaded headbands with the feather at the rear of the head, fringed moosehide dance tunics bearing detailed ornamental floral beading, and beaded fur bootees or moccasins. For dance, the hair is often worn in two pigtails fastened with decorative beaded discs. On each knee may be a cloth band bearing a "puffball" bobbin, and below each of these may be a circle of 6-inch tassles worn on the shins. From the V-neck of the dance tunic may dangle two or three bobbins.

The most common Athabascan men's dance movement consists of raising the two clenched fists level with the head about 12 inches away, and moving them up and down rhythmically in synchrony with the unchanging quarter-note beat of the drum. As an alternative to clenching the fists, men may grasp an upright colored feather in each hand, and move this up and down. The trunk leans alternately to left and right, and the feet stomp rhythmically up and down. The prevalent form of stomping is to execute two taps of the toe with each foot before changing. There is rarely any leaping from the ground, as in Eskimo dance. One foot usually remains solidly on the ground, bearing body weight.

Men will turn the whole body to the left and then to the right, performing this as a slow arcing rotation of the frontal plane; this is not carried out in unison. Men wear decorative beaded headbands bearing feathers at the front of the head, fringed moosehide dance tunics with floral beadwork designs, fur dance boots with beaded ornamentation, and valuable inherited necklaces of dentalia. Most dance costumes are of a brown color, and are trimmed in several places with hide fringes that "dance" during movement, as part of the visual effect.

The dance shirt of present Tanaina chief Shem Pete was made at Susitna Station about 1900. It was originally owned by Chief Ephim, the last chief of the Susitna Tanaina Athabascan, and Shem Pete's older brother. When Ephim died in 1916, it was potlatched to Big Chilligan. When he died in 1931, it was potlatched to Simeon Chickalusian, the chief at Tyonek. It is a dark blue wool shirt with stand-up collar, long sleeves, and red cuffs. It is fastened with shell buttons and with a red fastening-panel halfway down the front. Above the cuffs are 10 dentalium shells sewn in pairs. Twenty-eight dentalium shells are sewn down the front in pairs.

Chief Shem Pete's dentalium necklace was made at Kroto Creek about 1800. It is made of 39 dentalium shells separated by solid black beads. The attached pendant is made of 119 shells, with 19 in the bottom string and 20 in each of the next five strands. Between each string of shells are 60 opaque red glass beads. The bottom of the pendant is finished in 74 red glass beads and red woolen cloth.

Chief Shem Pete's dentalium wristlets consist of a string of loosely woven red wool folded over and sewn together on three sides. Strung on one side of the fabric are 4 single strands of sinew thread strung with alternating blue and black beads and dentalium shells. Centered on each piece is a shell button. They were made in Tyonek by Ely Stephan in 1905.

Chief Shem Pete's puffin beak rattles consist of thin, round, wooden rods wrapped with braided sinew. Suspended from each rod are 4 bunches of puffin beaks hung on separate rawhide thongs that are joined at one end and woven under the sinew wrappings on the rods. There are 20 puffin beaks on each rod. Feathers are fitted into the beaks. The rattles were originally used by a Tanaina shaman for healing ceremonies.

Chief Shem Pete's eagle feather headdress consists of eagle and goose feathers attached to a red woolen cloth headband with twisted sinew ties. The feathers stand upright, and some quills have fluffs attached to them with sinew. This headdress also was used for shamanistic healing rites.

If there are strangers present among the guests, men dancers will introduce the women dancers to them by name, between dances. The dance leader may call out "This is Ruth, my wife's mother," or "This is Mary, my brother's wife, and this is Sarah, her sister." Often, young toddlers wear dance costume and stand among the dancers near their mothers. Visiting male elders among the audience at a dance exhibition may jump out into the aisles and start dancing, or may join the performing dance team.

For the dancers, village participants, and audience, successive different dances are distinguished mainly by title, tempo, songwords, ancient dedication, and original composer. Each dance possesses its own dance song, the latter being melodically distinctive from other dance songs. Choreographically it may always seem to be the same dance; musically and emotionally it is not.

When the dancing takes place in a crowded community hall, as at an important memorial potlatch, the participants comprise almost the whole community in a tightly packed mass of humanity. They circle the hall as a body in irregular formation, clockwise direction. There is usually a small maneuvering space left in the center, for the drummer who is also the dance leader. He may move with or against the crowd; he provides visible and audible cues for the beginnings and endings of dances.

An important potlatch will last several days, with the dancing extending well into the early hours of each morning. By this time a kind of mass hypnosis has taken over that, together with the incessant pounding of the resonant drum, produces a degree of sensory overload and infects all present with elation and excitement. Such dance involves shifting boundaries of time and consciousness, perceptual distortion, changes in body image, and hypersuggestibility. Dancers may enter a euphoric state that serves as sanctioned "time out" from the problems of everyday life (Hanna, 1988, chap. 3).

Linear dancing for the Athabascan was reported early in the literature, and may be ancient. In the Upper Tanana line dance, there is one row of women and another of men, the two lines facing each other at a distance of about 20 feet. As the drumming commences, the two lines hop toward each other, one foot in front of the other without changing, in a jerky, shuffling gait. The hands are held on the hips. Each line, when about halfway toward the other, crouches down, each participant assuming a squatting position while still advancing. The crouch is only temporary, and the dancers rise slowly from this position, just before the two lines meet. When they meet, they do not bump or touch. The dancers nonchalantly pass through the opposing line, without special gesturing. After passing, the lines crouch again momentarily, and on reaching the extremity of the dance arena, turn and stand facing the other line at a distance, ready to begin again.

If this is a cultural survival of the Kutchin war dance witnessed by Jones (1872, p. 326), it has shown remarkable persistence and has diffused southward from Fort Yukon to the Upper Tanana villages of Tetlin and Northway. This is unlikely, for the Kutchin do not perform this dance. The Kutchin perform acculturated longways sets such as Nihk'iidoo (Eight Couple), in which two lines of alternating men and women begin by facing each other. This type of acculturated dance probably derives from Scottish jigs and reels introduced by Hudson's Bay traders. During fieldwork on the Shetland Islands in 1980, the present writer played tapes of Kutchin fiddling to Tom Anderson and Ian Burns at the town of Lerwick. They knew the tunes and named them; some of the names matched the Athabascan names for the same fiddling tunes.

It is interesting to note that in 1862 among the Canadian Kutchin to the east, Kennicott noted that "The figures were . . . Scottish reels of four and jigs . . . an Indian boy and the fat wife were the best dancers. The music consisted of a very bad performance of one vile unvarying tune, upon a worse old fiddle" (1942, pp. 109–110). The anthropologist Craig Mishler notes that when William Dall visited Fort Yukon in 1867, he observed that many inhabitants of the community were "from the Orkney Islands and the north of Scotland" (Dall, 1870, p. 103, cited in Mishler, 1981, p. 186).

In some regions of Alaska, the possibility of Russian influence should not be overlooked. A recent film on folk dance in the USSR shows several dances in which the participants crouch with hands on hips (Manefield, 1979). At Sitka in southeast Alaska and elsewhere there are enthusiastic amateur touring dance teams of Russian-American origin who keep up the Russian dances by rehearsing them and exhibiting them in Russian costume at dance exhibitions. On his arrival at St. Michael in 1842, Lt. Zagoskin was surprised to find the Yupik Eskimos performing the Cossack jump dance (Zagoskin, 1842–1844, in Michael, 1967, p. 113). Much of southern Alaska came under Russian influence at that time; even today the Russian Orthodox church is predominant in many communities.

The concept of dancing in two opposing lines may have diffused northward from the Atna Athabascan of Copper River. In 1954, Frederica de Laguna's informant described a Copper River dance in which two opposing lines of dancers advance toward each other. The informant stated that the dance went from Copper River to the Tlingit community of Yakutat (de Laguna, 1972, vol. 11, p. 899). In 1977, Tlingit dancer Judith Ramos gave the present writer an essay describing the present-day performance of the dance in Yakutat (Ramos, 1977). Copper River is about 100 miles south of Northway.

The Kutchin Athabascan reside in six main communities: Fort Yukon, Arctic Village, Venetie, Chalkyitsik, Circle, and Birch Creek. For them, Mishler lists five probable types of aboriginal dances, now extinct: (1) dances of celebration to welcome visitors, (2) memorial dances for the deceased, (3) shaman dances, (4) war dances, and (5) dramatic dances enacting traditional narratives.

One of the latter—the Crow Dance—persisted until 1922, the last time it was reported. Mishler considers that "This differential rate of persistence for each dance form illustrates that Gwich'in aboriginal culture was not immediately abandoned but only gradually replaced or transformed by more 'modern' dances backed by European instruments" (1981, p. 57).

Current acculturated dances among the Kutchin include Red River Jig, performed by one couple at a time; Double Jig, for two couples at a time; Four Hand Reel; Brandy (men facing women in parallel rows); Rabbit Dance, with five or six couples per set; Eight Couple, derived from the Highland Reel; Virginia Reel, which is a longways dance with two-handed swings rather than elbow swings; Handkerchief Dance, with the men connected to the women via handkerchiefs; Duck Dance, organized in three-couple sets; Broom Dance, a slow waltz; and Square Dance, performed in a large rectangle (Mishler, 1981, pp. 282–328).

These imported dances completely replaced aboriginal dance many decades ago and are very popular. In 1961 in the Canadian Gwich'in community of Old Crow on the Porcupine River, Asen Balikci noted "eight" and Duck dances (1963, p. 143). They were being performed by elderly Athabascan; their existence indicates a certain territory-wide persistence of the forms, which probably represent parallel development, for the Scottish traders were on both sides of the border.

In the Northern Games at Inuvik witnessed by the present writer in 1974, first and second places in the Fiddling Contest were taken by

David Ruben of Paulatuk and Tapwe Chretien of Yellowknife, with third place going to Noah Akhiatik of Holman Island. The Jigging Contest was won by Emmanuel Felix and Lilly Gruben from Tuk, David Lucas and Rita Allen from Yellowknife, and Alex and Liz Greenland of Inuvik. All the above were Canadian Natives.

The loss, wane, retention, and revival potential of a given cultural component is unpredictable. The cultural filter is one factor; a society already performing linear dances is likely to accept the linear dances of others, particularly if the latter are psychologically associated with prestige items of the contact culture—such as rifles. It is intriguing to note that Mishler, so well versed in Gwich'in music and dance, writes in 1981 that "The old-time fiddle music which once flourished almost everywhere among the Gwich'in but which I personally have seen decline in popularity since 1972 undoubtedly owes its origin to Scottish and Orcadian Hudson Bay Company traders and to French-Canadian voyagers of the mid-nineteenth century" (1981, p. 179). It is intriguing because, in 1987, the fiddling is undergoing expansion, with the older fiddlers like Charlie Peter teaching dozens of young men, and the dances performed more frequently than at any time previously.

Mishler's fieldwork among the Gwich'in ended in 1980. In 1983 the Kutchin fiddlers organized their first Annual Fiddling Festival, traveling to Fairbanks with their dance teams to perform. Every year from that time until 1987, over 60 fiddlers and dancers have traveled annually to Fairbanks for this spectacular Athabascan dance event, which draws large paying audiences over several days, at Eagles Hall. It attracts numerous Canadian Gwich'in fiddlers and dancers, who travel considerable distances. The present writer takes his university classes to it annually as part of an ethnomusicology course.

Whence originated the stimulus for revival? It was surely the very decline of which Mishler writes. Sensing the decline, and sensing the threat to a way of life that had long been theirs, the remaining fiddlers and dancers organized a strategy that would inject their tradition with new vitality. The strategy was one of arranging statewide exhibition and public exposure. Since that time, the fiddlers and their dancers have become known across the United States, appearing via film and video on television, and attracting new audiences. This in turn attracts more young Gwich'in to the form, who as their expertise matures make their substantial contribution to the borrowed heritage.

The Athabascan fiddling that accompanies the aforementioned dances is different to the playing of a trained violinist. The bow movements are extremely short, the bow is held at a steep slant, and the high pressure produces a scraping tone quality. The violin neck sits low in the crook of the left hand, and the violin neck points toward the floor. Double-stops are played with one left-hand finger, including double slides. The fiddlers invariably tap their feet loudly; this provides an intentional percussive accompaniment to the fiddling and aids the dancing. The music consists of continuous running eighth-notes, in typical Scottish folk fiddling style, except that Athabascan tunings are used. A noticeable harmonic characteristic is that the music is strongly triadic, and switches down a whole tone to the triad lying a major second below, later switching up again, as in, for example, the shanty "What Shall We Do With The Drunken Sailor" (not, incidentally, used by the Kutchin). Most of the fiddlers purchase inexpensive instruments, but some own handmade violins made in Alaska by self-taught Frank Hobson, Eskimo violin maker of Glenallen, born in 1901, now deceased.

To turn now to the Athabascan traditional closed circle dances, which feature the miming of an animal in the center, it is seen that these occur mainly among the Upper Tanana and Tanana in the east. They are performed also by the Chitina Dancers and the Copper Center Dancers of Copper River in the southeast interior, close to Tlingit territory. Informants such as Paul George of Nenana state that these dances originate from the animals in question, being transmitted to the Athabascan through dreams and visions while out in the foothills and on the lakes.

The closed circle dances divide into two main categories: (1) hunting episodes, and (2) legends and myths. In the Ground Hog Dance at Chitina, men dancers representing hunters encircle Ground Hog, who lunges at them aggressively. The hunters kill and eat Ground Hog. In a hunting mime performed north of Chitina at Copper Center, the Copper Center Dancers mime Spearing the Bear, featuring two dancers in the center of the circle. One is the dead Bear, and the other is Crow, picking at Bear's carcass and cawing loudly.

The Chitina Dancers present the Duck Clan Dance, in which mime depicts the story of Duck Clan Woman who marries a man from a different clan. Their outlook on life was so contrasting that they could not get along. In leaving the man and returning to her clan, Duck Clan Woman steals her child, but leaves certain items of clothing behind as a symbol of her actions. The husband comprehends her meaning and does not follow her.

Most of the known closed circle dances are shared by the Upper Tanana, the Tanana, and the Copper Center and Chitina Athabascan. Circle dances are common among many American Indian groups in the Lower Forty Eight; they may have been influenced by the circle made around a fire at night, after a day spent hunting. They may be inspired by the act of hunting, for in the period prior to the advent of the rifle it was necessary during the finishing-off stage for several hunters to encircle and spear the wounded animal. It should be noted that, when performed in a circle, the series of sequential actions comprising the mime will not easily be visible to an audience; in a dance exhibition context this partly nullifies the communicative function of the closed circle dance. Aboriginally, such a dance was primarily for the participants. It is noteworthy that Eskimo mimetic dance, which reproduces story details pictorially, is performed mainly in straight lines facing the frontal plane.

In much the same way that the Fort Yukon fiddlers and dancers endeavored to revive their 158-year-old musical form, Kutchin linguist and teacher Katherine Peter in 1980 founded the Fort Yukon Traditional Dancers, a revivalist group that has referred to the anthropological record and now performs the Crow Dance, in which the team circles and bites at one in the center who is miming being a fish (this is the dance witnessed by Mason in the early 1920s). Peter's group also performs the linear War Dance, the Legend of the Hunter and the Shaman, and the Gathering Dance. The team possesses 32 members and is stimulating renewed interest in traditional dance in the Fort Yukon region.

It is ironic that elements among the great American public tend to attach a degree of stigma to intentionally revived ethnic art forms, while the non-Western people who revive them do not. This constitutes a subtle form of paternalism: "where is our noble savage?" One of the most vital American Indian dances on the continent today, and certainly the most vital Indian dance in Alaska, is the Lower Koyukon Feast for the Dead (*hi'o* Stick Dance). It was suppressed with fervor by the Jesuits, and revived with equal fervor by the Lower Koyukon Athabascan.

THE LOWER KOYUKON ATHABASCAN FEAST FOR THE DEAD

Father Loyens provides an excellent account of Stick Dance history in his "The Koyukon Feast for the Dead" (1964). Marchiori provides an excellent contemporary description based upon his 1975 visit to Nulato in company with the present writer, at the time of the annual Stick Dance (1981). Marchiori additionally provides a lengthy culture-and-personality analysis of context, function, and meaning, some of it strongly Freudian, and some of it Frazerian. It is nevertheless a unique contribution to Lower Koyukon ethnography.

The present writer's most knowledgeable Stick Dance informant is Paul Mountain of Nulato, who has attended and participated in numerous annual performances of the ceremony, and in addition made a study of its details. The Stick Dance is usually held in March, at either Nulato

(1980 population, 350), or Kaltag (247); the two villages alternate. In some years it is not given due to insufficient economic resources; in some years (rarely) it is given at both villages. The event is a highly charged emotional and religious occasion, and perhaps for this reason it was frowned upon by certain of the early Jesuit priests. More tolerant priests came later, and the rite returned. Loyens, who wrote the best historical account, was unique in that he was a tolerant Jesuit priest for the region and a University of Alaska professor of anthropology.

The Stick Dance belies its simple name in that it is a massive, ceremonial complex involving mourning, spirit-placation, pole-dancing, drumming, singing, the wearing of dance masks, gift-giving, ceremonial dressing, and the feasting of 1,500 guests who arrive from neighboring and distant Athabascan communities.

For a year prior to the event the bereaved womenfolk mounting the Stick Dance make decorative beaded dance regalia and fine hunting garb with which to dress the small group of honored guests who ceremonially and mystically assume the identity of the deceased. For several weeks prior to the event the village hunters and the relatives of the sponsors amass large quantities of moose and other fresh meat for the week-long potlatching. For a month or two prior, women of the village carry hot plates of food to the honored guests in their homes; this food consists of the favorite fare of the deceased—their preferred dishes. The honored guests have been the pallbearers and the dressers of the body; knowing the food preferences of the deceased, they will say "I long for some beaver . . . I yearn for some bear." Mountain (1987, p. 1) states that this act simulates feeding of the spirits of the deceased.

When the special week arrives, an evening potlatch is held in the community hall every day, with the singing of slow memorial songs followed by traditional dance employing the customary washtub hand movement. Vast quantities of cooked meat are carried into the hall—far more than can be eaten. It is impolite to refuse this food, which is extended in large cauldrons to each person seated by the butcher paper on the floor. It is, however, permissible to take the uneaten food shares home. Small samples of food are placed in the fire as an offering to the spirits of the deceased (Esmailka, 1974). If the flames burn intensely, the spirits are ordering more titbits. If the flames are dull, the spirits are content.

On Friday, after the evening feasting is over and the pots have been cleared, the large body of main participants, comprising most of the Nulato population, return to the hall adorned in their fine dance tunics, beaded moccasins, and feathered headdresses. Mountain (1987, p. 2) states that in former times caribou antlers were used. Marchiori describes the wearing by older women of headdresses that bear a metal framework supporting antlerlike arrangements of feathers (1981, p. 79).

Slow, sad mourning songs and slow washtub dance movements are then performed to the rhythmic accompaniment of a pair of wooden clappers about 2 feet longer, beaten together by one of the men singers. These are followed by the thirteen "secret" songs that must not be sung at any other time. An ancient community legend relates the supernatural origin of these songs; they welcome the spirits into the hall. When the spirits are in, a thick circle of people forms around the perimeter of the inside of the hall, and the *hi'o* Stick is brought in. The *hi'o* is a spruce pole cut down by the men who are the honored guests, and stripped and decorated by women. The decoration consists of colored silk ribbons and fine, valuable local furs. Mountain states that considerable pains were taken to obtain real silk ribbon (1987, p. 2). The Stick is carried around the hall by men and women dancers to the accompaniment of song. There is no drum use until the last day. The *hi'o* Stick is set up in the center by being attached to a high skylight. Nulato dancer Paul Mountain considers that the pole is a link between the living and the dead (1987, p. 3). The men dance round it in an inner circle, and the women in an outer circle. The Stick Dance proper begins when the assembled participants form wheeling rows of dancers around the pole, moving clockwise and singing. The dancers are joined together by linked arms. Any gifts brought in after this point are seized by the wheeling dancers and danced around the pole to "consecrate" them, any premium furs being added to those hung on the *hi'o*. Gifts are sometimes rolled inside long rolls of calico, and danced thus around the pole, this symbolic linkage of the dancers replacing the linking of arms.

In the early hours of Saturday morning, the young male dancers strip the pole of furs and ribbons, climb it, take it down, dance it around the hall, dance it around the village, bring it back, and re-erect it. Midday Saturday it is taken down again, broken into pieces, and thrown onto the frozen Yukon River. It is said that whichever way the pieces point, that will be where the next Stick Dance will be held.

On Saturday evening (which is the penultimate evening), the gifts of blankets, furs, and other useful items are piled along one side of the hall; too modest a gift is thought to demean the recipient. The honored guests are fed; each with a brand-new bowl. The feeding must be ample, for the journey of the deceased persons' spirits is a long one. The nourishment must last the passage through the forest's underbrush and the various stages of ascent and descent. The sponsors then stand solemnly in a group to one side, while behind a green stretched canvas screen the honored guests change into new, lavish clothing provided by the relatives of the deceased. These guests must stand on a rug that separates them from earth. Mountain states that the dressing is seen as reincarnation of the deceased (1987, p. 5). The new clothing includes handmade rabbitskin parkas, calfskin boots with beaded tops, moosehide mittens, and hand-knitted socks with patterned tops. The old clothes are put into a large laundry bag and struck three times against the banks of the Yukon, to kill any lurking presence in the bag. The dressed guests stand with bowed heads for all to behold in wonderment. They exit without looking up, for an upward glance would allow the exiting spirits to take a living person with them. The spirits are now leaving the village forever. The gifts are then distributed to as many Stick Dance participants as possible, which takes about 4 hours. To facilitate maximum distribution, furs may be cut up into strips which will serve as ruffs.

On Sunday morning the honored guests make formal house visits, shaking hands with residents. On Sunday evening occurs the final ceremony, which is really separate from the Stick Dance proper. It is called the Clean Up Potlatch, and features Eskimo-style drumming, dancing, and singing, plus a special dance with feathered dance wands, which are wielded by participants called the Pointers of the Mask Dance; they sit on upturned Blazo crates.

First, some participants enter the hall with gifts, which are deposited across a suspended screen which lies over a long stretched rope. Then the drummer commences beating a single frame-drum, using Eskimo 5/8 and 7/8 rhythms. Women enter the hall carrying plates of food, which they put down temporarily near the screen. They then perform Eskimo-style mimetic dance motions to the accompaniment of Eskimo *ay-yai-yangu* song vocables, while the Pointers wave their feathered dance wands. There are two male Pointers, one at each end of the screen. They are the counterpart of the Yupik dance-leader who waves a dance staff near kneeling Yupik dancers at an Eskimo inviting-in. After the women have performed their Eskimo dancing, the roles are reversed, with the women wielding the dance wands and the men bringing in plates of food. Some of the dancers wear dance masks, and perform comic antics like Eskimo joking cousins at the inviting-in. The women use graceful, curving hand motions, while the men holler and stomp, flailing the fists. This mimickry of Eskimo dance behavior is considered very humorous, and is the cause of much laughter. When the two groups have completed this phase, the food is taken up and eaten by all, and the ceremony is over.

The aforegoing Mask Dance is not the only masquerade among the Lower Koyukon. A Mask Dance is performed outdoors on January 2 each year. In Nulato and Kaltag a canvas is loaded onto a sled and carried to each house by masked dancers who shake it. Food donations are collected in the canvas and taken to the hall for a potlatch. Mishler has shown convincingly that the Koyukon Athabascan use of dance masks came from the Yupik Eskimo of the St. Michael region (1974b, p. 5).

The Athabascan traditionally have a great fear of the numerous spirits in their human and natural environment. The Stick Dance helps to neutralize this fear. Dance ethnologist Hanna points out that "Dance may recount through kinetic discourses anticipated events that have potential anxiety or feared consequences. Dancing these events may help the individual to distance them and make them less threatening" (1988, chap. 2, p. 2). The act of dancing potlatch gifts around the *hi'o* Stick and of wearing comic dance masks at the Clean Up Potlatch may function in a placatory manner to establish a benign ambience between the dancers and the spirits, reducing apprehension and providing reassurance that all is well.

During the Stick Dance the names of the deceased cannot be mentioned; this taboo lasts until the week-long ceremonies are over. Their worldly goods are distributed, the recipients being merely intermediaries who receive some of the deceased persons' admired qualities along with the gifts. The lavish clothing of the honored guests serves the spirits well in the next world, for bringing finery from the old world establishes their status in the new. As the pallbearers and body-dressers take off their old clothes to receive new, they shed their identities and enter a transitional no-man's land of liminality, which they quit as they redress in ceremonial garb. Marchiori considers that the Stick Dance is an institutionalized prolongation of the mourning period during which the spirits pass through transitional stages, becoming distanced, and that the social oblivion of the deceased is accompanied by the social rebirth of the widow, who can then remarry (1981, p. 103).

The Stick Dance possesses several important social and religious functions. It lays to rest the wandering spirits of the deceased, and allows the bereaved to repay mortuary obligations. It provides for useful retention of the deceased's best qualities and skills, through a mystical transfer of identity to prominent local hunters—a sort of community reinvestment of "capital." It ends the long period of mourning and frees the survivors so that they can continue to face life. It allows villagers to repay various debts old and new, by contributing food and gifts toward the extensive potlatching. It provides an opportunity for nonrelatives to augment prestige by demonstrating liberality where there may be no obligation. The propitiation placates the spirits of the dead and also facilitates their passage through the corridors of time and space.

It provides an occasion for talented and creative dance-leaders to compose special dances and songs, and it is a cathartic release from winter confinement. Lastly, the momentous socioreligious drama brings together relatives and trading partners from distant Athabascan villages and reinforces social and economic ties between these villages.

DANCE TEAM SOCIAL NETWORKS

Many extended families retain and sustain their social cohesion and trade interdependence through participation in the community dance team, passing membership on from generation to generation. The Tanacross/Northway Dancers are one of the oldest established and most traditional of the Athabascan dance teams. Guédon noted their conservatism and cultural viability (1974, pp. 219–226). The members are Walter Northway, Lily Northway, Steven Northway, Emma Northway, Oscar Issac, Martha Isaac, Chief Andrew Isaac, Annie Sam, Ida Sam, and others. There are three generations of Northways here, the oldest of whom is 112 years old.

The Nenana Dancers comprise Paul George, Selena George, Winnie Charlie, Brian Charlie, Karen McManus, Dianna McManus, Tim McManus, Deanna Richards, Norman Richards, Rucky Richards, Louis Beltz, Amanada Beltz, and others. Another old established dance group, the Minto Dancers, comprise Charlie Titus, Sr., Annie Titus, Elsie Titus, Robert Titus, Denise Titus, Jon Davis, Rosie Davis, Evelyn Alexander, Melanda Alexander, Bobby Charlie, Norma Charlie, Randy Charlie, Angie Charlie, Keith Charlie, Calvin Charlie, Kathy Charlie, Rodney Charlie, Neil Charlie, Geraldine Charlie, Solomon Peter, Lorna Peter, and others.

The Kaltag Dancers comprise Cecilia Solomon, Garith Solomon, Daniel Solomon, Francis McGinty, Evelyn McGinty, and others. Involvement in the community dance team is thus a family avocation and reinforces the traditional kinship system by cementing centrifugal allegiances and, during the current period of rapid social change, providing a forum where kin cooperate in a traditional activity.

Membership in a dance team consumes time and effort, in a subsistence society where there is much hard labor to carry out in obtaining, skinning, cleaning, and preparing meat and fish. Long hours must be devoted to intricate beadwork that tests the eyes under poor light, and to sewing elaborate fringed and beaded regalia. Nevertheless, numerous Athabascan tradition dance groups are thriving. Membership in them brings rewards in the form of prestige, potlatch gifts, and subsidized air travel to urban centers for sightseeing and shopping. Many dance team members have aged relatives who are in hospitals or old folks' homes in urban centers; travel to a dance festival enables them to visit these relatives and to keep them up-to-date on news from back home.

The mere act of dancing embodies pleasurable sensations and brings aesthetic and emotional satisfactions; it also accommodates creativity needs. Performing traditional dance in the community hall uniquely epitomizes Athabascan-ness and brings with it a sense of belonging. Hanna points out that "Groups may turn to their cultural roots when confronted with the stress of change and negative contact with other groups" (1988, chap. 7, p. 1). At statewide Native congresses and political conferences to decide the future of Native lands when the present agreement runs out in 1991, Athabascan traditional dance functions as a nativistic emblem of group solidarity. It intrinsically (i.e., not necessarily with mime) transmits the message that there is to be no compromise on Indian rights.

In the early 1970s the present writer visited Chief Andrew Isaac at Dot Lake, near the Athabascan community of Tanacross. The chief described how Bureau of Land Management agents had been to his town council meeting, and thumped the table to demand right-of-way concessions for white hunters along ancient Athabascan river banks and trap lines. He described how the Indians around the table wept, refusing to comply, and afterward held a potlatch with traditional dancing, at which they symbolically affirmed their solidarity in maintaining their customary way of life.

The cultural survival of traditional dance within a given village, and the retention of the community dance team concept, is sometimes due to the enthusiasm and convictions of one dedicated individual. In 1979, Chief Shem Pete moved back to the isolated village of Tyonek on the far side of Cook Inlet, where dance had waned. Rallying those elders who still remembered the ancient dance songs in the indigenous language, and teaching the songs to a new generation, Shem Pete successfully organized the Tyonek Dancers and began performing at traditional potlatches. In so doing, he instilled a renewed sense of worth among residents, and evoked increased respect for the elders on the part of the young.

THE PROPRIETORY NATURE OF ATHABASCAN MEMORIAL SONGS

Athabascan villages have in a sense been placed off-limits to casual white visitors; the Tanana Chiefs organization has issued a fieldwork application form called Procedure for Agencies Seeking Information on

Villages within the Tanana Chiefs Region. Completing this form leads to a procedure in which the proposed investigator must state clearly his purpose, method, parameters, and expected results. It must, for instance, be shown that no other means of obtaining the desired information is available.

The Tanana Chiefs screening committee then contacts the proposed village, and informs the town clerk that Tanana Chiefs have been approached in good faith. It is then up to the town council whether the research visit should proceed. Advance notice is called for, and the Tanana Chiefs organization insists that copies of the results of research be supplied to the relevant town council.

The appropriateness of this screening procedure becomes apparent when the proprietory nature of many Athabascan songs and dances is taken into account. In the past, anthropologists may show up from the Lower Forty Eight, coming to a remote, traditional community, without having sought permission or given due notice, and then proceed to unintentionally disrupt social relations. In one instance, the researcher allied himself with a village official and proceeded to visit homes and ask questions with the use of this official as intermediary, only later to discover that the official was in severe disrepute in the village for dereliction of duty. Such outsiders sometimes coax and persuade dance-leaders into giving their time during busy seasonal subsistence periods such as the summer salmon runs, merely because it suits the academic timetable. They obtain songs, dance artifacts, and filming opportunities, without fair compensation for the subsistence time lost. They take the songs, artifacts, tapes, videotapes, and notebooks away, and the informants hear no more.

Tanana Chiefs now require that the village in question be provided with copies of such tapes, and with any published findings. It is this more reasonable procedure that has led in part to the Kutchin revival of traditional group dance, for the historical record is now in the local library for all to see. In 1974 the present writer returned to the village of Yakutat seven reels of audio tape that had been missing for 20 years, and that were much needed as mementos of the deceased.

Athabascan dance is not as proprietory as that of the Tlingit, who once used songs and dances as dowry for marriageable maidens, as compensation for drownings, and as trade items. The Athabascan dance composer marks special occasions by making a new dance, the supernatural inspiration for which he obtains via some unusual encounter in the natural environment, such as a bear appearing to nod, a bird that appears to be conversing in song, or a fish that seems to glow brightly. It may be for a memorial potlatch, an Alaskan governor's inauguration, or the dance team's out-of-state performance at the Spokane World Fair. Some Alaskan Native dance teams went to the 1984 Olympics at Los Angeles.

The new dance is run through at rehearsals; team members make any special "animal" costumes required. The dance enters the village repertoire, is performed before neighboring villages, and may be borrowed by these villages. This is permissible on the condition that the composer be credited at the time by announcing his identity, and by communicating the original dedication of the dance.

More proprietory than these are the old songs and dances that serve as mementos of deceased forefathers. A revered hunter is remembered either by the song he composed for a special occasion, or by a song composed in honor of him before or after his death. The song is associated with a dance in that the potlatch is the proper context for presenting the song, and optimum performance is where the old women do their washtub dance while the song is presented. The songwords for such a dance eulogize the deceased's best qualities, notably those relating to his hunting and fishing skills and the care with which he provided for his family. Inheritance of the song in question constitutes inheritance of the revered ancestor's attributes; performance of the song and of the associated dance mystically embodies the spiritual essence of the deceased—the magic of music helps to transfer it to the living. The song and the dance become a permanent reminder of his social and cultural achievements, and will later be performed at the memorial potlatch of their inheritor.

During the performance of a proprietory memorial song, the sequence of hand-and-body movements may appear to be the same as in any other performance, but that is not the point. The set of associated images is specific. The intellectual and emotional significance of the dance derives from its laudatory songwords, its sociohistorical origin, its ancestor-specific authorship, and from its patronal and patriarchal dedication. During performance the descendants of the dedicatee weep while sitting or dancing; the singing is extremely plaintive, with much burying of the head in the hands. There appear to be strong culture-specific elements at work, revealed in the high level of emotional response. However, there are also biological and physiological factors involved in this response.

Music is strongly associated with meaningful recall. Pitch and rhythm are received through the reticular system and transmitted to the cortex. The ultimate auditory receptor is located in the temporal lobe; the temporal lobe is close to that part of the brain which stores information related to perceptual judgement. Cyrus has shown that stimulation

Plate 1. Dance-leader Walter Northway of the Tanacross/Northway Dancers shows the large moosehide Athabascan drum and 'minim' beater.

Plate 2. Taken at the 1972 Lower Koyukon Athabascan Feast for the Dead, this photograph shows some of the rows of circling, wheeling dancers. Note the distinctive feathered headbands, which symbolize caribou antlers.

Plate 3. Tanana Athabascan dancers, showing typical dance costume.

Plate 4. Tanana Athabascan women dancers using feathers to extend movement into space.

of the temporal lobe evokes a high level of recall (1966, pp. 45–52). This may be one reason why music that was learned or heard at some meaningful event in one's past possesses the ability to produce strong emotional response years later.

The music of a given society comprises a discreet configuration of sounds unique to that society, by virtue of that society's distinctive sociocultural history. This configuration of sounds results from and is clearly identified by its particular combination of scales, intervals, melodic contours, and rhythms. More significantly, an accompanying set of learned meanings is attached to those sounds. During social and biological maturation, an individual must learn both the configuration of sound and the meanings with which those sounds have been imbued. Once learned, the configuration constitutes not only the musical heritage of a people, but a set of personal, nostalgic flashbacks and a family history.

This may be said to be accomplished as follows. Human neural tissue is by nature continuously active, with its own characteristic rhythms and synchronies of firing sequences, which can be recorded for the infant from the moment of birth. These patterns, which form a basic substratum of neural activity, are consistently broken into by sensory stimuli such as dance and music. Instead of supporting the rhythmic, long, slow waves already being discharged at birth, the internalization of the musical sounds has the opposite effect; it breaks up the established firing sequences and gradually changes them through life (Robertson-De-Carbo, 1974).

Melodies learned in one's past are permanently encoded with the meanings that came with them, and replay of those melodies brings on powerful recall of the emotional environment in which those melodies were originally embedded. Today, during the slow, sad songs and dances of the memorial potlatch, friends and descendants of the dedicatee frequently are overcome with sorrow, and are comforted by those seated nearby. To them, it is almost as if the deceased, in their fine potlatch dance tunics, exerted a strong mystical presence at the event, the song and the dance crystalizing their soul-essence. This all-permeating association of the music with the deceased is the basis for its proprietory nature; the music belongs to the descendants to the extent that the memory of and genetic endowment of the deceased belongs to the descendants, albeit the proprietoryness is not formalized.

SUMMARY

The cultural persistence of Alaskan Athabascan traditional dance is seen to vary not with language distribution but by geographical region.

The viability of the traditional form is strongest among the Upper Ta-nana near the Canadian border, where contact did not occur until the late 1800s. It is also strong among the Tanana and the Atna of Copper River. Survival of traditional dance traits is weakest among the Kutchin to the north, where the ancient forms are extinct. Reels, jigs, and fiddling were introduced there in the mid-1800s, and flourish, having recently undergone new impetus. The Tanaina of Cook Inlet and surrounds were influenced first by the Russian Orthodox church and then by prox-imity to the city of Anchrorage, with its spreading highway system; they have lost much of their heritage.

The Lower Koyukon, although long influenced by the Jesuits, cele-brate the Feast for the Dead (*hi'o* Stick Dance), which is the major Ameri-can Indian dance event in present-day Alaska. It possesses many im-portant social and religious functions, the most prominent of which are the termination of mourning and the release of the deceased's spirit.

The formal potlatch is the most common social context for Athabas-can traditional dance, where it merges with feasting, singing, and gift-giving in validating the fulfillment of social obligations and in marking community events. Traditional dance involves mainly hand and trunk movements, which are different for men and women, and occurs mainly in a half-circle, accompanied by a single drummer.

Distinctive, sex-specific frontier-style fringed dance costumes are worn, together with feathered headdresses. In the east and southeast there are closed-circle animal mime dances and line dances; both are probably of ancient origin.

Borrowing from the Eskimo population is seen only in the lower Koyukon region, where the final phase of the Stick Dance features Eski-mo-style dancing, drumming, singing, and mask use.

In many communities the dance team comprises members of old established families, and functions as a social network in which social, economic, and aesthetic roles are played out, allegiances are reinforced, and status is acquired and validated.

REFERENCES

Allen, Henry T. (1900). A military reconnaissance in Alaska, 1885. In *Compilation of narratives of explorations in Alaska* (pp. 411–484). Washington, DC:

Balikci, Asen. (1963). *Vunta Kutchin social change: A study of the people of Old Crow, Yukon Territory*. Ottawa: Northern Coordination and Research Centre.

Carlo, Poldine. (1978). Nulato: An Indian life on the Yukon. Fairbanks, AK:

Cyrus, A. (1966). Music for receptive release. *Journal of Music therapy, 3*, 45–52.

Dall, William. (1870). *Alaska and its resources*. Boston: Lee and Shepard.

de Laguna, Frederica. (1969). The Atna of Copper River, Alaska: The world of men and animals. *Folk, 11/12*, 17–26.

Endicott, Wendell. (1928). *Adventures in Alaska and along the trail.* New York: Frederick A. Stokes.

Esamilka, Violet. (1974). *The Nulato Stick Dance.* Unpublished MS, Music Department, University of Alaska.

Guédon, Marie-Françoise. (1974). *People of Tetlin, why are you singing?* Mercury series, no. 9. Ottawa: National Museum of Man.

Hanna, Judith L. (1979). Toward a cross-cultural conceptualization of dance and some correlate considerations. In J. Blacking (Ed.), *The performing arts.* The Hague: Mouton.

Hanna, Judith L. (1988). Dance and stress: Resistance, reduction, and euphoria. New York: AMS Press.

Hippler, Arthur. (1974). The psychocultural significance of the Alaska Athabascan potlatch ceremony. *The Psychoanalytic Study of Society, 6,* 204–234.

Johnston, Thomas F., Solomon, Madeline, Jones, Eliza, & Pulu, T. (1978). *Koyukon Athabascan dance songs.* Anchorage: National Bilingual Materials Development Center.

Jones, Strachan. (1872). The Kutchin tribes. In *Annual Report, 1866* (pp. 320–327). Washington, DC: Smithsonian Institution.

Kari, James. (1987). *Shem Pete's Alaska.* Fairbanks, AK: Native Language Center, University of Alaska.

Kealiinohomoku, Joann. (1981). Dance as a rite of transformation. In C. Card (Ed.), *Ethnomusicology II: A tribute to Alan P. Merriam.* Indiana University: Ethnomusicology Publications.

Kennicott, Robert. (1942). Journal, in J. A. James, *The first scientific expedition of Russian America.* Evanston: Northwestern University Press.

Kimball, S. T. (1960). Introduction. In Van Gennep, *The Rites of Passage.* Chicago: University of Chicago Press.

Kluckhohn, Clyde. (1968). Myths and rituals: A general theory. In Georges (Ed.), *Studies on mythology.* Homewood,   : Dorsey Press.

Krauss, Michael. (1975). *Alaska's Native languages and their present situation.* People paper. Fairbanks, AK: University of Alaska.

Loyens, William. (1964). The Koyukon Feast for the Dead. *Arctic Anthropology, 2*(2), 133–148.

Madison, Curt. (1986). *Songs in Minto life.* Videocassette. Manley Hot Springs,   : Madison.

Manefield, Thomas. (1979). *A people's music: Soviet style.* 16-mm color film. Journal films.

Marchiori, Mario. (1981). *The Stick Dance.* Unpublished doctoral dissertation for Centre d'Etudes Arctiques, Paris. MS in the University of Alaska Library (E78D2M3213).

Mason, Michael H. (1924). *The Arctic forests.* London: Hodder and Stoughton.

McKennan, Robert A. (1965). *The Chandalar Kutchin.* Montreal: Arctic Institute of North America, Paper No. 17.

Michael, Henry N. (1967). *Lt. Zogoskin's travels in Russian America, 1842–1844.* Toronto: University of Toronto Press.

Mishler, Craig. (1974a). *Music of the Alaska Kutchin Indians* (Record and booklet). Folkways Records (FE4070).

Mishler, Craig. (1974b). *The origin and meaning of the Lower Koyukon Feast for the Dead.* Paper presented at the Alaska Anthropological Association annual meeting, Anchorage.

Mishler, Craig. (1981). *Gwich'in Athabascan music and dance: An ethnography and ethnohistory*. Unpublished doctoral dissertation for the University of Texas, Austin.

Mountain, Paul. (1987). *The Stick Dance* (tape recording and MS). Music Department, University of Alaska.

Murray, Alexander. (1910). *Journal of the Yukon, 1847–48* (L. J. Burpee, Ed.). Ottawa: Publications of the Canadian Archives, no. 4.

Olson, W. M. (1968). *Minto, Alaska: Cultural and historical influences on group identity*. Unpublished master's thesis, University of Alaska, Fairbanks.

Osgood, Cornelius. (1936). *Contributions to the ethnography of the Kutchin*. Yale University Publications in Anthropology, no. 14, New Haven, CT.

Osgood, Cornelius. (1937). *The ethnography of the Tanaina*. Yale University Publications in Anthropology, no. 16, New Haven, CT.

Pearce, Tony Scott. (1985). *Musical characteristics of Tanana Athabascan dance songs*. Unpublished master's thesis, University of Alaska, Fairbanks.

Pearce, Tony Scott. (1986). Historical Athabascan music recordings. *Alaskan Folk and Traditional Arts Association Newsletter, 1*(1), 1.

Radcliffe-Brown, A. (1952). *Structure and function in primitive society*. Glencoe, IL: Free Press.

Ramos, Judith. (1977). Yakutat Tlingit dances. MS, Music Department, University of Alaska, Fairbanks.

Robertson-Decarbo, Carol E. (1974). Music as therapy: A bio-cultural problem. *Ethnomusicology, 18*, 35.

Ross, Bernard. (1861). Letter from Fort Simpson, April 10, 1861. Washington, DC: Smithsonian Institution Archives, National Museum of Natural History.

Szwed, John F. (1970). Afro-American musical adaptation. In *Afro-American Anthropology*. New York: Free Press.

Turner, Victor. (1965). Ritual symbolism, morality, and social structure among the Ndembu. In M. Fortes and G. Dieterlen (Eds.), *African systems of thought*. London: Oxford.

Whymper, Frederick. (1868). *Travel and adventure in the Territory of Alaska*. London: John Murray.

Zagoskin, L. A. (1842–1844). *The travels and explorations of Lt. Zagoskin*. Moscow: State Publishing House, 1956. (For new, 1967 translation, see Michael, Henry N.)

13

THE CEREMONIAL ROOTS OF TLINGIT DANCE

Thomas F. Johnston

This is a study of the role of Tlingit traditional dance in southeast Alaska. Month-long periods of fieldwork in 1974, 1975, and 1980 were funded by the National Endowment for the Humanities. Preparation of this and other papers was facilitated by sabbatical leave from the University of Alaska.

Tlingit dance occurs within three main social contexts: (1) the memorial potlatch in the home village upon the death of a relative, (2) the southeastern Alaska seasonal Native Brotherhood convention in a chosen Tlingit township, and (3) the seasonal statewide Native dance exhibition and art festival.

Within the memorial potlatch, Tlingit dance-dramas are a reciprocal formality performed by the Raven and Eagle moieties. Elaborate and valuable old dance regalia serve to display and elevate revered sib crests, while the mask-drama element serves to perpetuate sib origin myths and to explain relations with the spirit-world.

Within the Tlingit ANB convention in southeast Alaska, successive community dance team performances serve to affirm political solidarity and to renew ethnic bonds between Tlingits, including professionals and patriarchs whose work keeps them outside Alaska.

Within the statewide Native dance exhibitions and art festivals, Tlingit dance team performance serves to affirm ethnic identity and to display local community pride. Additionally, the dance team functions as an avocational voluntary organization that provides Tlingit individuals and groups with a variety of fulfilling social and creative roles such as dance composer, drummer, song-leader, artifact carver, and costume maker.

PREVIOUS RESEARCH

Although Alaska is one of the few remaining regions where American Indian dance traditions survive relatively intact and may be observed in rural potlatches and at urban dance festivals, there has been little research on the subject, and the literature is scant. In 1972, Frederica de Laguna completed a comprehensive sociocultural study of the Yakutat Tlingit, which included chapters on the potlatch, dance, and music (de Laguna, 1972, vols. 2 and 3). It is noteworthy that she considers that "of all the arts formerly practiced at Yakutat, perhaps that of music is still most alive, and song composers are still esteemed" (vol, 2, p. 561).

In the mid-1970s the present writer published a brief study of Tlingit dance (1975, pp. 3–10). Various ethnographies include some dance information. These include Krause (1885), Swanton (1908), Oberg (1937), McLellan (1954), Drucker (1965), Gunther (1966), and Garfield and Wingert (1979). Much interesting information on Tlingit dance regalia is to be found in museum catalogues, such as that of the Sheldon Jackson Museum at Sitka (Gunther, 1976). Lindy Li Mark completed a thesis on inland Tlingit music (1955), but does not mention dance. At the University of Alaska graduate student Dorothy Morrison is completing a thesis on the structure of Yakutat Tlingit music (1988). The present study is intended to focus on Tlingit potlatch dance traditions and dance style, and in so doing to broaden anthropological understanding of Tlingit aesthetic and artistic values. For, as Herskovits points out, dance is one of the universals that must be studied in order to have a holistic comprehension of any culture (1950, pp. 239, 438).

LOCATION AND SUBSISTENCE

The Alaskan Tlingit are the northermost group of the Northwest Coast American Indian culture, which includes Haida, Tsimshian, Kwakiutl, Niska, Gitksan, Haisla, Bella Coola, Heiltsuk, Nootka, Salish, Chemakum, Quileute, Chinook, Tllamook, Alsea, Suislaw, Umpqua, Coos, Tututni, Tolowa, Yurok, Hupa, and others. This culture presents somewhat of an anomaly in world anthropology. Most advanced cultures typically resulted from the increase in economic productivity associated with the development of agricultural techniques. The Northwest Coast Indian culture, although of the hunting-and-gathering type, was among the most advanced of North American Indians. It featured exploitation of rich maritime resources, elaboration of canoe navigation, artistic woodworking, and the potlatch system. Highly stylized artwork was featured on dishes, food boxes, canoes, houses, totem poles, dance costumes, musical intruments, and other cultural items.

The Alaskan Tlingit reside in a number of small towns on a 30-mile-wide strip of mountainous mainland and on an 80-mile-wide chain of richly forested islands: Baranof, Chicagof, Admiralty, Kupreanof,

Prince of Wales, and others. Knapp and Childe identify the following territorial groups:

Yakutat	Yakutat Bay	Auk	Stevens Passage
Chilkat	Lynn Canal	Kake	Frederick Sound
Hoonah	Cross Sound	Sitka	Baranof Island
Hootznahoo	Chatham Strait	Stikino	Fort Wrangell
Taku	Taku Inlet	Tongas	Cape Fox

(1896, p. 13)

The present writer conducted seasonal fieldwork at Yakutat in 1974, Hoonah in 1975, and Sitka in 1980 and made short trips to Ketchikan, Wrangell, Haines, and other Tlingit communities between these dates.

Traditionally, two kinds of canoe were in use: the large red cedar canoe made from a single log 40 or 50 feet in length, and the small cottonwood dug-out. Clan property consisted of salmon streams, hunting grounds, berry patches, sealing rocks, house sites in villages, rights to mountain passes, totemic crests, and shamanistic spirits (Oberg, 1937, p. 55). Songs and dances were also proprietory.

In the diet salmon was, and still is, important. The king salmon weigh up to 50 pounds, and there are sockeye, silver or coho, and the humpback or dog salmon. Use of shellfish includes mussel, sea urchin, oyster, and clam. Subsistence hunting is still followed, and use is made of rabbit, marmot, porcupine, black bear, mountain goat, and the white-tail goat. Women gather berries in season: thimbleberry, wild currant, soapberry, huckleberry, salmonberry, serviceberry, and high and low cranberry.

In addition to hunting and gathering, there were many economic opportunities for artisans who specialized in woodcraft. The Tlingit were expert canoe builders, chest makers, mask carvers, and totem pole carvers. These artisans might be housed and fed by the chief while engaged on a potlatch project. Many shamans sustained a livelihood by depending on healing fees, which were paid in food and economic goods. Skilled blanket weavers contributed to the sustenance of their families through the remuneration they received. Other Tlingit became shrewd traders. Precontact Tlingit society, with its stratification and its diversity, offered a variety of fulfilling and rewarding socioeconomic roles. In present times, the economic function of potlatch dancing has given way to new social functions, and the ancient formal potlatch roles—orator, dancer, composer, mask maker, and so on—have given way to dance participation as an avocational pursuit, with certain vestiges and survivals of ancient dance tradition remaining in place.

TLINGIT DANCE AT TIME OF CONTACT

Ceremonial dance has probably long constituted an important aspect of Tlingit culture: the Tlingit possess numerous different terms for the verb to dance, according to social context (Story & Naish, 1973, p. 63).

In 1741, Bering anchored at Yakutat and left various Western trade items there. The 1785 publication of Cook's journals describing the sea-otter herds opened the way for British, Russian, Spanish, and French profit-seekers (Gruening, 1954, pp. 1–8). Scientific expeditions came: in 1786 LaPérouse reports, "Before the chief came aboard, he appeared to address a prayer to the sun. He then made a long harangue, which was concluded by a kind of song, by no means disagreeable, and greatly resembling the plain chant of our churches. The Indians in his canoe accompanied him, repeating the same air in chorus. After this ceremony, they almost all came on board, and danced for an hour to the music of their own voices, in which they are very exact" (LaPérouse, 1799, vol. 1, p. 370).

In 1791, Alejandro Malaspina, an Italian commissioned by Spain in 1788, entered Yakutat Bay: "Two canoes of Indians shortly arrived alongside . . . as soon as they were close to the ladder all except the steersman stood up, and at the sound of a stentorian and frightful voice they all extended their hands together in the form of a cross . . . and began to sing what was evidently a song of peace and friendship" (Wagner, 1936, p. 247, cited in de Laguna, 1972, vol. 1, p. 141).

With Malaspina was the artist Don Tomás Suria; on Khantaak Island he reported, "They formed a circle around me and danced around me knives in hand singing a frightful song . . . in such circumstances I resolved to carry out their mood and I began to dance with them. They let out a shout and made me sit down, and by force made me sing their songs" (Wagner, 1936, p. 250, cited in de Laguna, 1972, vol. 1, p. 150). Suria could not know that the knives symbolically were to protect him from evil spirits during the dance and were a show of respect. De Laguna considers that Suria was being given the Tlingit dance role of Deer or peace-hostage, the central figure in a Tlingit peace-making ceremony, like that which ended the war between the Tluknaxadi and the Ganaxtedi (1972, vol. 1).

In 1794, Captain George Vancouver in the sloop Discovery, accompanied by Lt. Peter Puget in the armed tender Chatham, was sent to receive for Great Britain the territory that the Spaniards were to surrender in settlement of the Nootka Controversy of 1798. They explored Yakutat Bay and Khantaak Island, meeting the Russian expedition of

George Purtov. Purtov noted Vancouver's interactions with the Tlingit, and they are reported in Peter Tikhmenev's history of the Russian-American Company, of which there are translations in the Bancroft Library, University of California, Berkeley.

On Khantaak Island in 1794 two of the native inhabitants of the bay paid a visit to Vancouver's ship the Chatham: "After the usual ceremonious song was ended, they came on board . . . (later) the chief sent a sea otter skin to Purtov, and on his accepting this present, a loud shout was given by both parties; this was followed by a song, which concluded the introductory ceremonies . . . at Point Turner there were similar ceremonies of songs and dancing . . . the several chiefs occasionally visited Lt. Puget, who made them all presents of such articles as were by them considered valuable, and were well accepted . . . after an amicable discourse had been established between the two parties, they entertained each other with songs and dances, according to the different customs of each particular tribe" (Tikhmenev, 1863, vol. 2, suppl., pp. 60–63, cited in de Laguna, 1972, vol. 1, pp. 156–157).

While Baranof was at Yakutat in 1796, "the principal chief of that region appeared before him with a large number of people with their customary ceremonies, fully armed and dancing and singing" (Tikhmenev, 1861, vol. 1, p. 54, cited in de Laguna, vol. 1, p. 167). Baranof built a fort at Sitka in 1799, which the Tlingit burned, but the Russians returned in more strength in 1804.

In 1807, Langsdorff noted the Tlingit use of dance regalia: "The ermine skin around the head, upon the clothes, and sometimes held in the hand is a mark of luxury and wealth. The foremost dancer had in his hand a stick ornamented with sea otter teeth, with which he beat time. Some of the dancers had their heads powdered with the small down feathers of the white-headed eagle . . . the women sit by the dancers and sing" (Langsdorff, 1814, p. 114).

These early reports of Tlingit dance offer clues to dance style at the time of contact. Dance was a form of greeting, was preceded by elaborate formal oratory, and was often followed by gift-giving. Dance was lengthy, and often signified peaceful intentions. It was accompanied by ensemble singing, special regalia were worn, and there was a leader, who generally held a carved staff of office. Different tribes danced in different styles, and the women usually played a secondary role. The Tlingit had a peace-making Deer Dance in which a central figure was encircled, and in which everyone was required to sing.

The Tlingit possessed a barter economy; certain clans and villages had a monopoly on trade routes into the interior. The Wrangell clans held all trading rights with the Athabascan at the headwaters of the

Stikine River. The same was true of the Taku clans on the Taku River and the Chilkat clans on the Chilkat River (Oberg, 1937, p. 106). Chilkat dance blankets and abalone shell dance ornaments were among the most prized trade items.

Trading expeditions sometimes covered great distances; the Sitka, Hoonah, and Klackqwan potlatch dancers would occasionally travel 300 miles to reach the Haida and Tsimshian. In fur-trading times expeditions even went the 1,000 miles to Puget Sound. The Tlingit became canny traders with the Europeans, dyeing furs and delaying ships to sell them additional fish (Krause, 1885, p. 169). In return they obtained boat sails, rifles, and tools (Bancroft, 1884, p. 372).

In 1836, 4,000 Tlingit died in a smallpox epidemic (Bancroft, 1886, p. 560). Russian Orthodox priest Veniaminof noted that European vaccination usually provided immunity while the Tlingit shaman's magic dances failed, thus diminishing the shaman's traditional power (de Laguna, 1972, vol. 1, p. 177). The Crimean War and fear of British imperialism brought about a concession treaty in 1867, when the Russians, who did not really own Alaska, sold the territory to America for about $7 million.

Salmon canneries were built at Klawock and Sitka in 1878. Gold rushes in 1872–1897 turned Tlingit villages into boom towns. In 1877 a mission school was established at Wrangell, followed in 1880 by schools at Hoonah and Haines (Petrov, 1884, p. 3). Of considerable influence among the Tlingit was the Industrial and Training School founded at Sitka in 1878 by Sheldon Jackson. In 1881 geographer Aurel Krause and his brother wintered at Haines, Aurel writing a landmark ethnography.

A Southeast Alaska Convention met in 1881 to draft a note to Congress, and in 1883 the Organic Act provided for a civil and judicial district at Sitka, recognizing certain Tlingit rights (Tollefson, 1978, p. 9). Social change came as traplines operated by one man replaced cooperative hunting. Communal households gave way to a nuclear housing pattern and emphasis on the immediate kin group (Oberg, 1937, p. 56). The Alaska Territorial Legislature was established in 1912. When George T. Emmons was asked by President Theodore Roosevelt to ascertain Tlingit needs, he wrote, "He is not regarded as an Indian for he has no reservation of land nor receives any gravity from the government; however intellectual and educated he may be he is denied citizenship, so he can neither acquire land, locate mineral claims, nor take out a license as master, pilot, or engineer of his own craft" (Miller, 1967, p. 211).

To the south of the Tlingit, across the Canadian border, Kolstee reports similar cultural oppression of the Bella Coola: "The main force working against the potlatches and the winter ceremonials, and therefore against the songs, masks, and dances, was the church . . . beginning in 1883 a Methodist minister, the Rev. William Pierce, attempted to dissuade the Bella Coola from maintaining their ceremonial customs. . . . Pierce convinced Chief Tactalus to burn his whistles, robes, headdresses . . . the efforts of the missionaries were given official sanction in 1884 when Section 114 of the (Canadian) Indian Act declared potlatching illegal" (Kolstee, 1982, p. 3).

The survival of traditional dance depended on survival of the potlatch: "The nearest thing to an attack on the clan system was one directed at the funerary functions which are carried out by members of the opposite moiety who are subsequently repaid in a series of feasts, dances, and gift-giving" (Drucker, 1958, p. 65).

In 1880, 96% of Alaskans were Natives; in 1909 this dropped to 37% (Rogers, 1960, p. 198). In 1912, nine Tlingits met at Sitka to form the Alaska Native Brotherhood, and the constitution was drawn up in 1917, unfortunately adopting English as its official language. In 1935 the Tlingit-Haida organization was created, land claims proceeded (1935–1971), and in 1968 the U.S. Court of Claims awarded the organization $7.5 million, a sum used to push through further land claims. The Alaska Native Land Claims Settlement Act of 1971 virtually ended Alaskan Eskimo and Indian land negotiations in exchange for $900 million and 40 million acres of land, and authorized the creation of over a dozen Native-controlled regional corporations to administer enactment. The southeastern corporation was named Sealaska, and it received $173 million and 200,000 acres of land. Sealaska became responsible for administering nine small village corporations, each of which selected 20,000 acres of land along with a per capita payment (Tollefson, 1978, p. 17).

Of particular significance to the present study is the revised 1948 draft of the Alaska Native Brotherhood constitution; it adopted the commendable objective of "preserving history, lore, and art" (Drucker, 1958, p. 169). This was a reversal of previous attitudes. The fact that such an objective was needed illustrates the loss of important traditions that was occurring with increasing rapidity. Uncertainty surrounding the return of his lifetime investment in coppers and blankets caused a chief to think twice before potlatching. Going away from home to distant high schools weakened matrilineal ties, resulting in youths singing their father's songs. The language waned, so that Krauss writes: "Of about 9,000 Tlingits in Alaska, most speakers are over forty-five. Only in Angoon are there many speakers under twenty-five. There are virtually no schoolchildren anywhere now speaking Tlingit, and the total number of fluent speakers of the language may now be under two thousand" (1975). In the 1980s, however, the present writer noted certain instances where community elders are teaching schoolchildren ancient songs in Tlingit, and this may serve to stimulate increased interest in the present-day bilingual education program.

The Alaskan Native corporations are highly interested in preserving traditional dance, and they fund statewide dance exhibitions, folklore collection, and documentation. In southeast Alaska, the Alaska Native Brotherhood usually features several traditional dance teams at its annual conference.

THE TLINGIT CEREMONIAL POTLATCH

The meaning and function of Tlingit dance is best understood by examining its social context. De Laguna observes that "the potlatch stimulates the composition and performance of the finest songs and dances, the production and display of the most beautiful costumes, carvings, and paintings, including those of the house itself. Yet the significance of these transcends their purely aesthetic appeal, since they serve to symbolize the whole social order, the relation of man to man and of men to their totemic counterparts, while the oratory of the chiefs and the poetry of the songs evoke the legendary history of the sib ancestors and myths of the world's establishment" (de Laguna, 1972, vol. 2, p. 607).

The Tlingit ceremonial potlatch was a microcosm of Tlingit social structure, reflecting hierarchy and social class. For an American Indian group, nineteenth-century Tlingit society was extremely socially stratified, with chiefs, nobles, commoners, and slaves, the latter being mainly war captives. A tribal chief had more wealth, both hereditary and on demand from his followers, than a lineage leader, but he also had more patronage to distribute. A chief had to be wellborn, with no taint of slave ancestry. Orators and poets proclaimed his unblemished genealogy in which all remembered ancestors were the sons and daughters of chiefs. Tlingit chiefs had to be able leaders, haughty and proud, good speakers and good dancers.

The society featured complex matrilineal clan organization and two exogamous phratries: Raven and Eagle. These features made the Tlingit, Haida, and Tsimshian unique among Northwest Coast Indians. Exogamous marriage was linked with a belief in descent from common ancestors and an elaborate body of myth substantiating the belief. All Tlingit possess a family crest figure, usually a totemic animal or bird—some creature of the northwestern natural environment with which sib ancestors had experienced a supernatural encounter in the past. The totemic crest concept probably derives from the guardian spirit quest prevalent in many American Indian cultures.

Crest ownership carries certain mild taboos. Ravens may not keep pet ravens; Wolves may not pet wolves. Frogs exhibit a marked fear of frogs (McLellan, 1954, p. 87). Hat crests were so important that many dances featured only the movement of the crest over the top of a suspended screen, the rest of the dancer being invisible (de Laguna, 1972, vol. 2, p. 568). Dance-costume emblems of the Eagle phratry are Wolf, Bear, Halibut, Killer-Whale, Shark. Emblems of the Raven phratry are Frog, Beaver, Dog Salmon, Coho Salmon, Sockeye Salmon, and Mountain. An old Tlingit saying goes, "If Raven on back, then fish on head." Graphic distortion, simplification, and bisection are the adaptive devices of Tlingit artists, who practice nonrealistic conventionalization in depicting their clan totems on dance costumes.

Concerning a possible relationship between Raven the Tlingit phratry totem, and Raven the trickster in the folktales, Boas considers that "There is no connection between the Raven myth and the social grouping of the people, except the vague statement, that is not found embodied in any version as an important element, that Raven was the ancestor of the Raven clan" (Boas, 1916: 619). Tlingit dance, dance costumes, and dance masks, in addition to featuring Raven as sib totem, occasionally feature Raven as mythological figure: Raven's bringing of daylight, Raven's loss of his beak to halibut fishermen, Raven's journey in the whale, Raven's marriage to Fog Woman who made the first salmon, Raven's journey to the sky where he married Sun's daughters (Garfield & Wingert, 1979, p. 53). Jochelson early noted that the Raven cycle is widespread in western America and in Asia (1905). The Tlingit added phases accounting for Raven's birth and earthly life, and wove these into a unified epic by supplying motivation for his actions (Garfield & Wingert, 1979, p. 55).

Tlingit, Haida, and Tsimshian origin myths differ in one fundamental particular from those of the Kwakiutl and Bella Coola to the south of them, who reckoned descent through both parents but who also venerated ancestors. In Tlingit, Haida, and Tsimshian tales, human ancestors settled a new village and established a new lineage that preserved relationship with the parent group through names, crests, and myths that were imbued with great symbolic importance. In Kwakiutl and Bella Coola myths, a divine sky being established a village and yielded human descendants. Here, the tie between ancestor, locality, and all descendants was stressed (Garfield & Wingert, 1979, p. 18).

Ravens had to (and still have to) marry Eagles and vice versa; a young man observing a maiden's dance costume knew whether or not he could ever marry her. This is seen in the following dance song given to the present writer by Katherine Mills of Hoonah.

If the Eagles will sing, the Ravens will dance
She is an Eagle from the Eagle clan box house
To his Wolf
They looked upon me as a picture of my aunt
Like the spirits of a Tlingit shaman
They all went away
The Eagle clan from Birch Bay
Let us dream about you at times
His wife was of Chooka.

In this dance song are reflected Tlingit beliefs in the transfer of the personal qualities of the deceased (the aunt) to the young niece, and Tlingit bilaterality. Descent was, and still is, reckoned through the mother, individuals were ranked based on wealth and descent, and clan members amassed lavishly beaded ceremonial dance garments that testified to rank. The heir presumptive of a chieftainship in this society was presented formally at a potlatch with feasting, dancing, and gift-giving. Such a participant might have to demonstrate his understanding of Tlingit allusive oratory by "riddle-talking." Tlingit chiefs weave their sib traditions and folklore heritage into every potlatch speech, likening their crests to "great fires on the cliff" or "great forts." McLellan reports that the Angoon Decitan indicate that a potlatch will last all night by saying, "the tide still covers Raven's Halibut" (1954, p. 95).

De Laguna gives a detailed seating diagram for a Yakutat Tlingit potlatch (1972, vol 2, p. 631). Formal recital of the legendary history of the group served to validate its various privileges, and the guests served as witnesses. Tallymen counted the bundles of mnemonic sticks to keep count of the wealth goods presented (Drucker, 1965, p. 57). Such a potlatch was part of a lengthy, involved cycle of potlatching in which increasing status was achieved and much spectacular conspicuous consumption occurred, occasionally with the competitive burning of wealth goods such as canoes and Chilkat blankets. The true potlatch goods were the Chilkat blankets and large engraved copper shields. The latter were hammered out of placer copper obtained from Athabascans at Copper River to the west. These goods were never used for mundane purposes, but stored in elaborately carved wooden chests in preparation for the potlatch. Potlatch goods were derived from the surplus of economic goods through exchange. In addition to this bartering, one borrowed furs from brothers-in-law in order to trade them for coppers and blankets, got one's clan peers to do the same, then fulfilled potlatch obligations to society by distributing the accumulated potlatch goods.

At the potlatch the chief honored his own children and their lineage mates—members of the lineage of his wife's brothers—by formally presenting them, with much oratory and clan dancing. Orators would announce the honorees' assumption of hereditary names and titles, affirm their rights to crests, and arrange to have these crests tatooed on them.

The Tlingit potlatch would generally extend over several days, the formal initial reception of the guests commencing at the beaches and continuing to the steps of the clan house. The first day was taken up with prepared, poetic speeches by both sides, dancing by the host group, and feasting at which the nephews of the host served as waiters. The repast consisted of dried salmon, seaweed, boiled clams, sea urchins, and mussels, followed by salmonberry stalks and mashed soapberries (Oberg, 1937).

The second day was reserved for the clan dances of the guest group, and their numerous totemic crests were displayed with profuse oratory concerning their origin and mythology. On the third day of the potlatch, there were masked theatricals and psychodrama, using working models of legendary figures, their moving parts hinged and operated with strings. Rival shamans would perform slight-of-hand and walk through fire. These shamans were often Tsimshians, foreignness serving to heighten their aura of mysticism.

The potlatch would culminate with the formal presentation of gifts. The host stood before his elaborately painted house screen with the pile of gifts at his feet, and called out the names of the recipients by rank. Guests tended to be very sensitive concerning the quality, value, and symbolism of the gift offered them, perceiving insult where none was intended.

There were five main potlatch roles. There was the host, called Keeper of the House, and his immediate supporting house-group. Then there was the broader clan division from the home village and from nearby villages. Then there was the honorific role of the dedicatee, who might be a revered ancestor, a living patriarch, or a young prince. Then there were the guests of the opposite phratry, who comprised the house chiefs and their households. Last, there were the community residents of the host's village, who participated and benefited from the feasting and dancing. While the primary motive of the potlatch was personal prestige and power, it translated into clan prestige and clan power.

Tlingit rank was measured in wealth; a man was worth only as much as the bride gift given by his mother, and a clan was worth the amount of wealth given at its last potlatch, plus its former prestige value. A potlatch not only canceled old debts but created new credits. Oberg has outlined the four rules the potlatch giver must observe: (1) it must be given for the opposite side, (2) it must elevate the totemic crest of the giver's clan, (3) only the host gives gifts, and (4) a gift must later be returned in kind via a return potlatch, or the debtor's clan can lay claim to the creditor clan's crest (Oberg, 1937, p. 127). Potlatching was a complex social and ceremonial transaction drawing together economic goods, potlatch goods, totemic crests, group prestige, and the arts.

Among the Chilkat and other Tlingit groups during the period 1881–1882, geographer Aurel Krause gave much of his attention to Tlingit dance behavior. He considered that there were four main reasons for potlatching. He considered that there were four main reasons for potlatching: (1) birth and death, (2) successful hunting expeditions, (3) reconciliation between two quarreling groups, and (4) the completion of a new lineage house (1885, p. 162).

In her study "The Interrelations of Social Structure with Northern Tlingit Ceremonialism," Catherine McLellan noted six reasons for holding a potlatch: (1) as payment for funeral duties, (2) completion of a lineage house, (3) wiping off a shame, (4) public consignment of an insult to oblivion, (5) restoration of a redeemed slave to his former social standing, and (6) maintaining or attaining full noble status for one's self or one's children (1954, p. 78).

Names were very important to the Tlingit, the name embodying the essence of the person and his lineage predecessors. Thus potlatches were also naming ceremonies. Tlingit names are one-line poems, and should probably be considered an art form: "Sunshine glinting on the wet dorsal fin of the emerging Killer-Whale," "Raven flying out to sea cawing in the early morning," "Grouse making a robe for itself with its tail feathers," "Sunshine glinting on the white head of the eagle" (Carpenter, 1973, p. 288).

Krause writes that the potlatch had three main components: dancing, feasting, and gift-giving, and the recipients were socially obliged to return the gifts in kind with interest. Large blankets were shown to the assembly with ceremony, then cut up and distributed, so that every participant received some form of recognition. At the potlatch "the dances are sometimes done by men and sometimes by both sexes; even children do their part . . . rhythmic movements of the body accompanied by expressive and not unmelodious singing make up the dances. The dancers decorate themselves with colored festive regalia, gaily paint their faces or wear grotesque masks . . . carry wooden clappers, carved staffs" (Krause, 1885, p. 163).

In a Bear clan dance observed by Krause at Klackqwan, we see a kind of territoriality in the potlatch seating: "The house designated for the ceremony gradually filled up with spectators, the women squatting down along the walls, while the men took up the space around the fire, leaving only one side, the right from the entrance, free for the dancers. The dancers included the leaders of the community, among them old chief Tschartritsch, the most important head, not only of the Chilkat Indians, but of all the Tlingit of Alaska . . . one after another the dancers appeared, each one sticking his head in first and withdrawing again . . . with constant hopping back and forth, they proceeded to the space left for them to the right of the fire, up took up their positions there in a row . . . vigorous movements of arms and feet and various twisting of the body made up the dance . . . among the Chilkat we saw two kinds of dance, those of the Haida and those of the Athabascans of the interior. Each time the dancers came in singly and placed themselves in a row . . . stamping the feet, and pounding on boards with wooden staffs. The drums are often wooden boxes, decorated with carving and painting, or are like our tambourines . . . (there are) rattles which are made of two pieces and filled with pebbles . . . the children are introduced to the dances at an early age" (Krause, 1885, pp. 167–168).

From this we learn that Tlingit dance in the nineteenth century functioned to mark life-cycle crises such as birth and death, to mark the return of hunters, to "consecrate" the clan house, and to validate peace-making. The accompanying feasting and gift-giving functioned to redistribute wealth and as a prestige-acquiring device. Dance diffusion and borrowing was a cultural trait, the large carved box-drum was prevalent, rattles accompanied dance, and small children participated. In the aforegoing description of dance, the peeking back and forth of the dancers was probably a theatrical gesture, perhaps a pretense at ascertaining whether or not the dance arena was clear of evil spirits. The hopping back and forth was probably bird mimicry. The Chilkat in particular were and still are great dramatists; their dance employs elaborate animistic disguise, comic histrionics, and spoofing of shamans. Northwest Coast Indian potlatching, which in the literature is sometimes depicted as either a serious and/or a competitive ceremony, probably had its amiable or "fun" side. Helen Codere discussed this at length in a landmark essay, "The Amiable Side of Kwakiutl Life: The Potlatch and the Play Potlatch" (1956).

In the early 1960s Olson interviewed Tlingit elders concerning ancient potlatching protocol (1967, p. 66). He was informed that around 1880 Chief Kuxtite of the Tantakwan Ganaxadi gave a great potlatch in honor of a deceased clansman, with the Nanyaayih clan of Wrangell as honored guests, and the Tekwedi as home village guests. Dances were rehearsed, and a master of ceremonies was appointed to ensure that there were no affronts.

The Tekwedi home village guests lined up in front of the potlatch house and danced, after which the visiting Chief Ceke made a long metaphorical speech, idealizing the children of the host's clan and declaiming, "I take hold of their robes." The hosts then called out, "Chief Ceke, where do you wish me to throw this spirit?" Whereupon Chief Ceke responded, "Throw it where it belongs," meaning to the venerable head of the house.

In the potlatch house the guests were seated "where the sun rises," while the hosts were seated "where the sun sets." When one guest chief refused to eat the food served, the host exclaimed "Are you going to close the door to the land of the dead? If not, then eat!" This meant that if he did not eat, the host would boycott his reciprocal potlatch (Olson, 1967, p. 66). Olson goes on to report that it was desirable at an important potlatch to perform a new dance, the inspiration for which often came from non-Tlingit neighbors, such as the Tsimshian. De Laguna likewise reports that songs and dances were acquired from surrounding Indian groups via trade or intermarriage (1972, vol. 2, p. 569), and that Yakutat Tlingit shamans' songs had Tsimshian words because the spirits were thought to have emanated from that group (1972, vol. 1, p. 216). In many American Indian societies, the performance of music and dance is thought to embody supernatural power. This power manifests itself in the ability to transport, to transform, to mystically unite past and present, everyday world and spirit world. Using foreign songwords often heightens the aura of mystery at the event.

McLellan provides what she refers to as a synthetic sketch of a house potlatch taking place about 1900 (1954, pp. 78–82). It is useful for the present study in its step-by-step account of the action, and its placing of dance in social context. "A new lineage house has been built . . . the new chief and his sib-mates have collected sufficient wealth and food for the occasion . . . the local sibs of the opposite moiety are invited, and two out-of-town sibs are expected. During their journey to the host village the guests practice their songs and dances at every stop . . . necessary arrangements for song-leaders are made—one woman and two men from each sib—and special attendants are appointed for them. Then the visitors, dressed in dance costume and singing 'foreign' songs, are conveyed to the town in war canoes manned by young men of the host sib. There the out-of-town guests find the local sibs of their own moiety singing and dancing on the beach, thus marking the beginning of a sequence of rival entertainments which will last throughout the full eight days of ceremonial activity (McLellan, 1954, p. 79). At the University of Alaska Archives, there are several turn-of-the-century photographs showing Sitka and Yakutat potlatch dancers massed on beaches, greeting lavishly costumed potlatch guests.

McLellan goes on to say that "the second day begins a succession of formalities in which the host feasts the visiting and local guests in each of their three highest ranking lineage houses. In payment for this, the rival sibs of the guests moiety alternately vie with each other in singing and dancing. On the fifth day the actual potlatch ceremony begins. The host sib fasts, and now dons full regalia. All of the guests are properly seated, with the highest ranking in the places of honor at the rear of the new house, while the hosts stand by the door. All the food is eaten for the dead—not only for the dead chief, but for all ancestors of the host moiety. Other food which is put into the fire reaches the departed (McLellan, 1954, p. 80). Often, the hunters must kill game of a specific color, according to the chief's shaman's vision, for that will be more pleasing to the ancestor-spirits. Fire is the transportation medium for conveying offerings to the spirit world; the symbolism of fire and of blood accounts for red dyes on certain important dance masks.

McLellan continues: "When the meal is over, the host chief, wearing the most honored crest hat of his sib, initiates eight potlatch songs and dances, and begins in this way the collection of wealth which is to be distributed to the guests: furs, tanned skins, a valuable old copper, blankets, bolts of calico, and money. The chief calls on his people . . . they start valuable potlatch songs and dances in which they are joined by their sib-mates. The line of dancers dips and rises as the leaders lower and raise their ceremonial dance paddles to the drummer's beat. . . . The stories illustrated by the new carved lineage house posts are explained. . . . The new house chief assumes the illustrious name of his dead uncle . . . a new name referring to the potlatch itself is given to a favored son's son. . . . The guests must be suitably rewarded for the pallbearer duties they performed at the death of the old chief . . . the highest ranking are given presents based on finely shaded social status, measured in terms of wealth, character, past potlatching activities, and the intricate network of family connections. This takes two days" (McLellan, 1954, p. 81). Present-day Tlingit dancers still use carved, painted dance paddles to direct and communicate dance movements. The dance-leader drums, and the second and third officiants wave paddles indicating sib membership, and control the dancers' body height and floor movement with semaphore-like signalling. In former times, the dance paddles bore tufts of human hair from killed slaves, along one side. Today black yarn is used. Use of dance paddles is yet another symbol of Tlingit maritime subsistence.

McLellan goes on to say that "when the potlatching is finally concluded, the time comes for the guests to thank and comfort the hosts with formal speeches, and to cheer them up by dancing and singing in

their own ceremonial paraphernalia. Their return entertainment is
given the next day . . . the main emphasis is on dancing and singing a
thank-you to the hosts. Masked dances are performed by some . . . after
two more days of feasting the visitors depart . . . next winter they in turn
will invite their recent hosts to a potlatch. The aforegoing illustrates how
rhetoric, song, dance, and humor, as well as the trappings of sib regalia
and architectural ornamentation are woven into a Tlingit ceremonial"
(McLellan, 1954, p. 82).

In potlatching involving distant groups, regional reciprocity helped
to maintain amicable trade relations. De Laguna reports that "Yakutat
people regularly exchanged potlatch invitations with the people of Ka-
talla and Bering River to the southeast. Less frequently they invited
guests from Sitka and Juneau (1972, vol. 2, p. 613). Often, however,
bitter rivalry occurred among the visitors, disrupting trade relations—social problems outweighing economic needs. There were always two
groups of guests, usually two separate sibs. Each sib came with its own
chief and dance-leader. Even if there were only one sib of the guests
moiety present, this would be subdivided into two lineage groups (Swanton, 1908, p. 435). De Laguna points out that "these two groups of guests
came as rivals, 'to dance against each other' (*wute yaadulex*), trying to
outdo each other in beautiful costly garments, and in the excellence of
their singing and dancing" (1972, vol. 2, p. 614).

Protocol existed to limit and forestall mounting tension. Swanton
notes that "The contesting sides indicate that they want to dance in
peace by saying to each other 'I am holding your daughter's hand,' the
daughter of one Wolf dancer being the wife of another, and *vice versa*"
(Swanton, 1908, p. 440). Guests dancers were often apprehensive when
performing, fearing ridicule and disgrace for clumsiness. A jibe directed
against one guest group by the other could result in a mélée. Thus the
potlatch, while it united the moiety of the host, often divided the moiety
of the guests. The relations between two visiting Raven sibs would be
more strained than relations between all of the Ravens and all of the
Eagles present. In such instances, the role of the host was that of media-
tor, and he might address both sides, administering solemn admonitions:
"Your robe is ancestral. Will you dishonor the dead?" One dance-leader
informant told de Laguna that "If anybody make a mistake, they-re
going to have a big fight, going to use the knife" (1972, vol. 2, p. 615).

Crests were considered sacred and could serve to assuage offended
parties at the potlatch. Swanton reports that when a fight was imminent
between guests at a Chilkat potlatch, one of the hosts wearing a Raven
headpiece averted the fight by stepping forward and uttering the raven's
caw (1908, p. 440). Even today at a Native Brotherhood conference

attended by Tlingit attorneys from as far away as Washington, D.C., men who are strangers are bonded by shared crests on their dance costumes.

The aforegoing reveals much concerning the meaning, context, and function of Tlingit dance. Dance performance was not merely for self-gratification or recreation, but was a ceremonial gift to others, requiring a return dance later, in exchange. Dance could mean "We are showing gratitude," and it could signify "We desire good relations." Dance was also a marker, delineating stages in the potlatch process. A dance costume precisely pinpointed the wearer's authority and status within the social hierarchy for all to see: phratry, sib, rank, and assigned office at that particular potlatch.

De Laguna describes several Yakutat Tlingit potlatches in detail, giving informants' explanations of protocol, dance, and gift-exchange (1972, vol. 2, pp. 616–651). In these descriptions, the strong economic underpinnings of potlatching become evident. Tlingit ceremonial pot-latching was in many ways a crystalization of social, economic, and political structure in early twentieth-century Tlingit society. Later, the encroachment of mainstream culture wrought profound changes in the Tlingit way of life. One of de Laguna's informants stated, "and when they give all the dead person's things away to the opposite tribe, that means there is no money left for the probate fee or funeral expenses or to cover bad debts. All the people die intestate and that means a minimum fee of $150. There is also trouble between the old rule of inheritance and the present law" (de Laguna, 1972, vol. 2, p. 651).

Today in many instances, Tlingit lineage heads who have passed the years of their lives anticipating and formally preparing for a patriarchal role of power and plenty discover that the traditional potlatching lacks the necessary cooperative support; even when support is forthcoming, disintegration of kin structure and the influence of mainstream culture results in uncertain reciprocity. Potlatches today reflect many mainstream values such as the self-assertion of youth, the value of money, and the premium set upon time. Potlatch time-span has shrunk. The abbreviation of the week-long potlatch sequence and the elimination of phases of the complex dance reciprocity has had the effect of reducing emphasis on the opening dances of greeting, and stressing postpotlatch dancing. Tlingit society no longer fears aggression, no longer pays strong fealty to chiefs, no longer depends primarily on hunting subsistence, and no longer venerates crests to the same degree. Changes in potlatch function have brought changes in dance function. The rival group is now Alaska's white settlers, with their dominant middle class culture. Dance still integrates, still displays, still thanks, but its new primary function is that of affirming "otherness" in the face of assimilation.

Dance is an ideal vehicle for projecting a cultural model; it embodies culture-specific cognitive processes, values regarding acceptable posture, canons of taste in aesthetics, behavioral norms, music, and language. All of these are prime cultural markers, and all are essential components of dance. Carving and painting can be pursued alone, apart from one's group, but dance is a highly social activity, performed communally in ensemble, and its spirit of togetherness fosters the kind of social cohesion necessary to assert cultural identity.

TLINGIT DANCE REGALIA

More than among any other Alaskan Native group, dance accoutrements and accessories are, for the Tlingit, highly symbolic and form an essential component of dance imagery. Tlingit dance robes are not for warmth, fashion, modesty, or to differentiate the sexes. In depicting the revered sib crest they take on its totemic essence, embodying and recalling all sib history. Many crest objects such as Chilkat blankets and crest hats possess their own song and dance, dedicated to their glory.

In addition to appearing in regalia, Tlingit dancers wear distinctive markings in the form of facial paint. These are geometric designs such as raven's feet symbolizing moiety. Black means that the first stage of one's social potlatch obligations has been completed; black and red together means the second stage. Carved wooden cases used to be employed to carry a variety of small incised stamps with which to stamp the faces of dancers before a potlatch. Facial paint used to bear social meaning outside the potlatch. Early explorers, curious as to the physical appearance of Tlingit young women, first had to persuade them to wash their faces in the river. To the Tlingit, dance dress and face paint are not merely decorative or merely functional; they signify status and they carry class privilege.

We have mentioned two kinds of Tlingit drum. The first, the large rectangular box-drum, resembles the famous carved and painted storage chests in which the Tlingit customarily keep their valuable dance robes. The box-drum is taller and narrower than Tlingit chests, and threaded with cords by which the drum is suspended from the crossbeams of the clan house. A prominent guest would be invited to play it, while women sang, immediately prior to the distribution of the potlatch gifts. The drummer sits on the crossbeam and kicks the side of the drum with his heels. Krause gives a drawing of a Bear clan box-drum depicting a highly stylized bear, wolf, mountains, clouds, and eyes (Krause, 1885, p. 167).

Gunther gives a photograph of a Tlingit box-drum from Angoon (1966, p. 140). It shows Bear coming out of his hole, and on the other side is a circle surrounded by four bear's claws. On top is a broad, flat Killer-Whale dorsal fin painted black, white, and orange; at the base of the head is a Killer-Whale's head in profile.

The Portland Art Museum possesses the Tekwedi Killer Whale box-drum originally belonging to Chief Shakes of Wrangell. Killer-Whale is painted in black and red on each side of the box, in a circle. On top is a carving of the dorsal fin, inlaid with opercula and eight tufts of human hair. On each side of the fin is carved a human figure seated on a human head. This is the man Na-Ta-See who befriended a killer whale that was marooned on a rock, and who in turn was rescued by it when marooned and deserted by former friends. The design, painted in red, black, green, and white, represents the man being carried safely to the main-land by the killer whale (de Laguna, 1972, vol. 2, p. 632).

An excellent description of the artwork on Tlingit chests and box-drums is to be found in Glen Cole's "A Study of the Tlingit Boxes of the Rasmussen Collection" (1954). Birket-Smith (1936, p. 179) consid-ered that the ceremonial box-drums found among the Inupiat Eskimo of the northwest Alaska coastline derive from Tlingit box-drums. In view of the fact that there was minimal contact, this is doubtful.

The second kind of drum mentioned—the tambourine—is a flat, round frame-drum of considerable weight, bearing a painted moosehide skin. The skin was stretched overnight with rocks suspended from it, then fastened with thongs at the rear, like the spokes of a wheel. It bears the clan emblem, and is beaten with a short padded beater, unlike the Athabascan beater, which has a round hole in the beating end. Sib crests were sometimes painted inside the drum to avoid wearing away of the design. In a Raven drum beaten by Teet Milton at the Sitka potlatch in 1904, Raven sits on a rock (symbolized as a head), with two humpback salmon below, to represent the Humpback Salmon Stream with the big rock under which salmon swim (de Laguna, 1972, vol. 2, p. 632).

Tlingit dance staffs frequently depict a legend carved on the sides, such as that of the maiden who married Devil Fish (the octopus) and had to live at the bottom of the ocean. Dance staffs were used in oratory to emphasize climaxes in the speech, at which time they were thumped on the ground. Additionally, they were and still are manipulated in dance as pointers, extending dance movements in space.

The large blankets described by Krause were never used as blankets, but were in fact the famous Chilkat dance shawls, meant to be viewed wrapped around the moving dancer, who possesses ancestral rights to the design. Mildred Sparks of Haines possesses one of great value, which she preserves in a Tlingit storage chest and which she permitted the writer to photograph in 1974. Krause gives an illustration of a Chilkat woman working at her blanket weaving (1885, p. 140). Its long swirling fringes give the Chilkat blanket its indigenous name: "dancing fringe." The warp yarn is a double strand of twisted cedar bark covered with mountain goat wool, doubled and twisted a second time so that the bark cord is concealed. The woof is also of mountain goat wool. Colors are black, yellow, and blue green, in patterns on a background of natural white wool. The design is usually in three fields: a wide center field covering the back of the wearer, and a narrower strip on each side extending over the shoulders and visible from the front. A wide fringe finishes the side and bottom, and a narrow band of fur trims the top edge.

The pattern boards from which the women weavers worked were prepared by men, who painted the design on the board. The design showed only half of the whole, because the design was repeated on each side of center. Since the loom was an elementary one and did not have the warps fastened at the bottom, it was possible to weave the dance blanket in sections instead of moving across the warps. These sections were then sewn together with white embroidery, making the transition between the freedom of painting to the confined technique of weaving (Gunther, 1966, p. 13).

On the dance blankets one can observe today, the totemic animal is shown laid out flat revealing at once the whole animal, as though Tlingit experience in skinning was transferred to art. In one dance blanket described by Gunther, 18 squares outlined in black represent a Tlingit house front, and the design is the Tsimshian version of Gonakadet, the sea spirit. This blanket entered a San Francisco collection before 1880 (Gunther, 1966, p. 78).

Garfield and Wingert note that by the beginning of the twentieth century, the Tsimshian had forgotten the art of blanket weaving. Only the Chilkat Tlingit among all northwestern coastal peoples were continuing to make blankets (1979). By 1930, only a few of the older women remembered the technique. In an effort to revive the art, the Arts and Crafts Board of the Office of Indian Affairs employed these women to teach younger women. Chilkat robes survive today in museums and in the homes of descendants of Tlingit chiefs. They are regarded as priceless heirlooms, and institutional offers of up to $10,000 apiece are regularly rejected by these descendants. In 1985 the Fifth Annual National Heritage Awards appointed Chilkat blanket weaver Jennie Thlunaut a fellow. Jennie is 96, and is from Haines. She is the last of the older generation of skilled goat-wool weavers, and helped to make Chilkat blankets for numerous famous chiefs in the early twentieth century. She still uses her ancient loom and traditional technique.

Traditional accessories still used in Tlingit dance include the Chilkat blanket, dance staff, frame-drum, dance paddle, certain dance masks, and the rattle, of which there are two main kinds. Krause provided a drawing of the elaborate Raven rattle (1885, p. 168), sometimes called the "chief's rattle." Dancing with this delicately carved and painted musical instrument was considered to symbolize wealth and high status. Raven's head constituted that end of the rattle which is opposite to the handle. The main body of the rattle is complex, for the Raven's breast is almost invariably carved as the face of a hawk, with short recurved beak. On the other side of the rattle is usually a reclining masked shaman with his tongue outstretched, reaching toward Frog, who sits astride him. The shaman's tongue is sucking power (some informants say poison) from the Frog's head. Many Raven rattles, instead of Frog, depict a shaman torturing a witch. In this case the animal figure would be a dog, for the shaman's spirit dog detected witches. Turn-of-the-century photographs of shamans show the Raven rattle being held with the hawk's face uppermost and the shaman facing the ground; this, then, is probably the traditional position.

Another common form of chief's rattle shows Oystercatcher; this has a long elegant neck with a straight beak, and webbed feet tucked under the body. On the back is the head of Mountain Goat whose horns function as the legs of a human figure. Around the edge of the rattle wind the tentacles of Devil Fish. Among the Tlingit, goat horns and tentacles signify shamanistic power.

The second type of rattle used by the Tlingit is spherical; known as war rattle, this is shaped like a maraca and has a low-relief carving of a crest on one or both hemispheres, usually a bird's face, frontal view. This rattle is more common in present-day Tlingit dance because it is easier to carve and less expensive. An unusual variation of this rattle is one carved in the shape of a human hand, with separately formed fingers and thumb; the wrist is the handle (American Museum of Natural History E/1605).

It should be noted that Eagle is distinguished from Raven on Tlingit dance costumes by its beak, which is more curved; additionally, Eagle always exhibits a white head and tail. Bear is recognized by square ears, and claws that turn inward. Wolf generally has a tongue that curls upward, and erect ears. Thunderbird has a tuft of feathers projecting from the back of the head. Killer-Whale always has an enlarged dorsal fin. Shark has gill openings to the side of the teeth, and an upper triangle for a nose. Wavy lines often mean ocean; V's can mean bird flight formation. A large inverted V means mountain. In many cases the sib totemic crest appears only on the back of the dance costume; to distinguish moiety during frontal viewing, Eagle phratry members paint bear claws on the cheeks, while Raven members put raven tracks. In the coloring of dance costumes, brown means fall, white means winter, green means spring. Red and black have primordial symbolism related to blood and death. These colors all possess other meanings according to graphic context.

There are three main types of Tlingit traditional potlatch headwear, and these are still in use today. The first is the chief's hat, which consists of a carved wooden frontlet plaque with crest design in abalone inlay. It features use of ermine tails below and sea lion's whiskers above, the crown being filled with swan's down. Canadian swan's down is considered especially desirable. This down is bobbed and floated across the screen at the potlatch in order to "bring peaceful feelings" (informant Charlie Joseph of Sitka). Among the Chilkat in 1881, Krause noted the use of down in dance, stating "At the close of the ceremony, usually bird down is blown into the air" (1885, p. 169). Many dance masks have open mouths so that swan's down or eagle down may be directed at the potlatch guests through the opening.

At the turn of the century when intervillage potlatching peaked, lines of dancers faced each other on the beach welcoming arriving boatloads of other Tlingit. As the guests passed up the beach between the dancing lines, the down was wafted upon them; the chief's hat thus became known as the Friendship Hat. One chief's hat frontlet in the Sheldon Jackson Museum at Sitka is a carved wolf head with shells and teeth set in the mouth, green abalone squares set around the edge, sea lion's whiskers and woodpecker feathers on top, and ermine trailer behind and below (Cat.# I.A.423). A second such frontlet shows two carved heads, an eagle above a human head (Cat.# I.A.325).

Kathy Marks of the Mark Trail Dancers in 1974 states that the sea lion's whiskers on chief's hats are explained by an ancient Tlingit legend. In a storm at sea, a Tlingit canoe was blown a great distance off course, and was thrown onto a strange distant beach. It turned out to be an island covered in giant sea lion's whiskers. The hunters filled their canoe with samples, and finally returned to their home village, where they honored the ocean spirits who had saved them by inserting the whiskers into their potlatch dance hats.

The second type of Tlingit potlatch hat consists of a shallow cone of woven spruce roots, rather like a Chinese coolie hat. On top are worn small straw cylinders the shape and size of modern tuna cans. These are piled three or four high at the peak of the straw hat, and signify how many prestigious potlatches the wearer has given. Potlatch dance costume is thus seen to mirror precisely the social maturity of the dancer.

The third type of potlatch hat is of carved wood of a lightweight species, with a bulky three-dimensional carving of the totem—Bear, Wolf, Salmon, and so on—constituting the hat. It is carefully painted in small, curving, delineated panels, and worn while holding stiff, formal dance posture resembling theatrical, satirical cloak-and-dagger stance. This type of headwear derives from the Tlingit wooden helmets formerly used in war, and that were carved in the likenesses of fearsome devils. As battles became less frequent the helmet became a part of ceremonial costume, and the devils were replaced by clan crests.

We have described at length the Chilkat blankets and the crest hats; these are the two most important Tlingit dance accoutrements, socially, politically, and economically. One might add, of course, that their aesthetic excellence is great, bringing dignity and majesty to American Indian dance in a measure matched only occasionally elsewhere. Other Tlingit dancewear includes bibs, tunics, button blankets, and aprons. All of these exhibit clan totemic emblems painstakingly executed in elaborate colored beadwork and embroidery; some illustrate mythology. Each Tlingit village and town possesses its own collection of ancient legends reflecting local community history, real or fictional. A dance tunic noted by the writer at Yakutat in 1974 shows "White Raven Comes to Yakutat after the Quake." The dance tunic design illustrates how Raven stole water, then headed for Petrel's smoke-hole. Petrel then proclaimed, "May the Spirit of Fire Hold You in my Smoke-Hole!" Petrel poured pitch onto Fire, and so Raven became forever black.

The most striking dance accoutrement is the octopus bag, unusual in its four dangling, dancing legs. It is noteworthy that the Tlingit, with their histrionic skills and experience, bring to life the spiritual essence embodied in dance costume crests by having the costume *dance*—swaying blanket fringes, floating down, flailing apron legs. Spirits dance with humans in unifying communion, thereby maintaining good relations with the spirit world and ensuring the welfare of departed ancestor spirits and the protection of the human community from evil spirits.

The octopus bag is a beaded dance apron tied around the waist, with four wide straps descending to the thighs, parallel to each other and embroidered with white and colored beads. In former times it embodied a somewhat exotic symbolism because of its Devil Fish association. Although found among some American Indian groups in the Lower Forty-Eight, the Tlingit are the only Northwest Coast Indians to make them. The bag is of woolen cloth, usually red, and the stylized floral designs contrast with the traditional crest design.

Tlingit button blankets came into use in the middle of the nineteenth century when woolen cloth and pearl buttons were traded. They are navy blue with wide red borders on three sides, and derive their name from the rows of pearl buttons on the borders. Across the top is a lining in printed cotton, and ties to fasten the blanket under the chin. In Alaska today, the Haida of Hydaburg use these red and blue button blankets as their only dance uniform. One button blanket in the Sheldon Jackson Museum (Cat.# I.A.330) shows Raven split down the front and laid out flat, all in white pearl buttons. Another (Cat.# I.A.323), called "Land of Plenty Robe," was owned by Yakutat leader Olaf Abraham in 1910; de Laguna gives its symbolism: a bearlike face at the top symbolizes mountains at the head of a river, which flows into the mouth of a land otter. Above on each side are two heads symbolizing clouds; below are two large eyes, on each side are two wolves (1972, vol. 3, p. 1068).

Tlingit ceremonial dance paddles are of carved and painted wood, and have three main functions: (1) as insignia of office, (2) as pointers to give directional and spatial instruction to the dancers, and (3) to keep masked dancers out of the fire, for some masks are without eye-holes. Ancient dance paddles were long, but today's are quite short.

The dance masks are of three main kinds. The first are similar in shape to face masks but much larger, being suspended from the crossbeams. Dancers perform behind them, operating the moving eyes and jaws by means of pullstrings. The second type are tied with thongs at the sides or clenched between the teeth by biting on the dorsal bit. The third type are enormous, realistic wooden sculptures—carved or molded three-dimensional headpieces used for dance-dramas. They transform the dancer into a wolf, a bear, or a raven with an enlarged head—a sort of nineteenth-century Tlingit Sesame Street.

Tlingit dance masks derive from (1) totemic crests, (2) myths and legends, and (3) shamanistic spirits. One dance mask from Wrangell represents The Woman Who Laid False Claim (Swanton, 1909, p. 165); she improperly and illegally appropriated the fish and seal left on the beach by her son-in-law. A Land Otter mask from Yakutat depicts the legend of the drowned man who turned into Land Otter; fur is forming around the open mouth, which reveals sharp teeth, showing that already he is growing a muzzle. This is in the American Museum of Natural History (E/410), as is a dance mask representing Spirit of Devilfish (E/396). This mask has tentacles carved on the face, whiskers of bear's fur, and open mouth through which to stick one's dyed tongue or to blow down. There was formerly a crown of wooden horns on the forehead, representing supernatural power. Another dance mask portrays Spirit of Peacemaker, who intercedes between two quarreling sibs (E/401). The Tlingit believed that if Peacemaker were killed by one of the factions, his spirit possessed the power to cure the sick.

George T. Emmons collected a shaman's mask at Dry Bay prior to 1909. It depicts Bear's face, attached to which are four Land Otter heads with Devilfish tentacles for bodies; this is in the Burke Museum in Seattle (# TBM/WSM 2032). Tlingit dance masks are commonly carved from alder, and may feature very black eyebrows, very white eyes, black hair, dyed feathers, and red-stained cedar appurtenances such as a head-ring or crown. The masks possess incised line definition of detail and extensive polychromy. The shape commonly stressed is a wide geometric ovoid. Brows, eyes, nose, and mouth are strongly highlighted sculpturally and further emphasized by flat paint. Bold effects are achieved by "resultant line"—the consequence of the meeting of two planes of different angles, painted in contrasting colors. Tlingit masks appear to be designed mainly for three-quarter frontal viewing; straight frontal viewing flattens their sculptured surfaces. Bilateral vertical subdivision imparts symmetry.

In one Klackqwan dance mask, the head of a young raven has a movable jaw that opens to reveal the red lining of the mouth and a black margin. The areas around the eyes, the upper side of the beak, and above the eyebrows are painted in a green derived from copper, and the forehead and eyes are in black. A semihuman dance mask from Wrangell is carved of yellow cedar, with the nostrils, eyes, ears, and eyebrows inlaid with abalone. It has an eagle beak and is painted black, red, and gray green (Gunther, 1966, p. 129). Tlingit masks often have numerous movable parts: eyes move side to side, the jaw opens, a spirit in the throat may propel forward.

Tsimshian dance masks differ from Tlingit in that the mouth is generally a straight line, and often shows tension toward the sides. The area around the eyes is usually painted in a color highly contrasting with the remainder of the face, giving the impression of a smaller mask superimposed upon a larger one (Gunther, 1966, p. 129–134). The Tlingit, who made extremely artistic masks themselves, admired Tsimshian dance masks and employed them in shamanistic seances and at important ceremonial potlatches.

Ideally, all Tlingit dance accessories should be manufactured by the opposite moiety or ordered through them from Tsimshian artists. If there is only one skilled dance-hat crest carver in the community, he may carve for both moieties, but his wife is ceremonially paid for whatever is used by a sib of his own side. At every subsequent public display of the dance-hat crest, other wealth must be displayed, or it will lack full recognition (McLellan 1954: 88). This partly explains why present-day anthropologists are asked to pay for the tape-recording of Tlingit songs, and why payment is demanded for the photographing and filming of dance and dance regalia: behind the dance and under the surface of the music lies a complex economic equation, the bottom line of which is reciprocity and comparable compensation for inheritable sib proprietory symbols.

Tlingit masked dance is a form of iconic sign—the mask being a mechanism of transformation and the dancers being perceived as the spiritual apparition depicted. The psychodramatic realization of a key episode from Tlingit mythology proffers to the potlatch participants and the community a partial model of the Tlingit belief system.

TLINGIT SHAMANISTIC DANCE

Shamanistic dance was an important feature of precontact Tlingit society, for the shaman was healer, medium, and spiritual ally of his client. Franz Boas's documentary film of the Kwakiutl neighbors to the south of the Tlingit shows sequences in which shamans sing and dance over a stick patient (Boas, 1930). Tlingit shamans were often of Tsimshian origin, their alienness heightening dramatic impact. They practiced ecstatic trance, magical curing, mastery of fire, animal transformation, flight of the soul, rebirth from bones, control of the weather, prediction of hunting success, and other impressive psychodrama such as teleportation and extrasensory perception.

In a mid-nineteenth-century account by William Beynon, a Tsimshian shaman obtained specific dance powers from other shamans by bribing an influential chief with marmot pelts: "I went to the villages and each man sang his shaman power songs over me and put further dance powers into me" (cited in Garfield & Wingert, 1979, p. 47). A Tlingit shaman's credentials were usually derived from the claim that he had inherited spiritual powers from an uncle or older brother, that is, matrilineally, and endured the necessary initiation. To practice, the shaman needed assistants; these were invariably from his own sib but not necessarily of his own lineage (de Laguna, 1972, vol. 2, p. 670). Prior to exercising his powers, a shaman fasted, purged, and avoided cutting his hair; he also observed sexual abstinence, for women at times symbolize blood, which introduces danger and impurity into the rite.

The novice shaman went for a year into the mountains on a spirit quest. Additionally, important powers were acquired by cutting a land otter's tongue ceremonially; this effected transfer of the spirit. A famous Chilkat shaman encountered by Krause possessed much special paraphernalia, including drum, rattle, mask, staff, and so on, all kept in a special storage chest (1885, p. 196). Veniaminof reported that a shaman who wished to summon the spirits must practice alone for months, and rehearse the songs and dances to specific drum rhythms (1840, p. 41). In January of 1882, Krause observed a shaman's seance in Klackqwan, during which "two chests were lowered and raised through the smoke-hole . . . the third day the shaman performed a dance around the fire, wearing a colored dance blanket and holding a sharp knife in his hand" (1885, p. 202).

Olson's elderly informant at Sitka in the early 1960s remembered shamanistic seances and dance as part of secret society activities, an importation from the Tsimshian: "The Kiksadi danced . . . they painted their faces in the form of Raven's beak. They wore coils of cedar bark on their heads" (Olson, 1967, p. 119). In his "Tlingit Myths and Texts," Swanton gives Tlingit myths describing the mysterious adventures of shamans (1909, p. 217). Oberg is of the opinion that "Among the Tlingit, the shamans and their spirits were considered in a different category from the totemic spirits. They feared these shamanistic spirits which could be used by individuals to work harm upon other individuals. Totemism was social and integrative while shamanism was individual and disintegrative" (Oberg, 1937, p. 20). This statement may be too great a generalization, but it does point up the social problems of some shamans.

Drucker points out that "Soul loss was a mysterious malady to which North Pacific Coast Indians were subject. There was a general, not very clearly formulated belief in a subsidiary soul, whose departure from the body did not cause immediate death, but rather lassitude and wasting away, which was fatal if the errant soul were not recovered in time. Not every shaman could perform the feat of soul recovery; those who could were specialists. Sometimes an intrusive-object shaman recognized the disease and referred the patient to a colleague who had the special power" (Drucker, 1965, p. 90). Soul recovery was often a spectacular theatrical display. An important chief's soul would be discovered in a handful of eagle down at the edge of the village, and returned on a painted board representing the supernatural canoe used for the perilous journey. This might be acted out in masked dance, evoking awe and furthering the cathartic goals of the healing ritual. Communal anxiety over the chief's high fever sets in motion a religiously sanctioned coping mechanism in the form of psychodramatic catharsis—a public coming to terms with stressful frustration. In the shaman's imaginative and theatrical display, the purgative discharge of fear is an attainable substitute for inattainable victory over the dying chief's real problem.

Shamanistic dance and the ceremonial potlatch dance, then, transforms inchoate ideas into powerful imagery, which modifies phenomenal experience. The efficacy of the ritual dance in question in inducing the culturally prescribed response is dependent upon hypersuggestibility and the participants' learned faith in their religious constructs.

In 1987 the writer witnessed an extended shamanistic healing sequence, performed by the 30-member Gai San Dancers, an intervillage group, most of whose members come from Haines. The leader is traditional chief Austin Hammond, and the shaman is Jimmie Charlie. Jimmie states that he is a true Tlingit medicine-man, inheriting his powers in the traditional way from shaman ancestors. Other members of the team are Lillian Hammond, Elsie Lamont, Ruth Davis, Sam Jackson, Rick Johnson, and additional dancers. The shaman lay a red and blue button blanket over the patient, and shook his Raven rattle in one hand and a feathered dance fan in the other. Wearing a long gray wig and a crown of goat horns, he danced around the patient, singing vocables loudly, to the accompaniment of a constant drum roll by traditional drummer Austin Hammond. He administered a shell full of medicine to the patient. At this point, the healing rite took a humorous turn, becoming a spoof of the ancient shaman's theatrics. On swallowing the medicine, the patient suddenly sat up, belched, and fell back flat. The dancing shaman's apron then fell off (intentionally), whereupon the shaman desperately covered his crotch with his dance fan, standing knock-kneed. He performed a leap, then clutched his hip because of arthritic pain. He stood the patient up, danced him a few steps across the arena, whereupon the patient dropped dead. Turning to the dancers, the shaman hollered, "Can't win 'em all!"

Contrary to one's immediate reaction to all this, it was not a deviant performance. McLellan reports that "the spirit dances performed by laymen at potlatches are intentionally humorous imitations of shamanistic performance" (1954, p. 95). Thus the apparently uncharacteristic exhibition by contemporary Tlingit shaman Jimmie Charlie is entirely in accord with ancient tradition—Jimmie Charlie the shaman was spoofing his ancient confreres. Boas's film of Kwakiutl dance shows an audience ridiculing a shaman, demanding proof of his claimed powers. The harrassed shaman then rashly demands to be decapitated, disembowelled, and thrown into the fire, so that he can demonstrate his immortality (1930). The Tlingit possessed a fear of shamans and their powerful spirits; this fear was in part channeled and controlled by compensatory lighthearted satirizing of shamanistic ritual.

In precontact times the shaman knew his fellow villagers and their social problems. He was usually an expert herbalist and also a psychiatrist, eliciting their anxieties through questioning and deduction. He realized that in many cases of sickness, it was a matter of mind triumphing over the body. He tried to heal the mind with positive thinking and hypersuggestibility.

CONTEMPORARY TLINGIT DANCE TEAMS AND DANCE MOVEMENTS

The most famous and long-established Tlingit dance team in Alaska is at Haines—the Chilkat Dancers. Formed in 1959, they rehearse in their tribal house on the parade grounds of old Fort Seward. They are sponsored by the Alaska Indian Arts Inc., a nonprofit organization dedicated to the revival and perpetuation of Tlingit art and dance, and were originally encouraged to do this by their friend and founder Major Carl Heinmiller. Alaska Indian Arts is supported by the Alaska State Council on the Arts, Alaska State Travel Division, and the Alaska Visitors Association. They have displayed arts and dance at the Annual Intertribal ceremonials at Gallup, New Mexico (first prize), New York World's Fair (1964), Expo '70 in Japan (with the world's tallest totem pole, 132 feet high), and at Expo '74 at Spokane, WA.

The group possesses numerous priceless artifacts, including ancient Chilkat blankets, which they store in the old military hospital, where they carve dance masks, dance rattles, dance staffs, and dance paddles. The nearby theater is the dance venue where they mount public performances of ancient Chilkat dance-dramas. The present writer witnessed their dance dramas in 1975. In the Chilkat Bear and Raven dance, a revered chief is killed by a brown bear while hunting. Warriors discover his body and call the women to come forth to carry his body home in his Chilkat blanket. The warriors kill many bears while searching for the culprit, until Raven informs that the Bear has a large lock of human hair in his teeth, whereupon they locate him and exact revenge.

In the Cannibal Giant Dance, a huge monster devours Tlingit villagers for decades. Becoming aged, he switches to devouring the fish that women had prepared for the winter grubstake. Through a shaman's trick Cannibal Giant is finally overcome and killed. In the Chilkat village of Klackqwan stands the original totem pole of Cannibal Giant.

In the Tide Woman Dance, the Otter people—first people on Earth—were starving to death. Raven asked Tide Woman to send the tide out so the Otter people could collect clams. She drove Raven off with her Wolf helper, but the Otter people united against her and prevailed. This dance was originally of Haida origin, and employs several elaborate dance masks with movable parts skillfully operated by the dancers.

The Fog Woman Dance originates with the neighboring Tsimshian on the Skeena River, and depicts matchmaking. The tribal elders enlist spiritual aid in determining suitable marriage partners for the eligible young women. In the Ptarmigan Dance, the rhythmic courting steps of

Ptarmigan are depicted, in the spring when he is white all over. The dancers wear white dance tunics and manipulate white feathered dance fans. Mr. Ptarmigan attempts to attract Miss Ptarmigan, but has a competitor. This dance originates with the Athabascan to the west.

In the Spear Dance, the warriors make war against an offending group, and capture slaves. They decapitate the defiant leader. In the Haida Blanket Dance, the dancers compete in their dance steps over an extended period of time, becoming quite fatigued. The Chilkat blankets are brought out for this dance; the Ravens and the Eagles each choose a champion to represent them in exhibiting tireless footwork, which consist of miming animal and bird movements. Krause noted in 1881 that the Chilkat borrowed dances: "Among the Chilkat we saw two kinds of dances, which were distinguished as those of the Haida and those of the Athabascans of the interior, and which maintain their character even to the accompanying songs and the costuming" (1885, p. 167).

De Laguna noted of the Yakutat Tlingit that "the Tekwedi, who trace their origin to the far south, use Tsimshian songs, including some introduced into Yakutat only in the 1880s. The Kagwantan from Sitka via Dry Bay also have a Tsimshian song. The Klackqwan, on the other hand, have Atna walking, resting, and dancing songs, traditionally ones their ancestors had used at Chitina or had composed as they crossed the glaciers to the coast . . . similarly the sibs of Dry Bay, primarily the Tluxnaxadi and Cankuqedi have Athabascan songs obtained from the southern Tutchone on the upper Alsek. The Tluknaxadi also have some from the Gunana of the upper Taku" (de Laguna, 1972, vol. 2, p. 569).

McLellan reports that "One of the most successful acts of a Dry Bay potlatch in 1909 was the appearance of the Raven Tluknaxadi women clad in kimonos and wearing Japanese hats on Japanese-style haircuts—a bit of pageantry inspired by some shipwrecked Japanese who had drifted ashore the previous year" (McLellan, 1954, p. 83). The University of Alaska Museum possesses some Tlingit potlatch hats that are copies of hats worn in the nineteenth-century Russian Navy, except for beaded pendants suspended from the perimeter.

Tlingit proclivity for musical borrowing stems from broader social and economic customs centering on trade routes and bartering links, which in turn derive from navigational skills and the abundance of waterway travel. Although borrowing is common, it is nevertheless highly selective, materializing only where the Tlingit cultural filter permits the incorporation of alien music and dance, wherever power and prestige are thereby enhanced. Tsimshian songwords augmented the shaman's supernatural aura because they were incomprehensible. Another reason that Tlingit songs and dances traveled was that, as valuable property, they might serve as indemnity. If group A caused a drowning in group B, group A's song or dance might serve as compensation.

In the Chilkat dances just described as reflected the former role of women in carrying the body and in storing the winter food supply. They depict Raven as provider or depriver, and legendary figures such as giants, Tide Woman, and Fog Woman. A prominent element is the bipartite opposition of two forces, such as Ravens versus Eagles, humans versus mythical creatures, Tlingits versus unfriendly neighbors. Tlingit dance songs use both real words and vocables. Many of the apparently nonsensical syllables sung by the Chilkat Dancers in fact represent the cries, barks, and howls of animals and birds in the Tlingit natural environment. They reflect beliefs concerning the hunting spirits and the dominant role of the food quest.

The Chilkat Dancers were emblemmed potlatch costumes and ceremonial hats. They hold dance paddles, dance staffs, and Raven rattles. They maintain a half-circle, with the drum-leader on the end and certain solo dancers in turn in the center. The solo dancer in the center generally exhibits more extensive hand and body movements, and more extensive floor movement, because of his mime.

The dancers in the half-circle keep at least one foot on the ground, while the center dancer hops and leaps, often bringing both feet from the ground. A common solo foot movement mimics Raven: the feet are spread wide apart, leave and meet the ground together, and land heavily flat-footed, avoiding light toe-work, the meanwhile spinning around alternately clockwise and counterclockwise. Such a center dancer will wear a very large carved or papier-maché mask covering the whole head, with a 12-inch beak, movable eyes, and jaw. Such a mask is worn on the back of the head to project the beak in a diagonal, pointing upward. In former times the dancer's body would be covered with red cedar bark. For vigorous dancing the mask is tightly secured to the head, and is snapped jerkily up and down, and from side to side, in short, sharp alternation. If the bird is Raven, the solo dancer caws loudly, and may lunge at other dancers. On his arms he will attach yard-long black wings. Freedom of body movement and of floor movement deferred to crest elevation—dance framed the totem. The sacred emblem of the sib was tendered and displayed to the guests like the orb, scepter, and crown in the coronation of an ancient English king.

In the first (upright) dance posture, dancers did one of two things with their hands: (1) manipulate a staff, paddle, rattle, or drum; (2) perform hand movements. In these hand movements, decorative colored gloves were, and still are, worn for emphasis of motion—each glove bears five tassles which flail the air. The dancer vibrates the forearms and wrists, fingers apart in order to broaden the plane. Direction of wrist movement resembles that of a man speedily operating two safe combination locks simultaneously. This is done at chest height, and yields a blurred magical effect, drawing attention to the aura surrounding the hands.

Dancers using spherical rattles hold the handle straight up, with the rattle pointing toward the crossbeams, and shake them forward, often in a tremolo of continuous sound. This is done to highlight the most laudatory stanza-lines. Dancers holding Raven rattles hold the shaman side down, with the Raven beak pointing toward the audience, and move the rattle up and down. Seeds or pebbles in the rattles produce the sound, which acts as a sustaining filler between the staccato drumbeats. In some American Indian societies, seeds in rattles symbolize fertility.

Holding a carved object, and wearing a heavy cloak, the dancer will tend to dance in a style conducive to the purposes of these cultural objects. As we have already mentioned, rigid social structure and the mandate to glorify the crest probably determines aspects of dance style. Thus there are both psychocultural and physical determinants of dance style: learned attitudes toward class hierarchy, and empirical adaptation to the geometrics and inflexibility of cumbersome crest objects and ceremonial apparel.

The Chilkat blanket requires that the rear view be exhibited prominently, and that the fringes be spun and flared. The weight of the blanket requires that the dancer's hand or hands grasp the border at the frontal opening to prevent flapping and to forestall undignified uncovering of the body. Dancers can be seen doing this in Boas's film of Kwakiutl dance (1930). The Chilkat blanket determined the dancer's use of space. De Laguna notes that "these enveloping robes did not permit much freedom of motion . . . a Chilkat blanket also effectively pinioned the arms . . . most dances seem to have been performed on the spot, without stepping away, the body swaying to and fro, the arms moving from side to side, and the knees dipping" (1972, vol 2, p. 568). Except for the absence of the spinning of the fringes, the same remarks may apply to the button blankets.

Regarding the effect of mask-wearing on the use of dance space, it should be borne in mind that some masks had no eye-holes. Eye-holes were not necessary in a dance environment bounded by a suspended screen, a suspended box-drum, a crowded audience, and house walls. Sometimes the mask itself was suspended, limiting the mask dancer to the area immediately behind the mask. Sometimes the mask dancer stood on a bench to elevate the crest still higher; a tall screen obscured his body up to the neck, focusing attention on the movement of the mask. The bench naturally limited movement (Collins et al., 1973, p. 243). Hats determined dance movement. In the case of the chief's hat, the swan's down had to be kept in place within the crown until it was time to waft it toward the audience. In the case of the straw cone bearing cylinders, the latter must be restrained from tumbling to the floor. In the case of the carved wooden helmets, these had to be balanced; they were top-heavy, and they limited head movement. The dance drummer endeavored to keep all dancers in view so that they could catch his cues. He held the drum with the skin right-angled to the ground so that the sound traveled sideways; this meant that his beating arm made horizontal sweeps.

Contemporary Tlingit dance teams usually make dramatic entrances and exits in single file, commencing the drumming while still hidden from view behind a screen or doorway. Boas's film of Kwakiutl dance features similar openings and closings (1930). Krause noted among the Chilkat that "dancers came in singly and placed themselves in a row" (1885, p. 167). As each dancer appears he or she flashes a brief display at the audience, such as a leap, a left-right swing of the head, a sudden raising of the rattle, or a 360° revolution. Entrances and exits are performed to the accompaniment of special songs not used at other times, and that continue until all of the dancers are assembled in view, whereupon the dancers turn their backs on the audience in unison, and the song terminates, in readiness for the first dance proper.

At the Alaska Native Brotherhood performances today, there are the entrance and exit dances, the main body of half-circle dances, and the mimetic dance-dramas. Examples of the latter include the Spirit Dance executed behind a raised emblemmed screen, the Bow-and-Arrow Dance, the Canoe Dance, the Shaman Healing Dance (already described), and numerous other miniature dance-dramas, such as those already listed for the Chilkat Dancers.

In addition, there exists much Tlingit potlatch behavior, which resembles dance but is less defined. In oratory, there occurs much histrionic bouncing and deep knee-bends for emphasis. In Tlingit storytelling, which is a celebrated art, specialists like Walter Williams "dance" throughout the story, swaying, gesturing, standing on tiptoe, and getting down on the ground. In such storytelling, it is common for the reciter to slide to the left to depict the hero, then slide to the right to depict the protagonist, so that the storyteller's changing vocal pitches emanate from different directions. The audience perceives many successive small and large characters portrayed by the versatile, chameleonlike reciter, whose voice drops to a whisper, then dramatically increases toward a climax, body rising, chest puffed outward, forehead perspiring, arms spreading,

head thrown back. In Tlingit storytelling, oratory, psychodrama, mythology, and body movement merge into one impressive art form, formerly employed to validate chiefly privilege, now functioning to preserve Tlingit folklore.

Bill Holm relates Northwest Coast Indian dance to the plastic arts:
"The constant flow of movement, broken at rhythmic intervals by rather
sudden, but not necessarily jerky changes of motion-direction, characterize both the dance and art of the Nothwest Coast" (Holm, 1965, p. 92).
Dance, music, folklore, and art, with their shared deep-rooted origins
in Tlingit history and cultural experience, exhibit a subtle stylistic unity.
This unity may be said to be a crystalization of Tlingit aesthetic and
artistic values.

The Mt. St. Elias Dancers of Yakutat possess an extensive repertoire
of ancient dances, many of them dance-dramas, some of them borrowed
from neighboring groups. They were explained to the writer in a manuscript by Judith Ramos in 1977. Judith is the daughter of Elaine Ramos,
American Indian Woman of the Year for 1974, who is the great-grand-
daughter of Olaf Abraham, a celebrated Tlingit chief.

In the Yakutat Suna Suna Dance, Sun is implored to reappear from
behind rain clouds. The dance rhythm is slow, with gaps in the drumming. The dancers "look for Sun," and at the songwords Suna Suna the
dance movements become more vigorous. The movements consist of
scanning the sky, raising outstretched arms, moving to a crouching position and back, and finally seeing Sun, when the dance concludes.

The Yakutat Dish Dance is performed at potlatches, at which time
the assembled participants "sing and dance for their food" (Ramos, 1977,
p. 2). The dancers have already eaten their fill, so the dance is postpay-
ment, or thanksgiving. Everything is cleared and a large bowl of food is
placed in the center of the dance arena. The dance has two parts, slow
then fast. The dancers mimic Raven, eyeing each other and trying to
peck at the food first. In this part of the dance, the movements tend to
be individualistic. In the second part, the dance movements quicken,
and the dancers stand in place in a circle, trying to reach forward toward
the food. On a loud drum accent all of the dancers hop like Raven
toward the bowl of food, but just before arriving, they back. This is done
twice; the third time they all arrive at the food and mime pecking at it
together.

In the Yakutat Honey Dance, a ceremonially dressed doll represents
Honey, daughter of Shangukeite, of the opposite phratry. The dance is
said to have been made by a Tlingit whose betrothed left him: "Where
are you Honey, daughter of Shangukeite, when I need you?" In Yakutat
today, this dance is used by a lover at a community potlatch to show
respect and admiration for a girl of the opposite group.

The Yakutat Sa Tu Dance originates from the Athabascan Copper River region to the west, where it is still performed in its original version. In the Tlingit version, both arms are first thrown to the left at chest height, then brought back in front and moved to the right. The palms are open and face downward, the wrists oscillating in order to spin the glove tassles. In the next movement the arms are raised above the head as the dancer descends to squatting position. Once there, the arms are brought down. Finally all of the dancers rise in unison to standing position, throw the arms once more to the left, and let out a loud shout to mark the end of the Sa Tu Dance. The drumbeat remains constant throughout, and the dancers follow signals for the various movements from the drummer-leader.

The Yakutat Raven on the Beach Dance is in two parts, tide going out and tide coming in. The dancers act the part of Raven and sing in Tlingit, "Happiness fills me when the tide is out, and I feast on mussels." The dancers hop from mussel to mussel, pecking. In the second part, the tide comes in, Raven backs up, and projects a downcast expression with drooping wings.

The Yakutat Tlingit use spears in the three-part Spear Dance, which concerns two warring Copper River groups. The dance features varying dance tempos, face paint, and drumming like the sound of a rattle. In part one, the dancers form two files, lining up facing each other across an imaginary river and holding their spears. They desire peace but do not trust the other side. Part one is concluded by moving the spears from left to right. In part two the tempo quickens because the action becomes more aggressive—the dancers raise their spears up in readiness for throwing, lunging threateningly toward the line of dancers facing them. When the drummer-leader gives the signal, each line moves toward the river, but in front of each line is a peacemaker trying to hold them back. At the edge of the river they stop and dance slowly backward. This is repeated three times, whereupon both sides decide they have saved face and can initiate peace negotiations.

According to a Yakutat informant de Laguna met in 1954, this dance derives from an actual historical incident involving rivalry between a Klackqwan group and a McCarthy group at a Copper River potlatch. "It's against Indian law to use any kind of knife, when you dancing. But Klackqwan chief said they're going to cover with eagle feathers, so nobody see. So they went up to that McCarthy. They well prepared. The same thing—they're afraid we're going to have a war with them in that dance. . . . Then the guard reported the McCarthy people coming down already. And my tribe, they all run to our opposite tribe's house they so scared . . . They hold it this way, ready to spear.

When they said 'Hwii!' everybody charge for that canoe. But they stop
just on the water's edge and they change it again. They hold the spear
up again. That means no war. So the other ones in the water know it
then, there's no war, just dance" (de Laguna, 1972, vol. 2, p. 899). These
two descriptions—Judith Ramos's account of a present-day Yakutat
dance, and de Laguna's informant's account of a Copper River incident—tell much concerning the origin, diffusion, and choreography of
a Tlingit traditional dance. Here one witnesses its birth, development,
and adoption into the repertoire.

The Yakutat Jiixwaa Dance is in two parts; it concerns a boy who
turned into a fish, and the efforts of his lineage and their shaman in
trying to recover him. The dance rhythms are irregular and gapped.
He became accustomed to his fellow fish and afraid of humans. Kelp
and seaweed were growing on him. In part one, Jiixwaa emerges hesitat-
ingly from the ocean, hiding his face from his people, who are singing
to prevent him receding under the water. In the second part, Jiixwaa
dances toward his people, trying to pull the kelp and seaweed from his
face. The dance ends with his people encircling him so that he cannot
recede, and they lead him triumphantly back to their village.

In the Yakutat Paddle Dance, the manipulation of carved, painted
dance paddles becomes part of the dance imagery. The accompanying
song was formerly used with the Tlingit traveled on short waterway
journeys. A Frog screen is suspended low by screen-holders wearing
large Raven masks and floor-length button blankets bearing a Raven
design on the back. The Frog screen separates the dancers from the
audience, and the dancers paddle on their left side, extending the paddles over the screen in simulation of a long canoe. This is reversed for the
return journey. Boas's film of Kwakiutl dance shows a similar mimetic
sequence (1930). Boat building and canoe navigation were essential economic activities in early twentieth-century Tlingit life, and this dance
reflects that fact. Much Tlingit mythology derives from the strange adventures and mysterious encounters of mariners upon the sea; in some
dances the songwords and the screen design combine to tell the story.

The Yakutat Walking Dance is a contemporary dance dedicated to
Governor Egan at his inaugural several decades ago: "I will walk through
the mountains for you, Governor Egan." As they sing these songwords,
the dancers execute short forward dance steps while remaining in a half-
circle.

The Yakutat Rifle Dance is an entrance dance, and the performers
hold a hunting rifle. The dancers must make a formal entrance in pairs.
As each pair arrives at front stage center, the dancers continue dance
steps in place with raised rifles, facing each other in pairs while the rest

are still entering. About each ten seconds they turn and face a different dancer, then return to their former position. This turning back and forth is repeated until all of the dancers are in, when the dance concludes by lowering the rifles.

In the Yakutat Laugh Dance, the goal is to make the members of the opposite moiety laugh heartily. The movements of the women dancers suggest that the dance originates with the Copper River Athabascan to the west, for they manipulate chiffon scarves, which link the two hands. The hands are raised to chest height in front and moved rhythmically up and down about six inches. Men and women dancers each form a line and stand facing the other line. The two lines advance toward each other and the individual dancers slide by each other, slightly dipping as they do this. The process is then reversed in the other direction. Immediately following this, the lines change into a circle that revolves clockwise, the women dancers waving their scarves and looking at each other and laughing. In ancient times as well as now, different Alaskan ethnic groups derived considerable amusement from mimicking and exaggerating the dance movements typical of neighboring groups.

In the Yakutat Jumping Dance, the foot movement is sex specific and quite fast. Men dancers jump vigorously from side to side keeping the right foot in front of the left. The women dancers lift only one foot from the ground, and move that foot from side to side in front of the immobile foot. The dance is short because it is exhausting for elderly participants. It may have been influenced by Russian dance.

For the Yakutat Ptarmigan Dance, three participants wear special white dance tunics. A male dancer and two teenage boys imitate Ptarmigan and her two young ones looking for food. At a signal from the drummer-leader two boards are clapped together off-stage, and all three of the birds drop to the ground as if shot. The accompanying singing becomes quieter. As the singing picks up again the birds gradually return to life, reflecting the magical power of music, and Tlingit belief in reincarnation.

The Yakutat Elesowo Outside Dance is thought to emanate from the Athabascan Copper River region. It is performed outside the pot-latch house when the guests arrive for the ceremonial potlatch, hence is name. It is executed in two lines with the guests passing between the two lines, and concludes with hollering and whooping. In traditional potlatch protocol it immediately precedes the Coming In Dance, but the protocol is not always followed today.

In the Yakutat Whiskey Dance, an empty bottle is used as a dance accessory in a story that relates how a Tlingit hunter is disappointed in love because his beloved married another hunter of higher status. The man turns to drink; this is represented by upturning the bottle. Following this the songwords proclaim, "Now I believe that the earth spins, for I can see it myself!"

The Yakutat Money Dance immediately precedes the Exit Dance. All present are required to throw at least one dollar bill onto a pile of money in the center of the dance floor, and the dance continues until all have contributed. The dance is lengthy, for ample funds are desired. The dance-leader puts on a comic display, dancing up to prominent Tlingit personages present, such as the President of the Alaska Native Brotherhood, and fining such individuals for supposed or imaginary infractions of Tlingit potlatch protocol, such as not wearing a dance hat appropriate to their dance costume. In a way, this behavior is a spoof of Tlingit potlatch formality. At the conclusion of the dance, potlatch officials or conference organizers come forward and carefully count the money while it is still on the floor; it later enters Alaska Native Brotherhood coffers. This dance reflects the intrinsic economic basis of the ancient potlatching tradition, where wealth goods circulated and later recirculated in an endless cycle of reciprocity. It also reflects social and economic change, with the advent of a cash economy.

In the aforegoing dances are mirrored Tlingit maritime subsistence, Tlingit historical migration from the Copper River, diffusion of dance, the peacemaking function of potlatching, waterway navigation, and mythology concerning Sun and concerning Raven. To conclude the Yakutat group of contemporary dances we will describe the Goodbye Dance, which originated with the Atna of Copper River. Many Yakutat dances are from this region, because the Yakutat Tlingit probably migrated eastward from there to their present location. Many legends and myths recount the prolonged, hazardous crossing of a great mountain range lying to the west. The Goodbye Dance serves as an exit dance and is performed in a walking circle. The dancers vigorously wave tassled dance gloves as they peel off from the circle one after another, wave goodbye to the audience, and disappear behind a screen or doorway. The dance continues until everyone is out.

The Mt. St. Elias Dancers of Yakutat were founded in 1950 and are led by elders Mary James, Edith Rener, Ruth Jackson, Harold Bremner, Troy Bremner, Darin Bremner, Paul Henry, and Debbie Lekanoff, some of whom are the writer's longstanding dance informants. They utilize the Alaska Native Brotherhood Hall at Yakutat for their rehearsals, and perform at the annual ANB Convention in southeast Alaska, and other tribal occasions. The ANB rotate their meeting locale. Longtime Yakutat dance-leader Harry Bremner died while dancing in 1975; the present writer was greatly distressed to be standing nearby at the time. He was Chief of the Copper River Tribe of Yakutat, from the Raven Clan and the House of the Owl Bones of the Raven. Together with his famous brother-in-law Olaf Abraham he revived Yakutat Tlingit dance in the 1950s and performed for the inauguration of Governor Egan. His lineage dance costume bore floral patterns and a mountain, the former representing Earth and the latter representing Mt. St. Elias, the second highest peak in North America. It lies behind Yakutat. The tragedy of Tlingit dance is that many of its expert leaders are elderly, and the art is being lost as they pass away. Realization of this fact in the past decade has spurred leaders and educators to increased efforts in teaching Tlingit dance to the young.

The Mark Trail Dancers in 1974 comprised Johnny Marks, Kathy Marks, Jim Marks, Leo Marks, Bob Beirley, Austin Brown, Daisy Phillips, Rick Beasley, and Ralph Houston. One of their main features at that time was the Spirit Dance, which currently survives among other dance teams. Two members of the opposite moiety from the hosts stand and stretch a tall, painted cloth screen at shoulder height across the dance arena. The Spirit-Dancer or shaman wears a chief's hat and bobs swan's down across the top of the screen to transmit tranquility. To accomplish this he performs a leaping dance with arms outspread and head tilting alternatively backward and forward. In his right hand he shakes a Raven rattle, and on his face are painted moiety insignia in red and black.

In the Raven Dance of the Mark Trail Dancers, the solo dancer wears a large Raven head with various movable parts. Hopping within a circle of dancers and flapping his wings, he mimes pecking at a carcass and emits loud cawing sounds. The feet are widespread and the dancer makes two-footed jumps that twist the body around in clockwise and counterclockwise turns this way and that, landing heavily flat-footed and making a rhythmic thumping synchronized with the drumming. The trunk is hunched over, and the extended Raven beak alternately points up and down from sky to ground, and vigorously from side to side. At the ancient intervillage potlatches along the coast, the lead canoe would feature such a dancer in the prow of the boat as it approached the waiting hosts on the beach. This is shown in Boas's film of Kwakiutl dance (1930).

In the Proprietory Dance of the Mark Trail Dancers, each dancer steps forward in turn from the half-circle, in order to perform his or her Proprietory Dance solo. They must come forward in order of seniority and maturity, and be prepared to present their identifying matrilineally inherited dance. Each of these solo dances is different, and features personalized dance steps and the lineage song that accompanies them.

As each soloist concludes his or her brief act and steps back into the half-circle, the next steps forward. This continues until all members of the dance team have been featured in dance and formally presented by name, giving immediate descent. The dance is strongly reminiscent of the ceremonial naming and presentation of individuals who have been newly promoted in social rank, in those precontact potlatches following a death at the top of the social hierarchy. All ranks down the line are readjusted, and the inheritors' new status is redefined and validated in dance, symbolizing realignment of power. The dance used to be a rite of passage, wherein each solo dancer was symbolically separated from their past, traversed a no-man's land of liminality, received a new name representing an identity that had been transmuted to a greater or lesser degree, and then was finally reincorporated into society at the new social level.

The Gajaa Heen Dancers of Sitka are led by elders Charlie Joseph, Laurie Joseph, Donna Lang, George Ramos, Ethel Makinen, Annie Dick, Lizzie Basco, Esther Littlefield, and Maria Thiemeyer. The last two of these sew many of the beautiful Sitka dance tunics, doing so in exhibit at the Visitors' Center of the National Park Service in Sitka, where there is an extensive display of their colorful and elaborate artwork. In a performance witnessed by the writer in 1980, the following dances were presented.

In the Sitka First Migration Dance, the Tlingits are represented migrating down to the sea, traveling from the interior on the Stikine River. In the mythology relating the event, the Tlingit hunters and their lineages pass under a great glacier, enduring many hardships. The Second Migration Dance refers to the same migration, but describes the second phase, which is after they have passed the glacier: "Rush the boat out! Steady the boat!" The dancers swing their paddles in unison across the long, raised, painted Raven screen.

The Raven Spirit Dance derives from the ancient Guwakaan or Peace Ceremony, traditionally conducted at an intermoiety potlatch to reduce hostility, suspicion, and rivalry. In ancient times emissaries were sent to obtain supplies of the softest Canadian white swan's down for use in this dance. The Far From Home Dance was composed by a Hoonah woman of the Takdeintaan clan, when she was away from her home village and became possessed by an invasive spirit. These spirits were thought to linger in the forests near villages, and to haunt pathways and clearings leading to the village, waiting for unsuspecting travelers. They stole rides inside innocents, causing lassitude and weakness. Special shamanistic diagnostic dances were necessary to identify the origin and nature of the invasive spirit, followed by a dance curing ritual.

In a typical year's itinerary, the Gajaa Heen Dancers of Sitka perform at the Alaska Federation of Natives Convention in Anchorage, the State Legislature and State Museum in Juneau, the Tanana Chiefs and Fairbanks Native Association Annual Potlatch, the Southeast Alaska Arts Festival at Ketchikan, and the Kake Potlatch. Additionally, they perform frequently for passengers and crews on the Taku Ferry and on the LaConte Ferry.

This traveling continues an ancient tradition. It was through trade, travel, and migration that dance styles used to diffuse in precontact southeast Alaska. Olson reports that "Among most of the Tlingit tribes it was considered a great thing to perform a new dance or sing a new song. Many or most of these were derived from non-Tlingit tribes. Among the Chilkat the Gunana tribes of the interior were the chief source of innovation. At Wrangell the Raven clans got most of their new songs and dances from the Tahltan, whereas the Wolf clans, especially the Nanyaayih, used Tsimshian songs and dances. The Tsimshian were also the source of most of the songs and dances of the Tantakwan and Sanyakwan" (Olson, 1967, p. 67).

Contemporary Tlingit dance teams are active in Hoonah, Angoon, Kake, Saxman, Sitka, Haines, Yakutat, and elsewhere. The Cape Fox Tlingit Dancers are an extended family group who have migrated from Alaska to Seattle, WA. They were originally part of the Saxman dance team. Saxman is 3 miles south of Ketchikan, and was founded in 1894 as a site for a mission school serving Tlingits who had moved from Fort Tongrass and Cape Fox. The village takes its name from Samuel Saxman, a Pennsylvania-born schoolteacher who was lost at sea in 1886. Foty years ago the village elders formed the dance team in order to revive Tlingit local dance traditions. At Saxman today, old totem poles from the abandoned village at Cape Fox are preserved in Saxman Totem Park. When certain families moved to Seattle in 1969, they continued their dances at American Indian events of far larger scope and exposure then heretofore. These included the Pan-Tribal Pow-Wow and the numerous American Indian conferences held at the University of Washington and other centers in the northwest.

Contemporary Tlingit dance still follows vestiges of ancient potlatch protocol. First there is the formal Greeting and Welcome to the Guests, carried out with profuse oratory. This is followed by a short Christian prayer by the Alaska Native Brotherhood chaplain. The First Yeikootee (a short Tlingit ceremony with everyone standing) is next, followed by the Calling of the Names and the Serving. As guests' names are called, prepared dishes of high-quality fresh seafood are delivered to the various tables. This might include herring eggs, seal oil, halibut, venison

stew, hooligan, seaweed, baked salmon, crab, and fish heads. Then follows Money on the Drum, where a collection and subscriptions are taken.

The Naming Ceremony comes next, when new poetic names are
assigned to prominent achievers, who are honorifically adopted into
clans as a mark of respect; this might include whites. This is followed by
formal presentation of the money to the ANB treasurer. Everyone
stands for the Second Yeikootee. After several lengthy and colorful
speeches, there is a presentation of dances by the two moieties, whose
rehearsed and uniformed dance teams have spent weeks preparing for
the event. Awards are then given, followed by the Dedication, where
heirloom Chilkat blankets, ceremonial dance paddles, and perhaps a
large canoe are described in poetic laudatory terms, revered, and dedicated. Guests then make the Speeches of Appreciation; this is followed
by the Closing Prayer.

The performance of dance still symbolically affirms social relationships in Tlingit society, particularly those which cross socioeconomic
class lines. Ancient Tlingit values, partly by virtue of the strict social
stratification and formalized social roles, emphasized education and the
acquirement of knowledge via formal channels. The mother's brother
provided guidance and counseling to the mother's offspring, and each
chief possessed his advisory council of wise elders. "The higher the rank
of the child, the higher the standards to which he had to con-
form . . . their skills and accomplishments were praised by their elders"
(de Laguna, 1972, vol. 1, p. 514). Nineteenth-century white society also
valued education, and after contact the Tlingit cultural filter tended to
allow perception of compatibility in educational values. The Tlingit came
to accept, utilize, and incorporate American mainstream education into
their social system. Thus it is that today one notes many Tlingit politicians, attorneys, and business consultants in the Alaskan Native Corporations and in Alaskan politics. At the annual ANB Conference featuring
traditional dance, Tlingit professionals travel to Yakutat or Sitka from
all over the United States in order to seize the opportunity to renew old
clan ties and to renew their spiritual roots. However, successful and
powerful in the outside world, such Tlingit feel a strong psychological
need to affirm and reaffirm their cultural heritage.

THE DRUMMING ACCOMPANIMENT

One heavy moosehide frame-drum, together with one or more rattles of the Raven type or of the round type, plus the ensemble singing,
provide the dance accompaniment. The drum fulfills the most prominent rhythmic function, cueing the dancers' movements, indicating different phases of the developing action, and signaling beginnings, divisions, and endings of dances. The songwords function to outline the

myth behind the dance, and as a mnemonic device for remembering the sequence of dance movements, each of which may be associated in time and space with a particular syllable.

Tlingit dance drumming is not a constant unchanging beat, as is heard among the Athabascan to the west. It occurs not upon the downbeat but upon the upbeat (afterbeat), the songwords emphasizing the downbeat. Thus drum and voice obey different pulses. The drumming for a given dance will sometimes pass through several distinct phases: (1) brief drumming introduction, often in the form of a free tremolo, (2) even afterbeats, which in 4/4 time would occur on beats two and four, (3) gapped or spasmodic drum rhythm, and (4) imitation of a rattle. Particularly significant movements in the dance may be highlighted by silence, or in contrast to this be emphasized by louder drumbeats. There is sometimes singing without drumming, and vice versa, which imparts drama to the dance sequence in question.

The drummer usually possesses more freedom of floor movement than any other participant; the beating of the drumhead may emanate from left, right, rear, or front of the dance arena, in turn. The drum is not tuned to any particular pitch, but yields a deep resonant tone replete with numerous overtones. Tonal depth and quality can be modified in a general way by heating the drumhead with a firebrand just prior to the dance. The large circle of the drumhead perimeter frames the painted crest, and is yet another medium for elevating and displaying the sacred sib emblem at the ceremonial potlatch.

THE SONGS

Mark reports that the Inland Tlingit recognize several main song classes. (1) Myth songs; these occur within lengthy narratives, and are often sung by the "animal" characters in the story. (2) Hunting magic songs; these cause game such as rabbits and groundhogs to become ensnared in traps set by the singer. (3) Spirit power songs; these are owned and used by individual shamans. (4) Deer songs; these are composed and sung by hostage chiefs at peacemaking potlatches. (5) Lyric songs; these are Mark's most common category, and subdivide into clan mourning songs, children's songs, and miscellaneous lyrical songs.

Mark states that the songs are strophic and that 55.8% of the sample are tripartite, while 34.3% are bipartite in structure. The most common melodic ranges are a minor seventh and an octave. The most common melodic intervals are minor thirds and major seconds. Fifty-six percent of the melodic intervals are descending, 44% ascending.

The Tone of Greatest Emphasis (TGE) is usually a minor third above the lowest note used in the song. Melodic contour is undulating but ultimately descending, consisting of one or more arcs flattening out toward the end. Polyphony occurs sporadically in group singing, but only briefly, causing major 2nds and minor 3rds. The rhythm is isorhythmic but generally heterometric—the length of successive measures varies. Duple rhythms are more common than the triple. Syncopation is widely distributed, and dotted notes frequently encountered. All the songs in the sample have words, with vocables featured mainly in codas (Mark, 1955).

De Laguna writes that the Yakutat Tlingit recognize several main song classes: (1) shaman's songs, (2) children's songs, (3) peace songs, (4) songs of humor, (5) proprietory clan songs, (6) Haida mouth songs, and (7) dance songs. The ethnomusicologist who transcribed de Laguna's collected songs was David McAllester (de Laguna, 1972, vol. 3, pp. 1149–1369). These 103 Tlingit songs from Yakutat are the largest collection of transcribed, published Tlingit music; they are of great scholarly value and are published by the Smithsonian. Dorothy Morrison of the University of Alaska music department is currently analyzing their musical characteristics, in preparation for an M.A. thesis.

David McAllester considers that they exhibit the following tendencies:

(1) The only known polyphony in Amerindian music (parallel 4ths and 5ths, plus use of drone tones);
(2) The strongest rhythmic element of any known Amerindian music, with much syncopation;
(3) Descending overall melodic contour, but not cascading;
(4) Gradual rise in pitch during successive repetitions of a song;
(5) Some pentatonicism, with ccasional chromaticism;
(6) Transposition of complete musical phrases up or down a 4th;
(7) Frequent reiteration of single tones;
(8) Free melodic flow, with stanza divisions revealed primarily by the text;
(9) A song structure of refrain, stanza I (twice), refrain, stanza II (twice).

There is usually a beginning upward leap of an octave or a 5th, usually followed by gradual descent then another rise. Melodies are constructed and elaborated by being transposed upward or downward in short sections. In the contour of the melody, descending major thirds are common. Clusters of major and minor seconds are frequently found. Rapid repetition of the same note tends to impart forward motion and increase musical, emotional, and physical tension. Melody tends to gravitate toward, and climax at; a long held note. The use of microtones manifests itself as the flattening of pitches according to context, and as slides before notes and falls after. The melody is not divided into like measures, but shows a free, long flow of unequal measures.

Repetitions of the same dance song generally retain the original melodic contour, which is usually strongly downward. In her study "Music of the B.C. Northwest Coast Indians," Halpern observes that "as long as people are still in the vocal stage their scales show a downward trend. Later on, as instruments are added, the scales begin to move upward" (1968, p. 25). Gradual raising of the pitch may constitute a form of development, for at the successive higher pitch levels the music projects greater intensity. Intentional breath-taking is probably part of Tlingit melodic structure, for it imparts *stretto* or a concentration of musical energy.

Occasional part-singing is encountered, created by voices producing a parallel melody a 4th or 5th higher or lower; contrary motion is sometimes created by drone notes. Such polyphony is found in no other American Indian group; in this respect it is perhaps noteworthy that Mantle Hood suspects for some societies "a possible correlation between the principle of orchestration referred to as stratification and a hierarchical social structure" (1971, p. 58). The Tlingit are a stratified society.

Tlingit dance songs show a fairly consistent structure resulting from alternation of refrain and successive stanzas; the melody of the former finds itself expanded in the latter, often to allow for a new set of song-words. Halpern calls this type of composing logogenic—word-bound (1968, p. 25). To the investigator the texts appear rather fragmentary for several reasons. (1) The original Tlingit version at time of composition was allegorical and enigmatic, the audience being expected to possess a certain familiarity with the full story. (2) Old songs change over time—songwords become lost and meanings change. (3) A large number of the syllables are untranslatable because they are either vocables or archaisms. (4) There is difficulty in translating from Tlingit into English where the cultural equivalent, in terms of how people perceive life, does not exist. This applies to such Tlingit concepts as the humanization of animal behavior, the meaning of dreams, and the nature of the spirit world. Additionally, where real songwords occur, they may possess suffixed vocables, and have their inner vowels changed, as part of the formality of musicmaking.

De Laguna reports that the sib proprietory songs have Tlingit words, are sung by the potlatch hosts, and are considered extremely valuable. They are probably among the oldest known Tlingit songs, and their origins are ascribed to myths or legendary history. Specific sib songs are often associated with sib emblems such as named hats, Chilkat blankets, house screens, and canoes. Many such songs are named for the sib crest object: "Song for Crane Canoe," "Song for Thunderbird Blanket," "Song for Raven Post" (de Laguna, 1972, vol. 2, p. 569).

The dance songs are sung by the guests, who perform them as they enter the lineage house on the second day of the potlatch, and again after they have been paid. This last time provides a meaningful contrast in mood and tempo to the preceding laments and memorial songs. Enlivenment cheers the hosts and symbolically thanks them for the potlatch hospitality.

Among the Yakutat Tlingit, songs may come in dreams, and as the years pass by a song may acquire additional stanzas relating significant life-cycle events—the death of a parent, the drowning of a child. A Tlingit song may thus serve as a personal life history, and upon the death of the owner it may become a memento of that person. In 1974 the writer tracked down and located 14 reels of taped Yakutat Tlingit songs, the existence of which the villagers suspected but could not verify. Residents remembered their parents recording the songs in the 1950s, thus the tapes constituted valuable mementos of deceased persons. The writer found them in the archives of the American Philosophical Society in Philadelphia, and returned them to Yakutat at the annual ANB Conference in 1974. Such tapes add a new and wholly unique dimension to Tlingit musical tradition and to song and dance function, for in addition to performing proprietory sib memorial songs *about* the deceased, potlatch participants now listen *to* the deceased.

Another example of new dimensions is to be seen in the kinds of performing opportunities. In addition to potlatches, dance teams now perform at festivals, conferences, civic affairs, ferry arrivals, and other events that did not exist in precontact times. Dance instruction for the young has waned in the life of the extended family, but it thrives in the public schools. No longer is there a majestic chief before whom new dances may be presented, but there is the prestige of performing before thousands on television.

SUMMARY

The primary social context for the performance of Tlingit traditional dance is the ceremonial potlatch, of which there are several categories. Potlatch dancing is always communal and follows protocol governing group relations. A second important context in the past was the shaman's seance, where dance behavior was more individualistic. A second context today is the civic or statewide sociomusical event.

In form and content Tlingit dance exhibits general conformity to a given stylistic range featuring minimal floor movement and a degree of

Plate 1. Sitka dancers visit Klackqwan in 1904. The face paint indicates partial fulfillment of potlatch obligations.

Plate 2. At the Klackqwan potlatch in 1904, Sitka dancers adopt the typical Tlingit crouching dance posture.

Plate 3. Dance mask, Chilkat blanket, button blanket, and dance tunics at the turn of the century.

Plate 4. Potlatch dancers in Sitka in 1904. Note the large painted Raven drum on the right.

Plate 5. Entering the potlatch house in clan dance costume. Note the ermine cloaks and hats, and the octopus dance apron.

Plate 6. Potlatch dancers of the Killer-Whale clan entering another potlatch venue, in 1900. The ceremonial dance paddles served as staffs of office.

Plate 7. The Chilkat blanket was woven in the round, with mountain goat wool on shredded cedar bark. It's Tlingit name means "dancing fringe."

Plate 8. Sitka dancers with a large canoe and a carved house front indicating clan. Wolf always has protruding tongue; Bear always has square ears.

Plate 9. Sitka dancers arriving at distant Yakutat in 1900.

Plate 10. Three turn-of-the-century Tlingit shamans, each with the elaborate Raven rattle which bears a reclining shaman sucking power from a frog.

Plate 11. Tlingit shaman performing diagnostic dance in which he sniffs out the identity of the offending spirit.

Plate 12. Louise Peterson and Harry Bremner at Shark House at Yakutat in 1912, showing Chilkat blanket and wall carving.

Plate 13. Mary James at Shark House in Yakutat in the early 1950's. The costume on the left, and the cloak on the right depict familiar local legends. Local origin is indicated by the inverted V on the right, meaning Mt. St. Elias, which lies behind Yakutat. Mary holds a Killer-Whale fin from a box-drum. The column of four small cylinders on top of the conical dance hat indicate number of potlatches given.

Plate 14. Johnny Marks of the present-day Gai San Dancers, named after a mountain near Douglas Island. The button blanket shows Frog.

Plate 15. These Angoon children made their own dance costumes, and sing in Tlingit. The team travels widely in southeast Alaska. Photographs courtesy of University of Alaska Archives.

Thomas F. Johnston

Plate 16. The Tlingit Paddle Dance, showing Wolf screen, Raven mask, Raven crest on costume, and button blankets.

Plate 17. Hoonah schoolchildren make their own dance costumes and learn traditional dance from elders.

Plate 18. Hoonah women elders teaching dance to the young after school. Note the unusual square drum.

Plate 19. Haines traditional dancer Mildred Sparks shows a rattle and a drum, from her inherited crest heirlooms.

Plate 20. Yakutat dance-leader Harry Bremner rehearsing with Saxman dance-leader Martha Shields, at Yakutat in 1974.

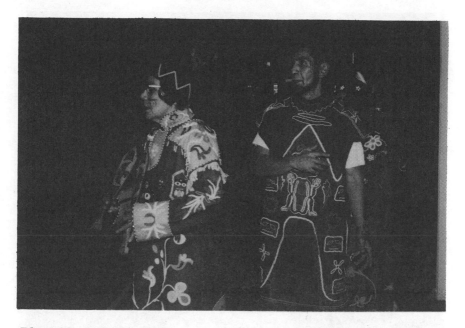

Plate 22. Yakutat dance costumes are distinguished by the inverted V, signifying Mt. St. Elias.

Plate 21. Yakutat Tlingit dance-leader Harry Bremner, in full dance regalia, including tassled mittens.

dignified rigidity. Enveloping regalia and weighty crest hats to some extent limit trunk and head movement; staffs, paddles, and rattles sometimes determine hand movement. When unencumbered, hand movement is mainly abstract, featuring the spinning of tassles on dance gloves. Mime occurs in special dance-dramas featuring animal mimicry, the wearing of elaborate symbolic masks, and freer floor movement and body movement, mask permitting. Content derives from sib origin myths, tribal legends, folklore, and historical incidents. Form and content remain little changed over the past century.

With regard to Tlingit dance function, it has been seen that the eighteenth- and nineteenth-century Tlingit greeted their first visitors with ceremonial dance. These visitors included LaPérouse, Malaspina, Suria, Vancouver, Puget, Purtov, and Baranof, some of whom noted this form of greeting in their historical journals. Tlingit dance thus appears to have been an enabling mechanism serving to facilitate harmonious social introductions, and probably also functioned to neutralize fear of the unfamiliar.

Within the context of the Tlingit ceremonial potlatch where rival sibs vied for status supremacy, it has been seen that dance could soften antagonisms and mediate. It frequently possessed an integrative function, serving Tlingit society in bringing about a degree of social cohesion. On the other hand, extreme dance rivalry between competing sibs could provoke hostility, becoming dysfunctional.

The most important Tlingit totemic crest objects were designed, not for wearing while enthroned or for wall display, but for dance. The Chilkat blanket was woven in the round for dancing, and the animistic essence of the totemic crest was brought to life mainly via symbolic movement. Dance was thus transformational, its powerful imagery evoking heightened perception of the revered crest.

Dance and the wearing of dance masks is a vehicle for depicting episodes in origin myths. It thus functions to validate Tlingit worldview and also fills an enculturative role in Tlingit society. In ancient times dance masks opened a doorway into the spirit world, and the wearing of the mask in dance functioned to mediate with the Tlingit pantheon of spirit deities. The same may be said of the shaman's masked dance of ecstasy. In dance, the feared shaman was sometimes ridiculed and lampooned; dance was therefore recreational and a release mechanism. Dancelike movement is still employed by Tlingit orators and storytellers to dramatize their recitations. Dance fills an expressive role, using many avenues to communicate. New dances are required for special occasions. Tlingit dance past and present marks notable incidents in Tlingit social and cultural history, such as the great migration, and gubernatorial inaugurations; here dance functions as a creative outlet for cognizant dance composers, and as a historical repository. Dance is a highly social activity and functions as an avocational bonding mechanism for small groups, such as dance teams based on the extended family.

In Alaska today, the once powerful Tlingit are a minority. The seat of state government is on their former lands, and the tourist ferries plough the waterways of their forefathers. In such circumstances, traditional dance serves as a badge of ethnicity, and its performance tends to instill cultural pride and to improve self-image. It is a truism that, while the Tlingit of today may, as individuals, enjoy access to material possessions and to a degree of personal security, their language and cultural heritage are threatened and their identity as a group is in question. The year 1991 is a terminal year for certain provisions of the 1971 Land Claims Act; traditional dance is being emphasized at the political meetings called to discuss the year 1991. Dance performance thus serves as a banner and a rallying cry in defense of traditional culture. Tlingit nativism joins with Athabascan and Eskimo nativism at statewide dance events—Eskimo Olympics, Native Arts Festival, Winter Games, Northern Games, ANB Conference, Elders' Conference, and the Fairbanks Native Potlatch—providing visible and audible cultural solidarity during a period of momentous change.

REFERENCES

Bancroft, Hubert H. (1884). *History of the Northwest Coast* (2 vols.). New York: A. L. Bancroft and Company.

Bancroft, Hubert H. (0000). *History of Alaska, 1730–1885.* New York: A. L. Bancroft and Company.

Birket-Smith, Kaj. (1936). *The Eskimos.* London: Methuen and Company.

Boas, Franz. (1916). Tsimshian mythology, based on texts recorded by Henry W. Tate. *Bureau of American Ethnology, 31st Annual Report, 1909–1910.* Washington, DC: Government Printing Office.

Boas, Franz. (1930). *The Kwakiutl of British Columbia: A documentary film edited by Bill Holm. Part 2: Dances and Ceremonial Activities.* Seattle: University of Washington Press.

Carpenter, Edmund. (1973). Some notes on the separate realities of Eskimo and Indian art. In Henry B. Collins et al. (Eds.), *The far north.* Washington, DC: National Gallery of Art.

Codere, Helen. (1956). The amiable side of Kwakiutl life: The potlatch and the play potlatch. *American Anthropologist, 58,* 334–351.

Cole, Glen H. (1954). *A study of the Tlingit boxes of the Rasmussen collection.* Unpublished master's thesis, Reed College, Portland, OR.

Collins, Henry B., Stone, Peter, Carpenter, Edmund, & de Laguna, F. (1973). *The far north: 2,000 years of American Eskimo and Indian art.* Washington, DC: National Gallery of Art.

de Laguna, Frederica. (1972). *Under Mt. St. Elias: The history and culture of the Yakutat Tlingit* (3 vols.). Washington, DC: Smithsonian Institution.

Drucker, Philip. (1958). *Native brotherhoods: Modern intertribal organizations on the Northwest Coast.* Bureau of American Ethnology, Bulletin 168. Washington, DC.

Drucker, Philip. (1965). *Cultures of the north Pacific coast.* New York: Chandler.

Garfield, Viola E., & Wingert, Paul S. (1979). *The Tsimshian Indians and their arts.* Seattle: University of Washington Press.

Gruening, Ernest. (1954). *The state of Alaska.* New York: Random House.

Gunther, Erna. (1966). *Art in the life of the Northwest Coast Indians.* Portland, OR: The Portland Art Museum.

Gunther, Erna. (1976). *A catalogue of the ethnological collections in the Sheldon Jackson Museum.* Sitka, AK: Sheldon Jackson Museum.

Halpern, Ida. (1968). Music of the B.C. Northwest Coast Indians. In P. Crossley-Holland (Ed.), *Proceedings of the Centennial Workshop on Ethnomusicology, Vancouver, 1967.* Vancouver, British Columbia: Government of the Province of British Columbia.

Herskovits, Melville. (1950). *Man and his works.* New York: A. A. Knopf.

Holm, Bill. (1965). *Northwest Coast Indian art: An analysis of form.* Seattle: University of Washington Press.

Jochelson, Waldemar. (1905). *Religion and myths of the Koryak.* Vol. 6 of *Jessup North Pacific Expedition.*

Johnston, Thomas. (1975). A historical perspective on Tlingit music. *The Indian Historian, 8*(1), 3–10.

Kolstee, Anton F. (1982). *Bella Coola Indian music: A study of the interaction between Northwest Coast Indian structures and their functional context.* Mercury series 83. Ottawa: National Museum of Man.

Krause, Aurel. (1885). Die Tlinkit-Indianer. Jena. First published in English in 1956 as Monograph 26 of the American Ethnological Society (Erna Gunther, Trans.). Page numbers in the text are from *The Tlingit Indians* (3rd printing). Seattle: University of Washington Press (1972).

Krauss, Michael. (1975). *Alaska's Native languages and their present situation.* People paper. Fairbanks: University of Alaska.

Langsdorff, Georg von. (1814). *Voyages and travels in various parts of the world 1803–7.* Parts 1 and 2. London. Published originally in German in Frankfurt, 1812.

LaPérouse, Jean. (1799). *A voyage round the world, performed in the years 1785, 1786, 1788* (2 vols.). London. First published in Paris, 1798.

McAllester, David. (1972). Recordings of Yakutat songs: 103 transcriptions. In Frederica de Laguna (Ed.), *Under Mt. St. Elias* (pp. 1149–1369). Washington, DC: Smithsonian Institution.

McLellan, Catherine. (1954). The interrelations of social structure with Northern Tlingit ceremonialism. *Southwestern Journal of Anthropology, 10*, 75–96.

Miller, Polly, & Gordon, Leon. (1967). *Lost heritage of Alaska.* New York: World Publishing Company.

Morrison, Dorothy. *Analysis of Tlingit music.* MS in preparation for a master's thesis for the Music Department, University of Alaska.

Oberg, Kalervo. (1937). *The social economy of the Tlingit Indians.* Originally a master's thesis for the University of Chicago, 1937. Monograph 55 of the American Ethnological Society, 1973. Page numbers given are from the first paperback edition; Seattle: University of Washington Press (1980).

Olson, R. L. (1967). *Social structure and social life of the Tlingit in Alaska.* Los Angeles: University of California Press.

Petrov. Ivan. (1884). *Report on the population, industries, and resources of Alaska.* 10th census. Washington, DC: Government Printing Office.

Ramos, Judith. (1977). *Dances of Yakutat.* MS, Music Department, University of Alaska, Fairbanks.

Story, Gillian L., & Naish, Constance M. (1973). *Tlingit verb dictionary.* Fairbanks: Alaska Native Language Center.

Swanton, John R. (1908). Social conditions, beliefs, and linguistic relationships of the Tlingit Indians. *Bureau of American Ethnology 26th Annual Report for 1904–5.* Washington, DC.

Swanton, John R. (1909). *Tlingit myths and texts.* Bureau of American Ethnology, Bulletin 39. Washington, DC.

Tikhmenev, Peter. (1863). *Historical review of the organization of the Russian American Company* (2 vols.). St. Petersburg. MS translation by Ivan Petrov in the Bancroft Library, Berkeley, CA.

Tollefson, Kenneth. (1978). From localized clans to regional corporation: The acculturation of the Tlingit. *Western Canadian Journal of Anthropology, 8*(1), 1–20.

Veniaminof, Ivan. (1840). Notes on the Atkin Aluets and the Koloshi. In *Notes on the islands of the Unalaska district* (vol. 3). St. Petersburg. In Russian. MS translation by B. Keen in the library at Yale University, New Haven, CT. Cited in de Laguna.

Wagner, Henry R. (Ed. and Trans.). (1936). Journal of Tomás de Suría of his voyage with Malaspina to the Northwest Coast of America in 1791. *Pacific Historical Review, 5*(3), 234–276.

INDEX